Visitors at My Door

Sabrina Fay Teiger

Radiant Heart Press
Madison, Wisconsin

The author has been granted permission to use the "Rainbow Bridge" © 2001 image on the cover by artist Willow Arlenea, who retains the copyright thereto. To contact the artist, please visit: www.designsbywillow.com.

The author has been granted permission to use the "KA" © 1998 image that begins each chapter by artist Francene Hart, who retains the copyright thereto. To contact the artist, please visit: www.francenehart.com.

The author has been granted permission to use *The Guest House* by Rumi © 1995 translated by Coleman Barks, who retains the copyright thereto. To contact the translator, please visit: www.colemanbarks.com.

To order additional copies of this book, please contact the author at 310-277-5881 or www..sabrinafayteiger.com

Published by
Radiant Heart Press
an imprint of Goblin Fern Press, Inc.
6401 Odana Road, Suite B
Madison, Wisconsin 53719
Toll-free: 888-670-BOOK (2665)

ISBN: 978-1-59598-0564
Library of Congress Number: 2007926624

Printed in the United States.

The Guest House

This being human is a guest house,
Every morning a new arrival.

A joy, a depression, a meanness,
some momentary awareness, comes
as an unexpected visitor.

Welcome and entertain them all!
Even if they're a crowd of sorrows
who violently sweep your house
empty of its furniture,
still, treat each guest honorably.
He may be clearing you out
for some new delight.

The dark thought, the shame, the malice;
meet them at the door laughing,
and invite them in.

Be grateful for whoever comes,
because each has been sent
as a guide from beyond.

~ Rumi ~

Translation by Coleman Barks, *The Essential Rumi*

Table of Contents

Preface

I was participating in a morning meditation held at a peaceful mind, body, and spirit resort when I first heard the poem, *The Guest House*, by Rumi. The moment I heard it, I knew it would play an important role in my life. When I decided to write a book, that poem came forth in my mind as the inspiration for the book and what its focus would be.

As I meditated on the poem, I set the following intention for the book:

> *It is my intention to nurture myself in the stillness of who I am and in so doing, open myself up to receive the visitors who knock at my door. This book has deep meaning for me, as it is an opportunity to open up to the messages, the teachings, and the inspirations that my thoughts/ emotions/experiences bring forward in my life. In taking the time to "invite them in" and listen to what they bring forward, I know I will come to a place of more peace,*

healing, and love ~ both inwardly and outwardly. As I come to more fully understand that I am not my emotions but the consciousness with which I hold them, it is my intended outcome to share these dialogues and reflections with others so that they, too, have an opportunity to listen to or reflect upon the visitors that come to their door."

This book has done exactly that. It has taught me how to stop and listen with my heart open. It has taught me to see and experience things in a new way. It has taught me that there are messages present in everything that our lives bring forward. It has taught me about awareness, conscious choice, and freedom.

The dialogues are simple and personal. I offer them to you as they unfolded for me. Through them, I learned about myself as a Human Being and as a Diving Being, both of which are worthy of praise, love, and celebration.

My greatest hope is that they inspire you to nurture yourself in the stillness, to give yourself the opportunity to blossom into all that you are.

~ Namaste

Introduction

Welcome, Dear One, welcome. I am so grateful that you have chosen to join me on this sacred journey.

I believe that we, as Beings, are a Divine part of the whole of Spirit. We have chosen to be here on this most amazing planet called Earth to learn, to remember, and to enrich the whole of our Being. The twists and turns our lives take are all part of this journey, and we all make our own way in our own time. To me, making my way home and birthing my authentic self is the same thing. It's the idea of having Heaven on Earth, for when I live from my authentic self, I am connected to Spirit. There is no separation. When I live from my authentic self, I experience joy and love, peace and compassion, gratitude and light. The way I experience life comes from within me, not from without.

I was a person who used to define herself externally. I relied on the opinions of others, their projections, judgments, and love to define my worthiness or take it away. I didn't claim my own power and felt I was a victim of my experiences. This journey has taught me that it is my birthright to see myself and stand up in all my beauty, in all my wisdom, and in all my light. This book has empowered me to see that when I truly show up, I light the way for others to do the same.

When I sat down to write this book, I sat down with the intention that it would be a simple book, written from my heart, and a tool for helping myself and others remember who they truly are. I wanted to stir the pot, offer up a new way of looking at life and the experiences we call forward as part of our growth and upliftment. I had no idea, nor was I attached to knowing, what it would turn out to be. I was committed to learning and opening myself to everything.

Over the course of nine months, I began to understand that everything, every thought, every emotion, every experience, carries a message for us if we are willing to receive it. I have learned that in order to receive the message in each experience, we need to slow down and actually listen; listen from our heart centers, not our heads. When I sat down with each visitor, I had no preconceived notions of what they were about or what they had to share with me, and each time, I was amazed at the wisdom and the love that poured through.

This book is a metaphor for me about life. It has taught me the truth behind the sayings, "It's not the destination that is important, but the journey," and "Don't judge a book by its cover." How often we miss the miracles and the mysteries that surround us because we don't take the time to learn. We don't step out of our preconceived notions about things, people, situations, experiences, or places. Too often, we think we already know. Too often we are in a big hurry to get where we think we need to go. This book is a gentle reminder to take our time and be open to the messages each experience brings forward for us.

I invite you to let go of what you think you know as you read this book. Since we all perceive and experience things differently, I am offering this book up as food for thought ~ as a way to encourage you to open yourself up to receive the gifts that are there for you. Some of what I have written may resonate with you, some may not. Either way, trust that what is true for you will show up to help you, and know that at your core, you are a Divine, wise, loving, joyful Being filled with light. You are on a most amazing journey home and reconnecting with your authentic self ~ here and now ~ is a beautiful way to get there.

I celebrate you and all that you are. I appreciate where you are on your journey, acknowledge you for moving forward, and embrace you with love and blessings.

~ Sabrina Fay Teiger
Los Angeles, 2007

This painting is meant to convey
SPIRIT or LIFE FORCE.
Its name is "KA" from the KA of the Mer-Ka-Ba,
which means "spirit."
Francene Hart © 1998

Gratitude

Gratitude blessed me this morning. She filled me with a warm sense of grace and love. I opened all the doors and windows of my home to let her in. It always amazes me how different the world appears when she is present with me. Everything seems possible. Every face I see is joyful. I am excited about my day and the miracles yet to unfold. I am uplifted. I am grateful.

G: Ah, Sweet Child, it is always such a blessing to embrace you and be embraced by you. I want you to know that every time you say "thank you" I feel your love. It is so radiant and warm.

S: It is such a blessing to feel you, to know you in my heart! When you are around, I feel so blissful, and I want to be surrounded by that feeling forever.

G: That is because gratitude is your way of connecting with home, with God, with All That Is. In those sacred moments, you let go of your perceived separation with Spirit and you feel a oneness with everything. That state of Being is truly blissful.

S: Oh, that is so true. I never want it to end.

G: The beauty is, it doesn't have to. Gratitude is a state of being ~ the more you say "thank you" and offer up gratitude for all aspects of your life, the more time you spend in that place of connection.

S: Sometimes, there are no words to express the gratitude I feel inside. It's almost as if I want to get down on my knees.

G: Child, know that words are not always necessary, but the way you open your heart to yourself, to others, and to Spirit is what matters. When expressed or felt, I touch all things. I spread around the universe, covering everything with a beautiful, lavender light. The echoes of a simple "thank you" resonate around the world, creating more joy, peace and harmony than you can ever imagine.

S: Well then, it is from this place that I would like to acknowledge all the beautiful Souls who carried me on their wings of unconditional love, compassion, joy, and support as I wrote this book.

G: That is beautiful, Sabrina. I would like to encourage you to start with yourself, for without your heart and your words, this would not have been possible.

S: Ok, then. I will.

I am grateful for listening to my heart and co-creating such a beautiful and insightful book. I am grateful that I opened to receive the messages that wanted to be shared. I am grateful for standing up in my magnificence and courageously sharing my gifts with others.

I am grateful for my husband, Douglas. He is an angel in human form who came back to love and support me unconditionally. He has given of himself both as a father and a husband. He has added his skills and creativity to enhance mine. He lifts me up in celebration of my successes and embraces me with compassion through my learnings. I am so blessed that he is my partner, my love, my balance.

I am grateful for my three boys: Zachary, Aidan, and Jared. These three magical Beings have loved me no matter what and have been my greatest teachers.

I am grateful for my parents, Ronit and Jack, my sister Camille, my brother Oren, their spouses and children, too. Each one has enriched my life in a unique way. I am truly blessed to be a member of this loving community we call our family.

I am grateful for Team MARS: Mike, Arriane, and Rahi. They held a sacred space of loving throughout the entire process of writing this book. They celebrated the highs and supported me through the lows on both the goal and learning lines.

I am grateful for my faculty reader, Dr. David Paul. His enthusiasm and loving support was the gentle wind that kept me on course.

I am grateful for Ron & Mary Hulnick, the staff, faculty, volunteers, and my fellow students at USM. All of these amazing people created a sacred community that held me through my transformational journey.

I am grateful for my writing group, Laurel, Linda, JoAnna, and John. Each one of these brilliant writers honored me with their gifts and supported me with love and encourage-ment to keep moving forward.

I am grateful for Kira Henschel of Goblin Fern Press. She believed in this book and graciously assisted me in the process of editing and publishing.

I am grateful for all of the artists who contributed to the first edition of this book and to those who still remain a part of this edition. Their art is uplifting and inspiring. There is a page at the back of the book that lists the art and website information of the artists.

I am grateful for my Guides, my Angels, my Inner Counselor, and the ever loving presence of Spirit. They surround me, protect me, nurture me, co-create with me, and love me with their gentle guidance and innate wisdom every moment of every day. I love them all so dearly.

G: I am grateful for you. I acknowledge you for stepping forward in all that you are and sharing your magnificent self with others! You are a gift to me, to yourself, and to this world.

... And so it is

Melancholy

Melancholy knocked on my door this morning. He wanted to keep me inside today. He brought with him gray skies and cold air, extra incentive to keep me indoors and under the covers. I wanted to shut him out and tried to push him away, but the clouds grew darker, the air felt colder, and he eventually persuaded me to let him in.

So I did. I decided that since he was going to be around for a while, I would invite him to tea, put a blanket around him, and find out all I could about why he was visiting today.

I asked him, "Melancholy, why did you knock on my door today?"

He answered, "Ah, your house had a huge welcome sign on it, encouraging and inviting me to come in." Thus began our conversation.

S: Why do you bring clouds with you when you come?

M: Ah, Sweet Child. I bring gray clouds with me as they seem
      to encourage people to stay indoors and reflect.
      Unfortunately, most people keep themselves so busy, even
      when indoors on a cloudy, gray day, that they miss the
      opportunity in my message.

S: What is the message that you carry for me today?

M: I am Melancholy. I come to visit when I sense you are
      looking for a change in your life but are stuck in the
      yearning. In a way, you can't see the forest for the trees. I
      feel you looking around at your life, your routine, and
      knowing, somewhere deep down, that things could be
      different.

S: But it seems that when you are around, it becomes even
      harder to make the change because I feel so down, so
      cloudy about things.

M: Yes, I understand that. Most people aren't willing to see
      the opportunity in reflecting on me or listening to what I
      have to say. Instead, they attempt to push me out. They
      don't like being in the space where I meet them. What they
      don't realize is that if they were to take the time to visit with
      me, possibilities would open up to them and movement

inside would take place. Once that movement or shift takes place, I am free to go.

S: So, you actually help me move through you, or this feeling that you bring when you are around?

M: Yes, that is correct.

S: How?

M: Just exactly by doing what we are doing, reflecting. Why do you think I'm here today?

S: Because I yearn for something to be different in my life. I yearn for the change to take place NOW. I'm impatient and unclear about what I want.

M: So, what would help you become more clear?

S: Knowing and manifesting what I want here and now.

M: What is stopping you?

S: The "shoulds," the "have tos," the responsibilities, the commitments.

M: Where is it inside you that says the change has to be "instead of" XYZ rather then "a part of" XYZ?

S: You mean like be more conscious about how I do XYZ and see the opportunity for change there?

M: Yes, that's a start. It's about evaluation and choice. Look at the difference in how you feel now that you are talking to me. That is the shift I am speaking of. In your life, you have things that "need" to get done, the responsibilities, etc. But how you go about doing them can make a big difference in your day.

S: So, what you are saying is that I have a choice in how I go about doing things throughout my day?

M: Yes, there is always a choice. Just as you made a choice to speak with me today, when in the past, you've tried to push me away or ignore me. Those are all choices, consciously made or not.

S: That's just it. I don't feel like I can consciously choose how I feel. Emotions kind of take over. I feel as if I'm a slave to my emotions.

M: Ah, but that is where you need to make your shift. Do you notice that you are talking to me, that I am an energy, in and of itself, that is outside of you?

S: Yes.

M: So, we, as emotions, are not of you. It's how you hold us in your consciousness that creates how you relate to us and vice versa.

S: I think I understand. Since I am speaking to you, I am affording myself an opportunity to make a shift in consciousness about you and about how I relate to you.

M: Exploring why I am around you and what message I bring offers you food for thought, which brings forward a shift in consciousness. And in bringing awareness to why and how you do the things you do, you can choose to change that.

S: What you are saying is that the choice to allow you to stay around or let you go is mine.

M: Well, yes and no. You have a choice to shift the way that you perceive yourself or the situation you are in. That shift in perception allows you to let go of the way you are holding yourself or the situation in your mind. You see, usually a shift in perception is accompanied by a shift from your mind or ego space to your heart space. In your heart space, you are accepting of everything that comes forward for you.

In your heart space, where you are right now, you don't have the labels. In other words, "melancholy" is a name your mind/ego gives me. In your heart space, I exist as a sign that you have an opportunity to look at yourself and see what learning is present for you. Do you understand what I'm saying?

S: Yes. My mind has learned to label emotions and perceive these emotions as positive or negative. Before I sat down with you, my perception of you was a negative one, one I wanted to "get out of." In speaking with you, I see that you are a very loving energy and that you are present with me as a way of letting me know that I have an opportunity for growth in front of me. It's kind of like a symbol on a map that says, "Stop here! There is something to be learned at this point on the journey."

M: Yes, I like that image. That is exactly what I am doing. And you, my dear, did stop here. What do you think you learned at this point on your map?

S: I learned that I have an opportunity every time I experience an energy shift to drop into my heart space to see what is going on. I am beginning to understand that my mind or ego looks at things it doesn't understand in a negative and fearful way.

From that place, Ego / Mind wants whatever is bothering it to go away, it wants to be in a positive place all of the time. Or maybe it's that Ego / Mind wants to feel in control all the time and when energies come in that shake things up a bit, it feels out of control. So, to be in control, Ego / Mind labels you and then feels it can deal with you.

My heart knows the truth: when energy shifts around me, it is just an opportunity for me to check out where I am and see if I want to continue on the same path or choose a different one.

It seems very clear to me that getting my heart space and my Ego / Mind space together would be very helpful. At least now, I am aware that dropping into my heart allows me to work directly with you from a place of peace and love, rather than from a place of fear.

M: You have done some great work with me. Know that all you ever have to do when you feel me around you is say "Hello, I remember you" and drop into your heart. Together, from there, we can move through anything!

S: Thank you for your teachings and for your love.

Chaos

Chaos knocked down my door today. They decided to visit whether I gave them permission to or not. Their presence was like that of a marching band, walking right through my bedroom. I heard loud, crashing cymbals and the unruly beat of a drum that let me know they were going to be around for a while. I didn't quite get it until later this morning when, after a series of mishaps, accompanied by yelling, attention demands, chores, and finally a breakdown into tears, I surrendered to them. I realized that in my desire to exercise control over them, I was just creating more Chaos.

So here I sit, alone in my closet with Chaos surrounding me and accepting that they're here. I have no fight left in me at this moment, so I may as well sit down and listen to what they have to say.

With these visitors I don't feel calm, but more antsy, more unforgiving of their disturbance and realize that this piece, in and of itself, is where the healing needs to begin ~ the unforgiving of the disturbance. For that is it, isn't it? Chaos has disturbed my peace, or rather my desire for peace today. They have turned me inside out and upside down.

S: Why did you decide to show up today in your loud and disturbing manner?

C: To get your attention.

S: Well, you got it.

C: We have to admit, it took a lot to get you to sit down with us. You are quite the determined fighter.

S: I didn't plan on your arrival today. In fact, I had quite the opposite in mind.

C: All the more reason. We, as it takes more than one of us to truly create the disturbing effect of chaos, are here to have you examine this need or desire to control things. It is difficult to control things when we are around, isn't it?

S: Yes, it is hard to keep it together, and I tried hard!

C: Why do you think being in control brings calm or peace to a situation?

S: That's a great question. It's just something I do. Being in control gives me a sense that I have a say in what's going on. And, if I have say in what's going on outside of me, then I have a say in what's happening inside. When I don't take care of my needs first, I try to control what others are doing so that I am then able to figure out what I need for myself. Unfortunately, I almost never get to that part.

C: Exactly. You woke up this morning realizing that we had come in, and instead of doing what you needed for yourself to remain calm in the chaos, you started tending to us and trying to control our loud voices. You are no match for us when you are off balance, as we feed off of each other's energy.

S: That is so true. As soon as I sat down here to talk to you, I felt a sense of calm and still do. I can say that more often than not, I tend to things outside myself first.

C: Then what?

S: Somehow I think that if I just take care of everything and everyone else, there will be more time for me. But the truth is, there is almost no time if I start that way. I know that, and yet I find it so hard to take care of myself first. If I did, everything else would fall into place.

C: But...?

S: But, somewhere inside, I feel as if I have to take care of
everyone else first, or I'm being selfish. However, on further
reflection, I realize and know in my core that taking care of
myself is self-loving and everything flows from there. If the
center is strong and nurtured, then all the spokes coming
off of it will be strong. And if something breaks, I will have
the strength to fix it because I feel whole.

C: Bravo. It seems as if today, we were loud enough to knock
you off balance. However, you made the effort by meeting
us here to center yourself and strengthen your sense of
peace through accessing your inner wisdom. We honor you
for that. The lesson we brought with us today has been
recognized and now we can go and leave you in peace ~ as
you have created the peace for yourself in the midst of the
storm.

S: Thank you.

C: We bid you farewell and are grateful you opened yourself
up to us and our teaching.

Miss Pissy

I am pissy. There is no doubt about it. When did Miss Pissy come into my space today? I don't know. My husband came back from running an errand and she just overtook me. I don't know how she got in or where the other parts of me are hiding, but she is still here. I think she locked them up and threw away the key, and the only way I'm going to find it is if I sit down and talk to her. I have resisted this all afternoon but now it's time or she'll hang around much too long. Being with Miss Pissy always leads to anger and mean behavior. When I try to ignore her, she finds a way to sneak in through the back door again. She seems to do whatever she can to mess things up around me. So, I guess it's time to see what she has to say. Here goes.

S: Ok, Miss Pissy. I know you are here. I feel you in my bones. Ohhh, I don't like myself very much when you are around, and I just want to get to the bottom of this visit so that you leave as quickly as you came!

MP: (*Laughing*) I love that I can rile your feathers so easily. What's up with you, my dear? You let me in. You had your doors wide open saying "Come on in if you dare." So, why not? I didn't realize the rest of you would be so easy to put away for a while.

S: What did you do with them?

MP: I gave them some chocolate and persuaded them to go somewhere else for a while. Then, I closed and locked the door when they left. Ha, ha. Now you are stuck with me.

S: Well, so what if I am?

MP: So what if you are. We could go back and forth like this all day if you want. Why don't we try to get to the heart of what's going on here?

S: What makes you think that something's going on?

MP: Because I'm here. There is always a reason I show up. Why don't you tell me what you think about it?

S: I think you are here to make my life and everyone else's life miserable. Because when you show up that's what happens.

MP: When I show up, your life is miserable and that affects everyone around you.

S: Yes, when I'm miserable it affects everyone around me and then I get blamed for that.

MP: So, you are responsible for everyone's mood? When you are happy, they are as well, and when you are pissy, so are they.

S: Yep, that about sums it up.

MP: Wow! You really hold a lot of power around people, don't you!

S: It seems that way, but I hate being the scapegoat. I hate that I allow people to put pressure on me to always be happy and nice and loving so that they can feel good.

MP: Would you say the same about yourself?

S: What do you mean by that?

MP: Would you say that when others around you are upset or pissy that you get that way, too, and blame them for it?

S: Ouch. I guess I do. It's just that when they get that way, I take it personally and then I get mad because I can't figure out what I did wrong to make them feel that way.

MP: So, that seems to be the crux of it right there. You tend to take things personally and that makes you pissy. That's why I'm here today. Why do you think it's your job to keep the peace or make everyone around you feel good?

S: Because everyone keeps telling me that.

MP: So, what does your intuition tell you?

S: That people are responsible for themselves, their behaviors, and their reactions. I hear that, but it's hard to really believe it since my whole life, I've been blaming others and they've been blaming me. I am learning about responsibility but how can I explain that to others when they look at me like I'm crazy? They just don't get it.

MP: I can understand how difficult it must be to try to explain a concept to others that you yourself are still a bit unsure of.

S: Yes. That is part of it. I am at the beginning stages of really trying to integrate this notion of responsibility into my Being. But what I find happening is that I get frustrated with others for not taking responsibility for themselves and then putting it on me.

MP: Ah, I understand. So, when you get pissy, you own your feelings and your attitude, but when others blame you for how you make them feel, you go even more into upset with yourself and with them.

S: Yes. That is exactly what happens. I feel like I can't win either way. I'm stuck in this place and can't get out.

MP: I really know how hard that is for you. May I offer some reflection on that?

S: Please do.

MP: You get upset. You take ownership for your upset, yet you find yourself met by another who is blaming you for how you have made him/her feel. Then you feel guilty for making that someone feel that way. From that place of guilt, you get further upset and make the other wrong for not being able to own his or her own feelings. Is that how it goes?

S: Yes.

MP: What would you like someone to say to you when you are feeling this way?

S: I would like them to acknowledge that I'm upset and love me anyway.

MP: Do you think that you could do that for the other person?

S: Oh, I see where you are going. My learning is going into compassion and not reacting to the other's reaction. But that is so hard for me to do.

MP: I understand it has been challenging in the past, but I encourage you to keep this conversation in your consciousness when you go into upset and see if it helps you. Blaming yourself and others only keeps you in this pissy frequency. I see how out of balance that makes you feel and in that place, you only tend to go deeper into the mire. Raising your frequency by going into a place of compassion for yourself or for the other person will help bring you right up and out.

S: I really hear what you are saying. I want to say that I will try it, but I know it is more important to put an intention out there. It is my intention to bring forward the energy of this conversation when I go into upset to help me jump into a different frequency and to remember that I am responsible for my upset, as well as my reaction to other people when they are upset. It is my intention to be compassionate with myself and forgiving of myself when I am out of balance.

MP: Great. I acknowledge you for setting that intention.

S: Thank you for staying with me through this. You're really not that bad.

Pressure

This pain in my chest won't go away.

    Seems it's found a warm place to stay.

I feel it rise and fall with each breath.

I've tried to ignore it and bore it to death.

But this pain has a life of its own that will thrive.

I've named it Pressure, this pressure to strive.

For all things come and go in their time.

Maybe it's telling me that now it is mine.

So, I sit here and ponder on this beautiful Fall day

What this Pressure has come here to say.

She has a message that wants to be told.

I'm ready to listen to what's new and what's old.

"Come sit with me," I hear her say.

"I'm here with you. 'Til we're done, I'll stay."

S: Good morning Pressure. I'm here with you now. I've tried pushing you away, thinking you'd go on your own, but I see you have no plans to go until we speak.

P: That is true. You called me in and asked me to stay, knowing I had a message for you. The truth is I serve no other purpose than to make you aware of how you are spending your days and how you are treating yourself.

S: What do you mean? I feel like I'm getting it all done.

P: Exactly! You are getting it all done but something is off if I've been called in.

S: You have been with me many times in my life. In the past, the best way to deal with you has been to go on a bland diet and sleep sitting up. Something tells me that's not what I need to do this time.

P: Well, let's look at why I'm here. What do you think?

S: I think I'm stressed but unaware of it and that's why it's manifesting in my chest, near my heart....Hmmmm.

I am going through the motions of getting everything done but without my heart in it! When I say this, I get choked up so I know it has meaning for me. I want to get all my work done and be a good mom and be a good wife and take care of myself. There is so much to do. Yet, sometime over the past few weeks, I've felt like it is all possible if I'm present for each thing. I have actually felt very calm and in the flow of things and that's why I don't understand why you are here.

P: You said something earlier about not doing these things in a heartfelt way, almost like you are on automatic ~ doing things because they need to be done rather than because you enjoy doing them.

S: But they do need to be done. I have to do my homework and reading. I have to go to the market and feed my family and my pets. I have to find ways to nurture myself and my husband. I have to volunteer at my children's school. I have to run errands to keep the household in order.

You know what? Just writing this now makes you grow stronger inside of me.

P: Do you realize all the "have to" statements in what you just said? No wonder I'm here. Truthfully, every time you say or feel this "have to," I grow stronger. You, yourself, are feeding me.

"Have to" carries a certain energy with it, a dense energy. That is what you feel mounting up inside next to your heart.

S: Oh, my! I am very aware that I often say I "have to" do things. I read once somewhere about shifting the idea or notion of "have to" to "love to." It just seems so unnatural for me to say "love to" go to the market, "love to" make lunch for the kids, "love to" do my homework....

P: Again, the tears come forward. What is that about for you?

S: Because inside, I know that if I can make the shift from "have to" to "love to," my life would be richer, my heart would be more joyful. The truth is, I have things that need to be done, where I don't have a choice of whether or not to do them. But I do have a choice as to *how* I do them and *when* I do them. I do have a choice "to love" to do them and to do them with gratitude.

Then, there are other things that don't have to be done at all, but I choose to do them, like nurture my husband, play with my kids, be creative, etc. If I make the shift and choose to do them with love or not do them at all, I wonder how my heart would feel. I have been present and in the flow, but have put the pressure on myself to get it all done, instead of checking in with myself about what I really need to do and how to do it in a loving way.

P: Do it with love or don't do it at all. Is that what you are saying?

S: Well, that seems like the ultimate goal. I'd settle for the awareness around how I'm doing things and then moving toward that goal and being gentle and loving with myself when I fall into "have to" mode.

P: I must tell you that I, as an energy, am self-inflicted. I respond to you and how you hold yourself, how you hold your responsibilities, and how much or little you live in a heartfelt way. There is only so much that your body can handle before it calls me in to flash the warning signals. I'm glad you took the time to talk today. And, by the way, I loved your little poem at the beginning. It seems as if you sat down to write that with love, not because you "had to."

S: I feel as if I can breathe easier. I want to make sure that now I don't put on the pressure to shift from "have to" to "love to" ~ that would be completely fruitless. Any suggestions?

P: I love you, Sabrina. I love your honesty and your insight into your nature. What if you see this as a gift you are giving your heart in gratitude for all it gives to you. With every beat, it sends love through your body. This love is what breathes life into you. You can just carry the love that beats through you out into all that you do. See it as an extension of your Being. Then it's not about the *doing*, it's about the *being*.

29

S: I really like that. It's a really beautiful image. Thank you so much. I am grateful that you stayed present with me so that I could hear you. Thank you for sitting with me through this exploration. Thank you for witnessing my shift. I invite you any time to whisper to me if you find I need a reminder here or there. I appreciate your wisdom and your gentle nature.

P"   One more thing before you begin to walk away. A very important piece of this is your breath. Pay attention to how you breathe. While I've been visiting, I've noticed that you have been breathing with the same energy as your "have to" way. Try breathing the "love to" way. See your breath as an extension of your heartbeat ~ of the love that is pulsating through you. Imagine the abundance of love that will fill you and emanate from you. Breathe in love. Breathe out love. It's all part of the same lesson.

S: Thank you. How very wise and insightful you are.

>   *Breathe in love, breathe out love,*

>   *From my heart,*

>   *into my Being,*

>   *Out to the world, and back inside.*

Should

I woke up this morning to my youngest son climbing into my bed. We had fun playing and romping around. The morning continued to unfold with its ups and downs but sometime after breakfast, on the way to the park, an unexpected visitor showed up at my door. The best way to describe this visitor is through a scene from the movie, *The Hitchhiker's Guide to the Galaxy*. Every time a person had an idea about something, he would get whacked in the face by a foreign object coming up from the sand. That's how I feel when this visitor is around. Believe me, this one I couldn't ignore. It did take quite a few whacks and a good cry before I decided I'd better see what was up. So, I opened the door to him. His name is Should.

Should walked in with attitude as if he knew best about everything. It took all my own restraint not to whack him upside the head a few times. I offered him a chair, not a very comfortable one, in the hopes that he wouldn't stay long. But, inside myself, I had a feeling that he'd be here for a while.

He sat down and looked at me as if I "should" be doing something else, like offering him something to drink or eat, but I was just not in the mood. I wanted to get down to business.

S: Ok, so here you are and I let you in. What's all the fuss about?

Sh: A little testy today, aren't you?! Shouldn't you calm down and take a seat!

S: There you go, telling me what you think I want or should be doing.

Sh: Yes, that's my job, and I'm very good at it!

S: You are very good at ruffling my feathers. I'll give you that.

Sh: That's only because you let me, and you are such an easy target.

S: What do you mean by that?

Sh: It's easy for me to tell you what to do when you can't figure it out for yourself, when you are stuck in the place of "I don't know."

S: That seems to happen often.

Sh: Yes, it does. That's why I like hanging around you. You make my job very easy.

S: And what is your job exactly?

Sh: I ~ what was the word you used? ~ whack you in the head with ideas to make you think about your choices and sometimes to push you far enough that you take the time to look at how you make choices for yourself on a daily basis.

S: Why do you care what choices I make?

Sh: Because I'm here to help you grow.

S: Well, I don't particularly like your approach.

Sh: I can accept that. However, I know what my role is, and I go about it with all I've got. I don't doubt myself and what I want to do.

S: Are you suggesting that I doubt myself?

Sh: I believe you doubt what you want for yourself and don't always ask for it when you do know.

S: That is true.

Sh: What's up with that?

S: I have all these ideas about what I want but then I hear your voice saying "I should do this or that."

33

Sh: And what if you stick with your way instead of following these "shoulds"?

S: I don't have confidence in my way and think that there are other ways that are better. I focus on what others would think of what I'm doing rather than just doing it.

Sh: Who is watching you and judging how you do what you do?

S: I am. I think there is a better way. I put pressure on myself, and assume that others do things differently. I am in complete judgment of so many things, and in that judgment, I open myself up for you to have a field day.

Sh: You sure do! I am right there with my infinite amount of suggestions.

S: I don't owe anyone an explanation of why I do the things I do, so let it go.

Sh: Now you are talking, Girl!

S: By throwing in your two cents to see if you can rock the boat, you give me the opportunity to choose what I feel is in my highest good. I let you rock the boat when I doubt myself. When I am sure of myself and/or willing to try something and risk the mistake (opportunity for growth), then what you have to say doesn't get to me.

Sh: That is correct. I like to come in and try to upset the balance. Sometimes I can. Sometimes I can't. That offers you a chance to look at where you are holding doubt about yourself and your desires and actions.

S: Wow! That's actually kind of cool, because if I'm willing, I can work on these areas.

Sh: You got it.

S: I apologize for judging you so critically before. You are not as bad as I made you out to be.

Sh: No, I'm not so bad. I'm great, and I love what I do. Nice talking to you today. Now, it's time to go and "whack" someone else. See you around.

Sadness

Sadness is looming nearby today. I feel her sitting around the corners of my eyes. She doesn't feel heavy or burdensome but more like a gentle pressure, just enough to initiate the formation of tears. They are ready to flow. Will I let them? A part of me wants to hold back because I don't feel like acknowledging that I am sad.

As I sit here, in this space, the tears begin to flow. I guess some part of me let her in just by acknowledging that she is near. It's not that I don't like Sadness. I guess I'm a bit surprised by her visit today. I thought things were going pretty well. I am curious to hear what she has to say to me.

S: Good morning, Sadness. What brings you my way, on this beautifully clear fall day? I guess I have tears to cry!

Sad: Oh, Sweet One, you invited me here last night when you went to sleep angry.

S: What do you mean?

Sad: You were upset with your husband and held on to it all night and into this morning. There was a part of you that wanted to let it go and tried to, but not completely. Under the anger that still remains is the sadness. That's why I'm here.

S: That is true. But what is this all about? I feel it so deeply inside and am afraid that if I let it out, it will be so much bigger than I am.

Sad: I encourage you to allow it to flow. Then we can talk. Let's just be silent together for a moment and see what comes forward. <silence and tears>

S: It is becoming so clear that how I act outwardly, towards others, is a reflection of how I treat myself internally. It hurts that I can be so unloving towards myself.

Sad: What a beautiful awareness. The tears I bring are tears of cleansing, of clearing, of purifying. They wash over you so that you can see life in a different way. The lives we lead and the experiences we have often bring with them so much debris. I am a way of sorting through that debris, sifting it so that what is left over is the pearl of wisdom that can be gleaned from the experience. If you are willing to open up to me ~ or to any emotion, for that matter ~ and reflect upon what is present, you give yourself the gift of insight and clarity. Take the time to stop and be present with yourself. Allow the tears to flow. See what comes forward as you did here today with me. You will be amazed at what you find.

S: By taking the time to visit with you, I have realized that outer reality is a reflection of inner reality. In other words, the way I am with others and the way I handle experiences that come forward in my life are a direct reflection of my own internal process. When I truly allow the tears to flow and clear away the debris, I am able to see what is being mirrored back to me. I need the tears for cleansing so that I can actually see the experience for what it is trying to teach me about myself and my own evolution. Thank you for that gem.

Sad: It is my pleasure.

Agitation

Agitation unexpectedly came by this morning. I turned around and he was there. I must have left the door open on the way to walk my boys to school. Like it or not, he's already made himself comfortable in the armchair by the window. Seems he is not going anywhere until I pay some attention to him. The truth is, I don't want to go through my whole day feeling this way so, I guess sitting down with him now is a good idea. Funny, for someone who brings with him this sense of agitation, he seems pretty calm. It's all about his effect on me, because I don't feel calm. I'm ready to scream, jump up and down, and pull at my hair.

"So, why don't you do that?" I hear a deep, husky voice say.

S: Do what?

A: Jump up and down, scream, pull at your hair. It might help you.

S: Yes, but you'll still be here.

A: Yes, I will. I have a lot to talk to you about, but we can approach it through your agitated state or in a much calmer way.

S: Ok, fine.

So, I do. I hit my pillow, and jump up and down and scream, yet this sense of agitation still remains with me.

S: Why did you decide to walk in today?

A: You left the door wide open for me. I saw this cozy chair and felt like sitting in it.

S: I know you have something to share with me, but I don't like that you are here. I feel yucky and want you to go away.

A: What are you agitated about?

S: Lack of communication, forced change, feeling as if I have no choice or say in the matter, seeing something I worked hard to build be destroyed in some sense. It's extremely frustrating. I want to handle this calmly but you are not letting me. You are stirring things up.

A: Am I? Or are you allowing me to?

S: What do you mean?

A: I am sitting here very calmly. You are the one who's allowing my visit to stir up all this stuff inside you. What's behind that?

S: I feel helpless, like I just have to accept change, and I don't want to. I want to deal with this situation but not in this tone, so I want to work through what's going on here.

A: I can only stir up what is inside of you that resonates with me and it seems as if there is a lot of stuff.

S: Maybe if you describe yourself that will help me.

A: OK. I create a bit of a storm inside by making your cells move around faster. This speed causes things to get stirred up. It sends up to the surface the toxins or the issues you hold inside so you can look at them if you so choose. That is what you are experiencing. You are stirred up and feeling this sense of movement inside, which is bringing your stuff up to the surface. Let's look at it together.

S: This is about change and lack of communication. So, how do I handle what I can't change or don't have the power to change? I don't like being told that things are going to be different when they affect me, and I feel I have no say. That's it.

A: So, when you can't control things, you get uncomfortable?

S: You got me, didn't you?

A: It's not about getting you, Sabrina, it's about offering you an opportunity to look at what doesn't serve you.

S: Yes, I feel out of control. Part of it is that when change is communicated before it happens, I am able to prepare and therefore accept it. When it's just dropped down on me without notice, I feel disrespected and find it harder to swallow. Sometimes, I internalize my feelings, and other times I voice my disapproval.

A: There are many people in this world who experience this lack of regard when new rules and regulations are just dropped on them. Like you, they either accept or revolt. Maybe, if you describe the situation with more detail, we can work through it in a more specific way.

S: OK. There is a new administration at my sons' school that is changing things around without communicating to the parents. I am a part of the Booster Club, which has worked very hard to co-create a sense of community within our school and did so with the support and blessing of the old administration. It is my perception that the changes being made are affecting this sense of family/community in a negative way. I am agitated by the situation because I feel powerless.

A: I hear you and I hear that these changes are seemingly detrimental to what you have created.

But let me ask how allowing me in helps the situation?

S: It doesn't, other than it makes me stop and question myself and what is present for me around this.

A: So, what options do you have in moving forward here?

S: I see that I have the opportunity to work this out with you inside myself so that I can find a way to deal with change gracefully. I can choose whether or not I want to share how I feel with others from a more centered and calm place inside. I can speak from a place of responsibility, rather than from an emotional place of blame.

A: That is very true.

S: I then have a choice as to whether or not I want to express how I feel to the principal and possibly gain a clearer understanding of where she is coming from. I guess hearing her side is important in helping me gain perspective.

A: That is a truly wise statement. So often, I come in because you aren't fully aware of all aspects of a situation; you choose to get upset before gathering information that might allow you to avoid the upset. Therefore, part of the opportunity here, Sabrina, is honoring your upset and working through it so that you are then able to sit down and look at the other side of the situation.

S: I really get that. I realize, so often, that my choosing to get

upset is almost instantaneous ~ someone does something I don't like and instead of checking in with them about it, I judge it and then get mad. It's all about communication, isn't it?!

A: Yes, it's all about the willingness to communicate, the willingness to see things from a higher perspective. Once you sit down with someone and express yourself and allow that person to do the same, a beautiful sense of flow is created.

S: I hear you. I really do. When I feel you inside, I know that I have an opportunity to check in about what is going on, as well as a choice about communicating to gain a clearer perspective. I may not understand or agree with the changes or the person, but I have more information to work with in my own process.

A: Sounds like you have found a way inside to deal with this. Your energy has shifted. I am still here, but you are no longer agitated. Bravo! You took the time to look at what came forward and brought forth healing.

S: Thank you.

A: You are welcome. If you don't mind, since I don't seem to be bothering you, I'd like to hang out in this chair a little longer.

S: Be my guest. (*Smiling*)

Judgment

Judgment sticks to me like glue. It actually has been with me for so long that it feels like a second skin. I don't think there are many things I've done in my life without some form of Judgment showing up. Oddly enough, I've never once sat down to ask it why it's here. Why it has chosen, or should I say ~ why I have chosen ~ to let it stay for as long as it has? It's a doozy. Something has come forward for me, and I can't seem to let it go because all I hear from Judgment is that I'm wrong. Fortunately, I have enough awareness right now to talk to Judgment and finally hear what he has to say.

S: I'd like to say welcome to you, but the truth is you've made yourself welcome for a long, long time. In fact, I can't remember when I first let you in. I must have made such amazing arrangements or provided the amenities of a five-star hotel to have kept you around as long as I have.

J: Ah, Child. It has been a long time, and I have been very comfortable here. I've gotten to know you very well and am a bit attached to you and your life. My job isn't always a fun one but it is a very important one.

S: Why is that?

J: Because without me, you wouldn't have learned to trust yourself or your decisions. Without me, you wouldn't learn how to ask the questions that help you stand up in all that you are. Without me, you wouldn't learn about discernment or compassion.

S: What do you mean?

J: You can only truly feel compassion for another being when you, yourself, have had similar experiences.

S: What does that have to do with you?

J: The best way to explain myself is for you to understand who I am. You chose to learn certain things and undergo certain experiences in this lifetime to help you grow and remember. When a soul descends, it has a lot of love and support around it throughout its entire journey. It might be hard for you to believe that you have chosen a Judgment Angel to put certain things forward on your path that you must work through.

One of your biggest life lessons is acceptance: acceptance first of yourself, how you act, who you are, etc., and then, acceptance of others. To be able to truly accept yourself, you need to face me and all of the "tests," if you will, that I bring forward into your life. That is part of why I feel like a second skin. I serve no other purpose than to be a guiding force. Until you are willing to look at me and what I bring forward, true acceptance is challenging.

The duality between judgment and acceptance is like that between happy and sad, good and evil, light and dark, etc. In this reality, there is not one without the other. It is up to you and your life's work to decide whether you give into and feed off the judgments or use them as a way to propel you forward on your growth process.

At certain points of your life, when you are ready, you begin to move from judgment to acceptance. I am here as a teacher. I do what I do out of love for you and out of respect for the lessons you came here to learn.

S: It's hard to swallow that these judgments come from a place of love, but when you explain what your purpose is, it's more palatable. It's also hard to believe that these judgments lead to self-acceptance.

J: Well, let's take the judgment you are holding right now over yourself and see what we can learn from it.

S: Ok. I don't feel like participating in helping out a family in need. I have volunteered my time and resources so many times in the past, and I just don't want to right now. I believe there are enough other people who are willing to help out. I just don't want to this time.

J: I really hear clarity around that. So what's the judgment?

S: I hear the words "compassion-fatigue" in my head and judge myself for not doing more. Here is the judgment: If there is someone in need, I should always be there to help. I help out so much. Sometimes, I just want to say "No, not this time," as I'm doing in this case. But you won't leave me alone.

J: There is something else, too.

S: Yes, if I choose not to participate, then others won't see my name on the list, and they will judge me for not participating. And, if something were to happen to me, they'd scoff and say, "We won't help her. She didn't help out when we needed her." Oh, I'm so good at creating negative future fantasy drama!

J: Wow! Did I come up with that one for you?

S: Well, I imagine you did if this is your department.

J: Ok, I guess I am a bit dramatic at times. Anyway, this is a perfect example of your willingness to look at this judgment. There is a part of you that knows what you are saying is not true, but a stronger part, which happens to be me, is giving you an opportunity to look at this. This is a big one for you. I honor the fact that this situation got you to sit down with me.

S: But what does all this have to do with self-acceptance?

J: You tell me.

S: I am very concerned with what others think of me. I often do things for that reason rather than because they're heartfelt. (Aha!) Acting so that "I look good" to others is not loving or compassionate. In this case, I am actually doing the opposite and being self-honoring. Why am I so concerned with how others see me?

Wait, it's not that! It's you. I am allowing you to cloud my world and projecting your voice onto others.

J: Bingo!

S: So, then stop it!

J: I can only stop when there is a sense of self-acceptance. We haven't gotten close to that yet.

S: OK. OK. There is a misperception caught up in this. Is that also your department?

J: No, but let's explore it.

S: The misperception I'm holding is that I should be available all of the time, do my best to serve others in any way possible, give money if I have it, give food if they need it, give, give, give because I can, and it's the right thing to do.

J: Wow! And you said I was dramatic. That's huge. Where did that come from?

S: Where did I think I had the resources or that it was my job to save the world? (*Big sigh*). The truth is, it's my job to take care of me and do all these things for myself. Somehow, I've externalized it. It's me who needs food when I'm hungry and me who needs to give myself money when I need it, and me who needs attention and service. I'm so busy trying to do that outwardly that I have nothing left for myself. WOW! So, of course I'm allowing the judgment in.

J: That's a great insight. One that was able to come forward because you were willing to sit with me.

S: The acceptance comes in when I realize that sometimes I am not in a position to give because I am taking care of my needs. This "down time" is crucial to my life and my ability to give! Acceptance comes when I am able to discern when I need to give and when I need to receive. The more I am able to reflect and relax, the more I have to give and the more my giving comes from my heart. The learning here is that it is just as important for me to take care of myself as it is for me to take care of others.

J: That is yet another brilliant insight into yourself and your process. Now, I can let this one go. Can you feel it lifting?

S: Yes, I can and I'm grateful for that. I'm grateful for the knowledge that each judgment is a projection of what I'm doing to myself. It doesn't make judgments any easier to swallow but does help me open up to dialoguing with you more often.

J: Thank you.

S: I've learned a lot about myself today and about how you serve me. I'm glad you are my Judgment Angel. You are a very kind one indeed.

J: My pleasure. The more acceptance and love you have for yourself and your needs, the less I will hover ~ and that's just fine with me!

Intimacy

The energy of Intimacy has been hanging around me. It keeps coming up in conversations and filling my heart with questions. The more I think about Intimacy, the more I wonder what her true nature is, especially in regard to me and my relationships. I believe Intimacy is something I dance around but have not experienced in her authentic nature. Now that I have the tools and the desire to know more, I am choosing to engage her in a dialogue. This is the first visitor I am inviting to come into my space so that I can learn more about what she represents in my life.

"Intimacy, Intimacy where are you? I'm calling to you. I'm sending you an invitation to come and meet with me."

I hear a sultry voice answer, "Here I am."

S: I am so glad you have come. I want so much to understand you and to get to know you. I feel that I am really missing you in my life and that in order to experience you fully, I need to engage you.

I: I am here, Sweet One. I am honored to be of service to you and to help you open up to me.

S: Can you tell me a little about who you are?

I: I am love at its core. I am multifaceted like a diamond. I am brilliance and I am shadow. I am what comes forward when you are willing to see all of yourself and share all that you are with others. I am the ecstasy you feel when you realize you are safe in my arms and have nothing to fear and nothing to hide.

S: Somehow, you seem unattainable.

I: Ah, that is a perception that many people have. Most people are quite afraid of me. I am always around, patiently waiting to be discovered and compassionately observing people as they struggle to bring even a glimpse of me into their lives.

S: Why don't you help them ~ and me?

I: It is not for me to do. It is for me to be there with you always, but for you to open up and discover me. Most people don't really understand what I am about. It is because you are ready to know and are willing to open up to me that you have called me forward. So, here I am.

S: Why is it so hard to know you?

I: Many believe that if they are close to someone physically or are engaged in a physical act with someone, they are being intimate. What they don't realize is one can engage physically and be disconnected. Expressing intimacy means being present ~ mentally, physically, emotionally, and spiritually ~ first with yourself, then with others. That is really the key. There is no way to experience intimacy with another unless you can experience it with and for yourself.

S: What does that mean?

I: It means that I come into your experience when you are willing to look at all the aspects that make up who you are ~ the light and the dark, the positive and the negative, the brilliance and the shadow. When you are able to accept, unconditionally accept, all parts of yourself without judgment, you walk into intimacy.

One of the best ways to experience intimacy with yourself is to look into your own eyes and really see yourself, see all the facets of who you are. The first step toward intimacy is being truthful about how you feel and how you see yourself. Then you move forward by learning to love and accept yourself and all your beautiful imperfections, and to celebrate all that you are.

S: But what about intimacy with another?

I: That, my Child, is one of the most beautiful, exquisite experiences you can have. Intimacy with another is created when you are willing to allow that person in to see and love you. You are saying, "I love myself enough to want to share all aspects of me with you." When you open this way, you are letting the other person know that you are willing and ready to experience all of who he or she is, as well.

S: But don't you exist on many different levels ~ sexual/physical, emotional, mental, and spiritual?

I: That is a good question. Yes, I can be experienced on different levels. I am most powerfully experienced on all levels at the same time.

S: Can you explain?

I: Yes. People think that they are being intimate when they have sexual relations, but that is a physical act. People can be physically intimate with one another just by looking into each other's eyes and becoming vulnerable. I am about opening. I am not present when you engage in sexual relations without opening yourself to another.

Let me explain further. I am really about opening yourself up unabashedly for yourself or another to experience. Therefore, I can only occur when all four levels are aligned. Physical intimacy can only occur if you are completely present with another mentally and emotionally. The spiritual component is a direct result of that alignment ~ whether being intimate with yourself or another. In that moment of intention, Spirit comes in.

The same is true with emotional or mental intimacy. All other dimensions of the self must be present and in alignment to share yourself with another. It is important to understand that when I say share yourself, I don't mean only physically. You can share yourself emotionally, mentally, and spiritually without engaging in a physical act. You can also be physically intimate with someone just by holding hands and being present and aligned on all levels.

Setting an intention to be present is another powerful way to experience me. If you set an intention to be intimate, then you are asking all parts of yourself to align and open:

Intention ~ Opening ~ Alignment ~ Intimacy

S: I hear what you are saying, but what if some parts still want to hide? What if I am not ready to see them myself, let alone share them with others?

I: More great questions. When your intention is to be
      intimate, part of that intimacy is open, honest
      compassionate, loving communication. It's the willingness to
      say, "Part of me is hiding. Part of me is scared to come
      forward..." instead of pretending that you are fully there.
      As soon as you are able to open up the channels and be
      honest about where you are, you are creating me, Intimacy.

      Once the honest dialogue begins and I am created, one
      never knows what can happen. Often you will see that
      those parts that were afraid the first time are not afraid the
      next. Sometimes those parts even come forward just in the
      moment of honestly communicating where you are.

S: So, it seems that you are really about showing up with
      myself and honestly communicating about where I am in any
      given moment. You are about creating a safe space for me
      to explore all of me ~ in love, kindness, gentleness. In
      compassion and celebration! Once I am able to do that
      with myself, I can set the intention to practice it with others.

I: Yes, exactly. I am always available to you if you are willing to
      be present and open about who and where you are at any
      given moment. It's when you try to hide yourself or "fake it"
      that you lose yourself. I have no expectations, no rules, and
      there is no right way to experience me. I am not about being
      perfect or powerful or beautiful or sexy. I am about being

honest. Even when you are feeling low or sad or miserable, I am about showing up that way and trusting whatever comes forward from that place in relationship to yourself and to others.

S: Wow! Not so easy to do.

I: Ah, Child. It is easier than you think. Personally, I feel it's a lot more work to hide behind a mask than to be who you are. People work very hard to live behind different masks so they don't have to show themselves for fear of not really being seen or of not being enough. The judgments run the gamut. The work begins when they can see and accept all of who they are and are willing to share that with others.

S: But it's scary.

I: Yes, sometimes it is. There is an opportunity in sharing the fear and trusting that whatever happens, you are loved. That is the beginning.

S: What if someone makes fun of me?

I: That is why I say it is so important to form an intimate relationship with yourself before you attempt to do so with others. When you love and accept yourself,

a) you will want to share yourself with others,

b) you will seek out those you can share yourself with,

c) you will love yourself no matter what, and

d) you will create intimacy with Spirit.

S: Why are people so afraid of you?

I: Because they are afraid to look at themselves, or they think they don't know how. They are riddled with so many judgments about themselves. It is a process. That is why I say setting intentions to begin is extremely potent. I am one of the greatest gifts you can give yourself and others. It takes time ~ step by step. For many, it means putting down the masks one at a time and being loving and patient with themselves as they go.

Know that you have endless amounts of support from Spirit. As you begin to peel back the layers, Spirit meets you with love and encouragement to help light the way. Experiencing me with yourself is like standing naked in front of God/Spirit and saying "Here I am." It means realizing that Spirit sees you and all that you are and loves you ~ all of you ~ no matter what.

S: If Spirit loves me no matter what, I can learn to love myself no matter what. I can learn to love others and let them in to love me, too!

Compassion

Who is here today surrounding me? The sky is gray. It's a rainy day, and my tears seem to be flowing with the rain. These are tears of sorrow. That is clear to me. But the feeling that comes with them or blankets them is the feeling I get when I feel someone else's sadness or pain. It's a mixture of sorrow and love and that feels like compassion ~ the ability to love someone through the sorrow. In this instance, I am loving myself through my own sorrow. It has been a tough week, filled with joy and laughter, yet combined with heartache, anger, and pain. Now, here you are. I can feel that you have something to say. Please, sit down. I am grateful for your presence. Let's talk.

C: Thank you for your willingness to sit with me today. Thank you for opening your heart to me today, for it is in your heart that I wish to be present with you. You have gone through a lot and worked through a lot this week. You have dug down deep inside yourself, shone a light in some dark places. My sense is that it has been hard to bear.

S: What has been hard to bear is not so much the memories, but how I speak them ~ how much anger there is inside and how judgmental I am toward myself for how I bring these memories forward.

C: I believe that's where I come in. It is difficult to feel compassion for others when you are not willing to allow it into your life for yourself. You have been very hesitant to allow me in to comfort you. Why do you think that is so?

S: I don't feel deserving of compassion. I don't know how to be gentle and loving toward myself when I'm in a place of hurt. I almost feel that if I inflict pain on someone, I deserve to feel the same pain. Intellectually, I understand that I'm not responsible for the pain of others, but if we are all interconnected and they feel pain, I feel it, too. I'm sensitive to it especially if it's been inflicted by my actions.

I need to be loved right now because I don't feel loveable. I feel ugly and mean. I feel lost. I feel alone and am looking for someone to embrace me in love. Here and now, you are that someone. I want to be held by you. I want to allow the energy of you in to wash all this stuff away.

C: Child, you do tend to harden yourself towards love ~ love from the people who surround you. Why is that?

S: Such a good question. What comes up is that I feel I don't deserve it.

C: But why?

S: Because I feel like I've hurt many people. I feel like I'm a mean, hard person. I feel like I'm selective in whom I love as opposed to letting my love flow freely. I'm not even sure I understand or know love in its purest sense.

C: I don't believe that to be true. I know that you have experienced love ~ the essence of love ~ and I also know you give it to others, but don't allow it into you.

S: I send love out, but I don't really open to receive it. I'm too busy sending it out. I give, but again I give it selectively. Therefore, I receive it selectively, too. I guess it's also hard because love isn't something I feel I can or should have to ask for... I shut it out so much. That's a very painful realization. The truth is that I can't experience it if I don't open to it and I can't give it if I can't experience it.

C: Opening your heart to me and allowing me into you is a very important step. I acknowledge you for taking it and encourage you to acknowledge yourself for that as well.

S: I do. I'm so grateful that I took the time to open to you and to allow you in. I so desperately need you. How do people see me as such a loving Being when I don't feel that way about myself? I don't believe them because I don't experience it unless I'm in my spiritual community. Why is that?

C: You are all surrounded and supported by Spirit. This field helps you see each other as you truly are. You, yourself, feed off of this love and see yourself as part of the whole. I know there are other times in your life when you feel it, too. It's just when you are in the place you are now that you tend to feel that you always live from this place. You and I both know better. Sometimes, when you are stuck in the mire, it's hard to gain altitude and see things from a higher perspective.

S: Yes, when I'm down, I tend to polarize and see everything about myself from this place of despair. Thank you for reflecting that to me.

C: The truth is...

S: The truth is that I am multifaceted and at this moment, I am seeing myself and my life through my judgmental filter.

C: But remember what Judgment spoke to you about?

S: Yes, he helps me discern the truth. The reality is, when I'm in a certain place or surrounded by a certain emotion, I see my whole life through that filter. It's a skewed perspective. That's what I'm doing here. It's important for me to remember that otherwise it's easy to go into "poor me" mode. Thank you for helping me clarify that.

What is coming forward now is that when I'm in a place of strength or clarity, I don't make room for you. I was able to let you in when I was in a vulnerable, emotional place. Why is that?

C: That's a good question. I operate on the heart level. When your heart is open, you allow me in. When you move into your head to gain clarity, you move out of your heart and into a mental or intellectual state. I don't function there. The idea for you then is to be able to align the two so you can gain clarity and have your heart open, so that the heart and the head are functioning together.

S: I see what you mean. I can feel when I shift out of my heart place and into a mental place. It usually happens when I can't access my emotions. Is it possible to align the two?

C: It is possible to live from your heart space and interact with yourself and others from that place. The mind is a very valuable part of your existence. However, it's not a place through which you learn your lessons. Lessons are truly learned when love and compassion are applied to the experience. In other words, it's not enough to understand something mentally; it is crucial to your growth that you embrace it from your heart.

Alignment comes when the heart embraces what the mind understands. That isn't always easy to do. Like now, we are speaking to each other from a mind space, whereas we began our conversation from a heart place.

S: The difference is clear and palpable. How do we get back to the heart space?

C: Close your eyes. Put your hand over your heart. Set the intention to go into your heart and see what happens.

S: Yes. Now I feel you in a different way. I get an image of a heart embracing my brain. I am embraced by you and no conversation is necessary.

C: The next time, when you are in a mental place, try doing the same thing and see where that takes you. Observe how you handle yourself and others from there.

S: I will.. (Sigh).

C: You are getting it. You are piecing the puzzle together. It's a process and you are asking the questions and opening to the learnings. There is a lot to be said for your desire to grow. It's an honor to be a part of your process.

S: Thank you. It's hard and beautiful at the same time. I am grateful for your presence today. I really opened myself to feel you. You are warm and loving and cozy. Heart and Mind, Mind and Heart, Heart Space. Let my heart do the talking. Let my heart lead me on. Thank you. I am grateful for this visit. I am grateful that I opened to your loving.

Expectation

It's my birthday today. I took my boys to school and didn't hear them say anything to me about it. Oh, that's when you jumped right into the picture in no time at all. The expectations started coming and I heard myself say to them "How would you feel on your birthday if I didn't say 'Happy Birthday' to you...?" As soon as those words emerged from my mouth, I knew you had arrived.

When I came home to my three-year-old son singing "Happy Birthday" to me, I smiled inside. It was in the shower that I realized I had an opportunity to talk to you. So, here I am, ready and willing.

S: Hello there.

E: Hello back.

S: I kind of figured out what's behind your visit.

E: Do tell!

S: Well, I realized that somewhere inside, I was coupling my kids' love for me with their "doing" something to recognize my birthday. How ridiculous is that?! I know my kids love me.

E: That's true. They do love you and because they love you, you expected that they would honor you by expressing that somehow.

S: Yes, I guess so. But I figured out quickly today that if I honor and celebrate myself, then everything else is just icing on the cake.

E: Why do you think you allow me in as often as you do?

S: I don't know that I allow you in, but you are around. Why do you come around so much? Tell me about yourself.

E: I am the mirror of how you believe things are supposed to be. You have been raised in such a culture that takes pride in defining right from wrong, a culture with traditions and rituals that are "supposed" to be followed. I merely hold up the reflection of those things for you to examine. It is you who chooses whether or not you want to or need to define yourself through them.

A part of you does, and therefore holds the expectation that things "ought to be" a certain way. Then you define yourself and your surroundings by that. There is another part of you that knows better, that knows that how you hold yourself, no matter what is around you, is what counts.

S: I hear you clearly. I never thought of a birthday that way before.

E: It's not the birthday as much as the rituals or the "shoulds" of how you are celebrated on your birthday.

S: Isn't it nice or important to have both?

E: Yes. It is nice to have both. To feel the love that others have for you is a gift.

S: Yes, it's a gift, a heartfelt one at that. Gifts are given when they are given, not because it's a birthday or a celebration. A gift can be given just because. The expectation of it takes away the value and takes away the spontaneity. If I hold an expectation, I lose being open to receive. Having an expectation blocks receiving something in a different way. When I expect something, I open myself to disappointment and then, I might not see the gift when it comes in its own way.

E: There is another reason why I am with you as often as I am.

S: The crux of it is that when I expect things, I give away my power. I get totally caught up in needing to be validated for what I do.

E: Tell me more.

S: A few days ago, a friend asked me to design a flier for him. I was happy to do so. I created something great and called to tell him how excited I was and that it was done. I asked him to check it out and call me back. He hasn't called and I'm not sure if he's even opened it or not. I had an expectation that he should have called me to acknowledge the work I did for him, and he didn't.

E: Did you do it so he'd acknowledge you or because you wanted to help?

S: I did it because I wanted to help and it was totally heartfelt. I was just so excited about what I'd done. I wanted him to share in the excitement.

E: I really hear how proud of your work you were. What puzzles me is why you diminished your own excitement by waiting to hear from him. Why was it not enough that you did what you said you would do and were proud of the result?

S: These are good questions. This goes deep for me. It's not enough that I liked what I made for him. I needed him to like it. I needed him to validate me and acknowledge my work.

E: Why? If he did or didn't, was that a reflection of you?

S: No.

E: Let's try this. I, more often than not, lead to disappointment. Why? Because when you place the energy of me on
something or someone, you are anticipating a future event
rather than just being present in the moment. You take
yourself out of the flow and into a place of needing to know.
It's another form of wanting to control the outcome, instead
of just allowing things to play out as they will. In doing so,
you end up making certain assumptions about yourself and
the situation. When I'm around, it's a signal that you are not
being present and flowing, but needing to know and control.
Give it up to God. Do you hear me?

S: Yes, I do. If I choose to do something, I can choose to do it
lovingly, without strings attached. It's important for me to
look at this. If I have strings attached, I'm setting myself up
for disappointment because the outcome is dependent on
others who may or may not see things the same way I do. It
seems that the heart of the matter is me not believing in
myself or my own work enough, so that I look to others to
validate and acknowledge me. If they do, great and if they
don't, I fall into upset. I'm giving my power away, not only in
that moment but until I get the approval or disproval from
others.

E: Exactly. And all that time in between is spent in upset and
in self-doubt.

S: What you're saying, then, is to choose to do the work with no attachment, praise myself for it, and then let go. But there's still a voice that says, "Well, if I took the time to do it, he should take the time to look at it and acknowledge it one way or another."

E: I hear that voice loud and clear. Did that part of you do it for the response or do it out of the kindness of helping another? It seems that part of you needs to hear the acknowledgement from yourself!

S: Yes, I get that.

E: As with the other scenario involving your children, you expected things to happen a certain way and when they did not, it threw you off balance.

S: That is true. It is the whole control versus flow concept I've been working on. You are a form of control. Doing something and letting it go keeps me in the flow and allows the miracles to unfold. That is the other part, isn't it? When I hold expectations over people or situations, I don't allow for miraculous events to unfold. I am so busy looking for what I expect that I miss everything else around it! I get focused on the minutiae instead of the opportunity.

E: That's it! When I'm around, you have the opportunity to look at what you are trying to control. Then take it one step further, and see if you can let it go and flow with what is unknown.

S: I can set an intention to flow when I sense the need to control. That takes a load off! Thank you.

E: You are most welcome. Imagine a gentle wind blowing. Things that are stuck in control, in expectation, hunker down and don't budge. They want to know it all and want things to stay the same. Things that are free and flowing are carried by that wind on a miraculous, unfolding journey. Which would you rather choose?

Joy

Joy came flitting in today like a 4th of July sparkler, lighting up my heart as it danced and crackled. That's the feeling I have around me today. What would a life lived through joy look like? Would it sparkle and shine? Would it feel magical and uplifting? Would it be possible to really allow it in and to invite it to stay, taking up permanent residence in my heart? I'd like to know. What is it about this feeling that we love, that we yearn for? What really happens inside when Joy comes to visit? I want to know and here's my opportunity to find out.

S: Joy, oh great and delicious energy that you are, please come sit with me. Please come teach me about yourself.

J: It would be my pleasure. Thank you for opening yourself up to me.

S: You have this effervescent feel to you, radiant yet soft. You glitter in the light of the sun. Can you tell me about yourself and why I feel so good when you are around?

J: When I'm around, your heart is open to possibilities. You see the world through your heart rather than through your thoughts or your mind. You don't filter things but allow the simple beauty of them into you. You open your entire body to me and that's why you often feel a tingle from your head to your toes. I am part of your authentic self. When I'm around, the glasses through which you normally see come off. Your heart knows joy, love, compassion, and gratitude. Your true nature dances at its freedom.

You see, I am not something that exists outside of you. I am you at your core. In this moment, you have removed the walls and the filters that often keep me tucked away inside. I am always there. Interesting how you asked at the beginning if I could find a way to "take up permanent residence in your heart." The truth is that I am already there. I am your birthright. How do you think you acted differently today to allow me to shine through from within?

S: I connected with my angels. I allowed myself to be embraced and loved by them. I listened to their messages of love and encouragement and you were right there as a part of them, a part of me, and a part of the entire experience.

J: The "me" in you connected with the "me" in All That Is.

S: Yes. I experienced a sense of oneness. Whenever I have that experience, it brings me great joy. But it seems to happen so infrequently. How do I connect with you more often?

J: How do you think?

S: By opening my heart and connecting with All That Is.

J: Yes, those are wonderful ways. However, experiencing me also comes from surrender and trust, surrender to where you are on your journey and trust in who you are. You have had several dialogues with other visitors like Expectation where you found out about control. Control functions on a lower frequency of energy. Joy, Love, Gratitude, and Compassion function on much higher frequencies.

When you get caught up in the "have tos" and the "shoulds," the expectation, the judgment, the "not enough" energies, you are functioning from a much lower frequency. There is no room for me to be there. However, when you surrender to the flow and trust in yourself, in your angels, in Spirit, you raise your vibration and open up to energies that function at higher frequencies. You literally lift yourself up.

S: The reason people want to "bottle you up" is that they need you when they are in the lower frequencies. How do we jump from lower to higher in order to reach you?

J: Great question. I can't change my frequency to move into a lower one, but *you* can shift into a higher one. That's where awareness and choice give you freedom. If you are aware that you are vibrating in a lower frequency, you can ask for help. I'm not saying it's an easy shift. Sometimes it takes a while, especially when you are not willing to give up your perspective or your need to be right.

S: You're saying that when I'm allowing a lower frequency to consume my energy and I bring my awareness to it, I can choose to raise my vibration. I can choose to let you in by shifting up into you?!

J: Yes, with some work. It's about choice. You can choose to stay where you are, or you can choose to lift up. For example, the other day, you were upset with your husband. You stayed in that mood for a while and then I observed you shift into joy. What happened for you there?

S: I realized I was mad and decided I didn't want to stay there. It didn't feel good. All too often, I stay there too long. So, I made a choice. It wasn't easy because I had to get all my parts in alignment, but I decided that being together was more important than being "right" or "wrong." I giggled, walked over to him, put my arms around him, and said, "I don't want to be angry." I made a conscious choice, which resulted in us being embraced by joy and laughter.

J: Excellent! You see how it's possible. You said a very important thing about conscious choice. Being aware brings your consciousness to a situation that then allows you to stay there or move out.

When you choose to exist or spend time in a higher frequency, the possibility of a love cycle is created:

Joy -> Gratitude -> Love -> Joy

Remember, you are a Divine Being having a human experience. Having human experiences also brings you down into different energies, which is part of your learning. As you evolve, you learn how to raise yourself back up or even back into your authentic self's nature and live from there. Again, it's so important to remember that when you're down, you keep yourself there through judgment, criticism, expectation, etc. This places you in a cycle of pain and despair. Consciousness and choice around that will free you.

S: So, I need to be willing to open the door and choose to stay at higher frequencies in order to experience you. You never leave. I shift in and out of you depending upon which cycle I am running through.

J: That is true. I am always here. Today, you were in a high enough frequency to recognize I was around. That is what brought us together.

S: I'm so grateful. Thank you so much.

J: No need to thank me. Acknowledge yourself for your choice. Remember, you are never alone. Even when you are in a lower energy, your angels are around to help, as is Spirit. Most important, remember that I, Joy, am inside your heart ALWAYS. I am never lost to you. I exist inside and can be magnified by joy in others, as well as by joy in connecting with Spirit.

Serenity

I'm sitting in my backyard with the sun kissing my face and the soft wind stroking my skin. I feel so blessed, so peaceful. This is my time; time for me away from all the rest of the world. My kids are at school, my husband is at work, and I am taking advantage of it. Most of the time, I keep myself busy shopping, doing homework, volunteering, driving the kids here and there, etc. I seldom allow myself to be in nature, to feel her blessings and allow peace to embrace me from within. In this moment, even with the trash trucks off in the distance and my animals whining for attention, I am focusing on me.

I often ask for restoration to come through sleep, but sitting here, I realize that restoration also comes through honoring these moments of quiet. It is important that I give myself permission to take time out for me. I am worthy of opening to the stillness that is within and around me. In this quiet time of restoration, my breath flows more naturally, and I realize that if I don't take care of myself, then I can't take care of others. This seems to be one of my hard knock life lessons!

Who is it that sits with me today as I enjoy this time? I feel something around me. Can you share yourself with me?

Ser: My name is Serenity. I bring with me the peace you feel inside yourself when you choose to stop and let me in. You have chosen to stop participating in the hectic day-to-day life that surrounds you and take a break for yourself.

S: What is so important about this idea of restoration? I thought it came through sleep and that allowed me to keep going. But sleep is restorative for my body only. I am more than my body and this sense of restoration and the serenity it brings with it fuels my heart. It feeds my soul. It is imperative to my well-being.

Ser: Your words are wise. You live in a society that praises speed and accomplishment, a society that doesn't quite understand the benefits and the great need for restoration, peace, and serenity. Relaxation is frowned upon as time wasted, as selfish. But for those who truly understand the importance of restoration and peace, therein lies the jewel.

S: What do you mean?

Ser: You were a part of the masses in terms of your thinking and
     actions until a while ago. You lived your life in a fast-paced,
     keep busy, 'don't stop until you drop' mode, for that is what
     you were taught. Yet inside, there was a part of you
     yearning for rest, for peace, for contemplation. Now that
     you have tasted the magic of the stillness, you have a desire
     to share this discovery and the wisdom within it with others.

S: I realize that people need to discover this on their own.
     However, many seem to be uncomfortable with this peace
     and quiet, and therefore avoid it.

Ser: Yes, that is true for several reasons. Some see it as selfish
     and some don't like what comes forward for them in the
     peace. Many people think they find restoration in doing
     things that please them, such as playing sports, dancing,
     painting, etc. While these things may be very nurturing, they
     are different than just being with oneself in the quiet of
     one's heart.

     This sense of quiet opens the heart and allows truth to
     surface. For many, this is very uncomfortable and what they
     tend to do is judge themselves rather than love themselves.
     They see where they could make changes in their lives, but
     it seems too hard to make these changes. They think it's

easier to stay in the doing, rather than "being." In the long run, the peace that needs to come forward is expressed in different ways, through illness, arthritis, injuries, etc. Often, these experiences get the person to slow down and look inside in an effort to make different choices.

S: I find it hard to believe that this is all in service to getting a person to sit quietly, to restore. What is it we are trying to restore?

Ser: Balance.

S: What do you mean by that?

Ser: Equilibrium of heart space and mind space, bringing the two parts into balance. People live in mind space 90 – 95% of the time. The body can only support that for so long.

S: How so the body? The body is the machine. Isn't it the soul that seeks love and peace? What part of us really needs this sense of restoration?

Ser: The soul doesn't *seek* love and peace, It *IS* love and peace. You see, when the body takes a break, it allows the soul time to soar. The soul has an ability to regenerate every cell inside the body when it connects to All That Is. It brings forward light, healing, love, and wisdom. When you are so busy "doing," there is no space for wisdom and grace to come forward.

When you stop, you create a space for them. Most of the time, it is in this quiet space that people receive messages, come up with solutions to problems they've encountered during the day, have epiphanies, etc. This experience is what I refer to as Grace. Grace can only be felt in the space where you surrender to Being, rather than getting caught up in the "doing."

S: I hear you. I find serenity when I take a break from the "doing." In this place, I experience my Being, my connection to All That Is. This connection brings forward restoration and regeneration.

Ser: Exactly. The sense of serenity and restoration promotes wholeness and well being. It reminds you of who you truly are. From this place, you are ready to move onward and upward on your journey.

S: God Bless You. Peace be still.

Resistance

This morning I am here with Resistance. I did not want to get out of bed and go to my exercise class. I kept hitting the snooze button over and over until it was almost too late to go. Then I sat and thought about it. I'm resisting. I don't feel like going but I'm really giving myself permission not to go. There was no Should voice, which is a relief and a measure of growth. It was simply a matter of choice.

Then, I thought about my Pilates class and the emphasis placed on physical resistance. The more resistance I use, the stronger my muscles get. I use enough to make me work harder but not so much that I stop myself because I can't push through it. These thoughts make me wonder what role Resistance plays in my life? How does it serve me? When does it help me grow stronger, and when do I allow it to stop me completely?

R: I'm so glad you brought these questions forward. You make such an important point about me.

S: Hello there. You just kind of popped right in.

R: Yes, I did. I've been hanging around since this morning wondering if you were going to pursue your line of thought.

S: So here we are.

R: So here we are.

S: Can you tell me more about yourself?

R: Sure. What would you like to know?

S: Well, when I am exercising, I am bringing you forward to help me focus and work my muscles. Sometimes I feel you when I'm facing a challenge or a choice. Is there a difference between when I call you in during exercise and when I feel resistant about moving in a certain direction?

R: There is a difference between the two. In the first example, you and I are working together. You call my energy forward to help push you as far and as hard as you can go to get physically stronger. You determine the level of resistance you want to use. In the other case, I am coming forward to help you in much the same way, to grow. You didn't actively or consciously engage me. You didn't call me saying,

"Resistance, come push me into an uncomfortable place so I can grow." However, your heart and soul did.

S: What do you mean, my heart and soul did?

R: You have come here to grow, to evolve. If your life always stays the same, there is no room for growth. It is your soul's nature to grow and it is my job to push you into an experience that will cultivate growth and learning. Your mind and your ego are complacent when things stay the same, when they are known. Your soul says, "OK, there is an opportunity here. It's time to make a change." In the natural order of things, change happens all the time. Often, when you are at the helm of the change, or "in control" of it, you do it without resistance. When change comes in the back door, many people tend to go into resistance about it. People tend to resist what is foreign to them. It seems scary. It seems much easier to keep things as they are.

S: What I just realized is that when I exercise, I want my body to grow stronger so I consciously call you forward. In a way, I perceive that I am in control. However, when you show up without me having chosen you, I get frustrated and often scared, as if I don't know what is going on or am no longer in control.

R: That is very true. I am linked with fear in the consciousness of many. Fear of the unknown goes hand in hand with control, stubbornness, and the notion that "no one can make me do this." The need to control comes from the ego space. The ego wants to be the decision-maker and is suspicious of things that are different. The soul knows that growth and change are its natural state and therefore seeks them out.

S: I guess the question then becomes: "How do you affect the mind in this type of situation?"

R: I act like a force field pushing up against you.

S: The more I think about it, the more I realize how prevalent the concept of you is in our vocabulary. I talk about resistance in terms of strengthening muscles. I say "my resistance is low" when my body is ill; I become resistant to a drug or an illness; I resist advances by not allowing myself to feel or embrace the feelings others have for me, etc. In a way, you are important on both ends of the spectrum. I need you to help build my muscles and grow. I need you to help me fight off disease and illness in the body, but I push up against you when it appears you are taking me out of my comfort zone.

R: Seems tricky, doesn't it? You want me around when it appears I'm helping you, but push up against me when I make you uncomfortable.

S: Aha! I just got it. I am always pushing up against you. You are a field of energy that comes in and creates a safe place for me to do just that. In my body, when I am sick, the illness has to push up against me. When I am exercising, I encourage my muscles to push up against you. When change needs to happen in my life, you are there again, providing an opportunity for me to examine it all, to look at where I am and where I am being asked to go.

By pushing up against something, I have an opportunity to grow. Sometimes, I push to exhaustion. Sometimes, as soon as I feel you there, I give up and stay curled in a ball. Sometimes, I surrender to whatever it is that brings forward the change. You are just the wall of energy. How I hold what I want in my consciousness determines how hard or impenetrable you are. If I choose to fight tooth and nail to stay the same, you become as hard as brick. If I choose to question you and ask why you have come forward, you are much more malleable and easier to penetrate.

When the body is ill, it doesn't have the strength inside to hold up an impenetrable wall, so the resistance is weak, just as when I feel resistant to a situation. The degree to which I am resisting is determined by me, by the relationship between my mind/ego and my heart/soul in regard to the choice at hand.

R: Wow, Sabrina! You're really getting it all on your own. The degree to which the heart and the mind can communicate about things also can determine the degree of resistance present. The key to what you said is that you, and you alone, determine the strength of the resistance. I am neither positive nor negative. I am energy here to serve your growth and evolution.

This morning, when you were resisting going to class and you said that you didn't hear any "should" voice, you were comfortable making your decision and didn't need to bump up against too much energy.

I encourage you to remember that even when you resist something strongly, you are given an opportunity to ask why you feel the need to be in control and ask what it is that you are afraid of in the situation. Are you afraid of self-judgment? Are you concerned with what others will say? Are you filled with doubt about something that feels right to you? Are you pushing yourself to do something that isn't in your best interest? All of these questions are things to think about when you bring me into your consciousness.

S: Thank you so much for your presence today and for holding space for me to uncover your depth and your meaning. I truly appreciate it.

R: My pleasure. You did most of the work here today.

S: Yes, I did, but your energy around me was aiding the process.

Earth Girl / Soul Self

Who am I? I have been asking this question forever, it seems. Who am I? I ask again as I sit here turning it over and over in my mind. As I sit here meditating, I hear two voices very present with me. One voice says, "Go left," the other, "Go right." One voice is gentle and loving; the other is controlling and judgmental. Which one do I listen to? Who is guiding me? Who is living this life here? It seems so confusing at times. Sometimes, I want to escape to a place inside that has no voice at all and just be. I know that if I choose to open a dialogue, I have a chance to gain more clarity. Truthfully, I recognize these voices. They are those of Earth Girl, who is my mind, my ego, and Soul Self, the voice of my heart.

SS: Who are you, Earth Girl?

EG: What do you mean, who am I? I am you, silly.

SS: Well, you may be a part of me, but you are not the whole of me.

EG: What are you talking about? I am you. You live here, you are me. Maybe I need to ask you who you are?

SS: I'm your Soul Self. I reside in your heart center.

EG: Oh, so you're the one who keeps coming in and changing things so they move in a different direction. You see things from a different perspective, which disconnects me from what I believe to be true.

SS: Is that what it feels like to you when I'm around?

EG: Yes. You think you run the show and you do things very differently, but it's my show. Who are you to be interfering?

SS: I hear how upset you are with me. What is it about me that upsets you?

EG: Well, I don't understand you and when you are around, it's like I don't exist. Everything I've worked so hard to create seems to be wrong or unimportant. When you come in, it's all about love, love, love. I don't believe that all the time. There's a lot of shit to deal with in this world.

Half of the stuff you say, I don't believe. It's all very confusing and there doesn't seem to be room for both of us here in this body.

SS: Well, there is a lot of validity to what you say. I am about love, joy, and peace. I am about seeing and living from a different perspective, but I need you. I respect you, and I honor your role here.

EG: You do? Then why do you come in and negate all the things I say and do?

SS: I offer a different perspective. Sometimes what you say and do only keeps Sabrina down. You rule her world through desire and control and negativity.

EG: What is wrong with that?

SS: It's not that anything is wrong with that. You are entitled to all of your experiences and ways of being. It's just that I offer up a different way, a more loving, compassionate way to look at those experiences.

EG: But when she listens to you, I am gone. She doesn't listen to me and I don't like that. She's supposed to listen to me.

SS: Sounds like it is really important for you to be in charge.

EG: It is.

SS: Does it feel like if you're not in charge, you're not worth anything?

101

EG: Yes. When you're in charge, then I have no job. That's why I resist you.

SS: Well, how would you propose we co-exist?

EG: Everything goes through me.

SS: Is it that you want what you perceive to be the power?

EG: Yes, I do.

SS: I don't need or want power.

EG: How do you get her to listen to you? How do you pull her away from me?

SS: I don't pull her. She has free will. Whereas it's important for you to believe that you are running the show, she really is. She really has the choice of who she's listening to, you or me.

EG: I am going to keep her busy so that she doesn't have time to listen to you.

SS: I think you are doing a great job with her.

EG: You do? Then why can't you just go away?

SS: I can't go away because I am the part of her that connects her to Spirit and to all other life forms. You see, Earth Girl, you and I both play very important roles here in this body of Sabrina. You are her Earthly guide. You help her

navigate through her experiences here on this planet. You
keep her safe. You help her learn. You give her the ability
to feel, touch, smell, taste, and see. You are a beautiful
vehicle for her and for me, and I appreciate you deeply.
You are her connection to this beautiful planet.

I am her sixth sense, her connection to Spirit and the
essence that exists in all things. It is actually very important
for the two of us to work together. Something inside me
tells me that your hunger for power and your need to be in
charge is because you feel threatened by me. There is no
need for that. I am not trying to take anything away from
you. In fact, I have been trying to connect with you. I have
been trying to get your attention so that we could have this
conversation and find a way to work together that benefits
us all.

EG: I was afraid that I wouldn't exist if I let you "take over." The
truth is, I always feel good when you are around.

SS: In my way of experiencing things, there is no such thing as
taking over. For me, it's about creating a sense of
community and working together for the highest good. I
know that you want the best for Sabrina and this life she
has here. I know that you feel your job is to protect her from
harm and that often, you see change as scary or harmful.

But I assure you that what you want and what I am about is what is best for her.

EG: I didn't realize that. I guess because I'm so into the power thing, I thought you were as well, and felt as if I had to defend it with all I have. Defending my power meant that I was in charge of everything and I got really frustrated when I would yell and scream and she'd still listen to you.

SS: You are very good at yelling and screaming. You are very good at a lot of things, but if we find a way to work together, think of all the great things we could learn and experience.

EG: But how do you suppose we can work together?

SS: Well, as I said, you have a very important role of guiding and navigating on this earthly plane, while I work on many other levels. Instead of being afraid of what you don't know, you can check in with me about it. Now that you know I have no intention of hurting you ~ or her ~ we can talk things over. I can learn from you, and you can learn from me. How does that sound?

EG: I'd like to try. Maybe you could give me an example of something that would help me understand what you are talking about.

SS: Ok. Let's see. Let's say I have a message for Sabrina that is coming from nature. I send her a message through her heart or intuition that she needs to go on a hike or be outside somehow. It is your job to get her there. It is up to you to get her dressed and fed and out the door. It is your job to help her walk and to use your eyes to help her see. I may continue to send messages your way about where I want you to go and, if you trust me, then it will be a magical experience for all of us.

EG: I get it. But it sounds like you are running the show, and I am following your directions.

SS: Fair enough. The need to be the leader is not what feeds me, but I see that it's important to you. When you crave something, or want to do something like eat a cupcake or go run on the beach, I will love you through that experience and celebrate your desire.

EG: What if you don't agree with what I want to do?

SS: Remember, it is about communication. Sometimes, I may get a sense that there is danger ahead. In that case, I would send you a signal about that. It is up to you to listen or not. The truth is, Earth Girl, you are running the show down there. It is my job to help steer you. That is why it would be so amazing if we could work together. Think of the possibilities. I encourage you to check in with me when you feel sad or unimportant. My job is to listen to you with my whole heart and send you the love and support you need, no matter what!!

EG: I think we could make a great team. I am so glad we had this conversation and look forward to working together to co-create an amazing journey ahead.

SS: You are surrounded by love, Earth Girl. You are blessed by Spirit and your very being is celebrated by the angels and the people who surround you.

Acceptance

Each morning, I set a clear intention to be more accepting of myself and others. Today, as I was meditating on acceptance, the Serenity Prayer came floating into my consciousness. The prayer ~ *God grant me the serenity to accept the things I cannot change; the courage to change the things I can; and the wisdom to know the difference* ~ has touched my heart and continues to do so every time I read or hear it. My life lesson, and I do believe the life lesson of all of us, is Acceptance. We live in a world that is filled with mystery, chaos, and sadness, but also a world filled with miracles, beauty, and joy. Our world is multifaceted.

As I reflect on this prayer, I realize that Acceptance is about flowing. Acceptance, or the wisdom to understand the difference between the things we can and cannot change, is about trusting that something bigger than ourselves is at play here.

I am learning to accept rather than judge because there is a Divine Plan at hand that I don't necessarily understand. The need to understand often comes with the desire to control. If I understand why something is happening, then I can figure out how to change it, how to stop if from happening to me, or how to bring it forward in my life.

I hear a voice come in from nearby:

A: You have such wisdom to share with others, Sabrina.

S: I'm glad you think so. I am so fascinated by you. I know deep down how beautiful and fulfilling a life lived in acceptance and grace would be and I yearn for that.

A: Child of Grace, your heart's desire to find me is admirable, and I support you in your journey to find that peace within yourself. Just as Compassion and Joy are innate parts of you, so am I.

S: You feel like the hardest one to live by. Life seems so unfair, so unbalanced, most of the time. I know there is much beauty and many miracles around, but it seems I tend to focus on the Chaos and Sadness because they are so much more prominent. That is hard to accept. Sometimes I feel that if I accept things, I'm just "allowing" them or not doing anything to help things get better.

A: Where in your consciousness did I get paired with non-action?

S: I don't know. Those thoughts came forward as I was speaking with you.

A: Nowhere do I define myself as complacent or non-active. I am actually a very powerful energy. I am an energy that sheds light over this world. My "M.O.," if you will, is to come from deep down inside your authentic self and raise you up to gain a higher perspective. When you see things from that vantage point, you see the many different aspects at play. You may not understand all that you see, but you trust that *all is as it is*. Judging, fearing, or rejecting things, people, or ways of being that you don't like do not serve you.

I often witness that people don't want to accept the things they don't understand. They feel threatened by them because they feel out of control. Here, it is important to remember and understand the Serenity Prayer. There are things that can be changed; there are things that can't. Learning to accept both situations is wise and important.

S: But, it seems that if I accept, then I agree or condone. If I accept, then I am not willing to fight for my beliefs. If I accept, then I am wrong and you are right. If I accept, then I lose the battle...

A: Here is another perspective. If you accept, you are peaceful. If you accept, you bring more love and compassion to the world. If you accept, you are free and open to the miracles that may come forth from the situation. If you accept, you just might see a different point of view. If you accept, you flow with Spirit and get closer to unconditional love for yourself and others, no matter what they may say or do.

There are two sides to every coin, my Dear, just as there are two sides to every argument. You see life from your own unique perspective, through your own filters. These filters have been molded to fit only your set of eyes over the course of your life's experiences.

There are some who will choose to see life as dull, chaotic, and miserable, while others will see it as beautiful, miraculous, and peaceful. The array of perspectives is multifaceted. You can flow and accept, be compassionate, loving, and graceful. You can control and expect, be judgmental, get angry, and become agitated. Or, you fall somewhere in between.

I am not saying that one way is better than another. They are just different; they exist as polarities. Polarities are crucial to existence. Without one side, you wouldn't understand the other. You can learn and grow from experiencing both polarities. Acceptance has no labels, no boundaries, no lines that it crosses, no limitations. It is only when you label things as right and wrong that I get lost.

When God created, He/She didn't create with judgment, but with love. All things were created in love because God is love. I come in when you put down the labels, when you stop making things right and wrong, and embrace them for what they are: two sides of an experience.

S: I hear you, but it seems hard to teach acceptance when someone you love is hurt by another or when a country is devastated by atrocity.

A: Child, I never said it was easy. I come forward when you gain altitude and see life's experiences from a higher perspective. It is very difficult to accept sometimes, but therein lies the growth. My energy doesn't judge any thing, any person, or any process. I wait patiently.

Your soul knows me. I am a part of its core. Remembering that and teaching it to your mind, which is where the labels come from, is the challenge. Pay attention to how you feel in situations when you fight to control things. Seek first to accept, then to understand.

S: I realize that my heart or Soul Self is trying to teach this concept to Earth Girl, and Earth Girl is having a hard time getting it because she sees things as black or white. Acceptance is next to Godliness and we are Divine Beings, so our ability to accept is innate. It's getting that across to our Ego self....

A: Let's look at it this way. You live on Earth, which exists based upon a system of right and wrong. Even though God created polarities to gain a clearer understanding and integration of self, it was mankind that labeled them and created a system based on punishment and reward. God accepts that as part of your growth, as well as Earth's evolution. The mind, or Earth Girl, may label things as good or bad, right or wrong, but by communicating with the Soul Self, she learns to rise above and accept that things are what they are. Earth Girl learns to send love, light, and blessings.

S: Accepting means loving myself for where I am, loving others for where they are, and trusting that wherever that is, is perfect.

A: That is accurate.

S: You have so much wisdom and many, many teachings. It will take time to digest what we just covered. It is my intention to sit down with you again to gain further clarity around this life lesson. Thank you so much for teaching me about yourself today.

A: Blessings to you, Dear One, for your desire to grow and evolve and for seeking to understand the energy of the First Law of Spirit.

Motherhood

I awoke early this morning from a dream I was having about one of my sons. I can't remember exactly what we were doing together, but what woke me was the word "Motherhood." It wasn't part of the dream; it was a voice booming from within and from overhead. It was silent, yet as loud as loud could be. There was not doubt what it meant or why it was there. The Divine Mother (DM) was with me and she wanted me to get out of bed and write about Motherhood. So, here I am.

I am the mother of three amazing boys. I love being a mother even though it is the most challenging job in the universe. Before I became a mother, I thought it was the ultimate job. I couldn't wait and thought it would fulfill me completely. I had my children and kept waiting for the fulfillment. I am busy. I am loving. I am the teacher I have always wanted to be. I have healthy children. Yet, I still yearn for more. I yearn for time alone. I yearn for sleep. I yearn for peace.

My children have taught me about so many things. They live in the present and have reflected to me how much I live somewhere else, in the future, in the world of what could be or in the world of "if I just had a few more minutes to do this." I often shake my head, realizing that I'm missing out on the joy of what is happening in the Now.

They have taught me about authenticity. They have taught me about love and they have taught me about laughter. They have taught me about forgiveness and moving forward.

So, why am I writing? I constantly ponder what my job is really about.

I know that my sons are gifts from God. I know they chose me, as I chose them. I know that each one of them comes in with his own curriculum, his own life's work, and his own personality. I know that it is my job to love and support my children and to keep them safe from harm while they are on their journey. They are not mine, but they came here through me.

How do I love and support them and allow them to be, to explore, to engage in this life without curbing their freedom? How do I teach them without imposing my patterns on them? How do I nurture them and discipline them without stunting their growth?

How do I not take their actions personally? How do I do all of this and not lose myself to it?

I am a great mom, but often hard on myself for how I mother. I am constantly asking myself why I do the things I do or say the things I say like, "Don't go outside barefoot; it's cold…" when five minutes before, I had. Why is it OK for me, but not for them? Where is that line crossed?? Help.

DM: Oh, Sweet Mother. You have no idea what a good mom you are. You are so filled with love and your children know it in the core of their Beings.

S: I feel like I'm always saying, "No." I feel like I'm disciplining more than I want to or should be. I don't understand my job so much these days, especially as they are getting older.

DM: Yes, the job of a mother seems to be ever changing as your children grow and challenge life in many ways. You see, children are not challenging you as much as they are challenging life itself, wondering what it's all about. Wanting to know how far they can push and pull things. Life is like a science experiment to them, yet their science is different. They are not bound by the results; they are motivated by growth. They are curious, innocently curious about everything, including you and how you react to what they do

117

and say. You are their safety net. They know that you love them no matter what, therefore they know it is safe to test life around you, for you will catch them.

S: I get caught up in wanting my own time and finding that I get upset so easily, especially when it's chaotic here.

DM: Ah, but you've had your dialogue with Chaos already. And what did you find?

S: That taking care of myself is of the utmost importance, that trying to control Chaos only makes it worse, but flowing with what is happening and finding my center in it is imperative.

DM: That is true. Your children are here to explore. Think of them as founders of a new land, a new way of living, for to them, that is what this life is about, especially when they are young. The way you see things and live your life is a wonderful gift to share with them, but not meant for you to shove down their throats.

S: But I feel the need to protect them.

DM: From what?

S: That's a good question. From life experiences that aren't so positive. When they were younger, I wanted everything to be easy and wonderful. I wanted to keep them sheltered from the harshness "out there." In talking to other moms, I realized that struggle and adversity are just as much a part of life as happiness and joy. If I protect my children from the more challenging aspects of life, they won't be prepared for the "reality" of it when they grow up.

DM: I believe you already know that it is how you are with them when they go through the bumps in the road that is most important. Do you love them and support them? Do you listen to what they have to say? Or are you too busy talking? Are you too busy trying to live life for them?

S: When you asked that last question, I got that there is a fine line between living life for them and losing myself to them by constantly being there and doing things for them. As the Divine Mother, how do you participate in our lives? How can I be more like you in my own mothering?

DM: As the Divine Mother of all things, I witness life unfolding. I understand in my core that all that is happening around me is Divine! The struggle to bloom, which both flowers and people do, the laughter at being tickled, the love shared between two as they embrace, the hurt knee after a scuffle...I don't judge one as being more important than another. I don't judge behavior. I sit back and watch with love.

S: But I can't just sit back. I am responsible for them. It is my job to keep them safe. It seems I don't understand how to balance intervention and witnessing. I feel so exhausted from doing so much with them and for them.

DM: I sense your frustration with mothering. So much to do, so many tasks... Who creates that for you?

S: I do.

DM: So, maybe you need to ask yourself why have you created so much to DO in your life, and does all of that take away from your mothering or enhance it?! You see, you can act in a similar way that I am describing. A part of you knows when it is time to intervene and when it is time to sit back and observe, just like the ebb and flow of the ocean. You have that tide running through you. Be willing to listen to it. You are doing it. You are listening. You just don't realize it.

Remember, children are here to explore and discover. I don't take what they do personally, and I think mothers often do. My love has no judgment and no conditions. It sees when you fall and sends you more love to be able to deal with what is present for you. I am an energy that is part of your make-up. Just being aware of that will help you in those trying times.

S: I hear you, but the reality of it seems so different. You are above us, below us, around us, but you are not here, physically with us.

DM: That is an illusion, for what is truly real? That is a question worth asking yourself. What is it that truly matters here? What is it that you truly want to give your children, teach your children? Is it what material or physical world reality lives by, or is it a balance of understanding that physical world reality operates one way, while Spirit lives in acceptance and love of all things. How do you want them to move forward in their lives? What is your behavior modeling for them and how do you incorporate the laws of Spirit into their daily life experiences?

S: These are all teachings I'm striving to live by. I am caught between Earthly mothering and Divine mothering. I am caught between teaching them about the labels Earth runs by and modeling how to live within these boundaries from a higher, more enlightened perspective. How can I teach them what I'm trying to figure out myself?

DM: Teach by being truthful; by accepting yourself and where you are on your journey; by loving yourself no matter what, and by not defining yourself and your learnings through Earth-bound definitions. You are doing just fine. I see how you stand back up after you fall and move forward again. I feel the love that emanates from you for your children. I acknowledge your questions and your exploration, for you are a guiding force for them here. You offer them that which you seek yourself. You are a gift to them because you are willing to learn from them, as well.

S: Thank you. I acknowledge that I am doing the best I know how to do in each and every moment.

DM: Yes, you are, and it is important for you to realize that your children are doing the best they know how in every moment as well. Remember what you learned through your dialogue with Acceptance. Use that wisdom as your guide. Love yourself as much as you love them, for through that love and acceptance, you will all flourish, grow, and evolve.

Your children chose you because they knew you would provide them with a strong foundation. And, from where I sit, you are doing just that. You, Sabrina, are a seeker who is looking outside for the answers that are within. I encourage you to trust the depth of your inner knowing, for you are a Divine Mother. You carry my energy in your very Being. I acknowledge and honor you for all that you are and for your strong intention to be of loving service.

S: I am grateful for the richness I feel inside of myself as you fill me with your loving.

Perfection

Such richness and wisdom has come pouring through in these dialogues. I am grateful to have been graced by each and every visitor. I feel so full inside. Everything around me seems to be "perfect." Yet, as that word comes out, it seems so loaded to me. I wonder why?

It is my intention to learn more about this energy of perfection. I want to help others understand how things came to be and how our need to label and to define led to a misperception of it. How do I explain this? How do I share with others what has become so clear for me in my heart? Help me here. I am asking for a visit from someone out there. Who will it be?

"I am here, my child. Ask and you shall receive. You have opened up your heart to me with a clear intention of sharing something beautiful with others, something that will help them on their way. I feel it is of such importance that I, myself, have chosen to speak with you today."

S: Oh, my! I am surrounded by grace, and I feel you. Who are you?

God: I am God, Goddess, All That Is. I am the mother/father of all things. I am love and acceptance, joy, and compassion. I am within you, sweet child of mine.

S: I felt you as soon as you entered my space or should I say, as soon as I opened myself up to the awareness of you. I feel so blessed, honored, and grateful that you, yourself, have chosen to speak with me.

God: Child, you have manifested something very sacred and special with this book, and I honor your work. I honor your purity of heart in your desire to share your wisdom for the highest good of others.

S: Thank you. It is so important for me to share the wisdom I have come to know so well. It has helped me so much and I want to pass it on to others, even if it only helps a few.

God: You write from such a place of truth and loving that even if your words only resonate with a few, the energy behind the words will affect many. It will touch the depths of their hearts and echo in the chambers of their souls.

S: My intention when sitting down to write was that the energy of the words sprinkle over the reader like magic fairy dust, opening them up to remember who they authentically are. Thank you for acknowledging that.

God: So, my Child, your intention today was to write about perfection. How may I assist you?

S: Throughout my life, I have strived to be perfect. I wanted to do whatever it took to be a perfect daughter, friend, wife, mother, Being. I kept stumbling over my faults and flaws, which constantly seemed to stand in the way. When I looked at myself, they were all I could see. I have heard it said that anything created by God is perfect; perfect in its imperfections; perfect because it is of You. But our definition of perfect here on Earth is "flawless."

Through my own inner work, I am beginning to understand that the labels and definitions we impose on things can be very different from the energy of what they really are. I want to help people understand that and see beyond the label or definition of perfection. I want to understand why that word is used when applied to us as your children and what energy it holds for you. I want to help others lay down their expectations of yearning to BE perfect and see that they already are. Can you help me with this?

God: (*Smiling down upon me*) You have asked a very interesting question about perfection, how it relates to what I have created and who you are as Divine Beings. As Divine Beings, you are whole. Perfection also can be defined that way. There are many reasons a soul chooses to incarnate and to experience life on Earth. Life on this planet offers the most diverse, complex, and colorful opportunities through which a soul can experience itself.

Remember the dialogue you had between Earth Girl and Soul Self? Soul Self is whole, as are all of the souls that exist here and everywhere. When you chose to take on a body and become Earth Girl, you came into a world based on labels and definitions. That is how it functions. This Earth plane is not one that breathes life through intuitive experiences, but through material/physical world reality, and as such, things/experiences need to be defined. This "reality" needs concrete borders and boundaries for things. That is what makes it such an amazing educational/ evolutionary experience. These borders or definitions are what you and many others are getting stuck on.

You see, I am Love. I exist in a constant state of love, therefore, I see, breathe, and experience everything ~ EVERYTHING ~ through love. I experience you and every other Being as whole, as perfect because I love you as you are, no matter what. You are a part of me. When you step outside of me and forget where you came from, you live in a world that is defined with words and labels. By defining things, you have labeled the polarities we have co-created as being perfect or imperfect, good or bad.

Acceptance taught you that polarities just exist; they are neither good nor bad, positive nor negative. When you live through the eyes of your Earth Girl, you get caught up in the struggle to define yourself according to these polarities. When you remember who you are, a Divine part of me, your need to define falls away because you know yourself. That knowing has no need for words or definitions. It just is!

S: I hear you. I understand what you are saying but... (*Sigh*)

God: What is that big sigh about?

S: It's just in the translation I'm saddened that we have created a world that seems so harsh, so filled with rigid definitions and judgments.

God: Ah, Child. Your world is full of potential. It offers such amazing, brilliant opportunities for people to grow. It is filled with beauty and majesty unlike anywhere else in our existence. Remember that you chose to be a part of it. Each of you did, just as you are now choosing to remember who you are and share that with others. Imagine as you continue to embrace yourself in your authenticity and share yourself with others, they may choose to open up as well. In that opening, the world around you as you know it, as you have co-created it, will change.

Another way to say it is that, in your wholeness, you chose to come here to experience how much you could expand, to see how big your loving could grow under circumstances that are only present due to the dynamics of Earth. This is a true testing ground of your ability to love yourself and others in the face of adversity and challenge.

S: But does that mean that we can only expand our loving through struggle and challenge?

God: No. However, on Earth, that is what many of you believe. You can expand by lovingly and joyfully celebrating yourself and others in the face of anything.

S: You said something earlier about choosing to remember who I am. Is that a choice? I thought that when we enter this physical world reality, we agree to forget and then make our way through attempting to remember.

God: That story comes from the need to define things in order to understand them. A Soul never forgets itself. It always knows itself. It always knows from where it came and what it is made of. When it chooses to be born into physical world reality, it is gifted with an Ego. See the Ego as a guiding force on this plane because the Ego is of this place. The Ego's job is to help you live life to its fullest potential.

S: The Ego seems to lead us away from who we authentically are.

God: Because the Ego is easily influenced by its surroundings and by the information it is fed, it lives by the definitions and boundaries this Earth plane has set up. It doesn't understand that you are boundary-less.

S: So, how do we begin to balance what the Ego teaches and what the Soul knows?

God: Great question. There is always the opportunity for the Soul and the Ego to work together.

S: It seems as if so many of us awaken to ourselves so much later rather than sooner in life. Why do some know themselves before others?

God: Faith, trust, belief, circumstance, curriculum, awareness. There are many reasons. You see, the Soul is aware of the Ego, but the Ego needs to learn from the Soul. Depending upon your curriculum and the lessons you have chosen to learn, and how you choose to learn them, determines when you choose to awaken to yourself.

S: How do you mean ~ choose?

God: The Soul is very patient and always there sending and receiving messages to the Ego from Spirit. However, the Ego can choose to listen or not. Some Egos are very strong and have been taught to be threatened by things they don't understand or cannot see. Others are more willing to explore the unknown. The choice I spoke of earlier is for the Ego to learn to trust what is coming forward from the Soul. If Ego and Soul choose to work together, they will help one another learn and grow. There is no timeline in place for when that happens. For some, it takes lifetimes.

S: We have gotten off track from where we started this conversation.

God: The way I see it: we are just where we are. How wonderful we have had an opportunity to explore together.

S: I have so many questions. There is so much I want to know and share. I don't feel like I've answered the questions clearly enough.

God: Child, it is not for you to answer the questions, but to breathe life into them by asking. Questions continue to live on. It is in the exploration of them that you get closer to home.

S: Do you have any parting words to share with me, with us?

God: Know that you, each and every one of you, are a Divine part of me, and in that, you are perfect. Know that I love and cherish every precious aspect of you. Know that life offers its polarities for you to experience so that you gain an appreciation and acceptance of all sides of things. Know that in your wholeness, you don't need words to define you. Know that I am with you, around you, within you always, and you only need to shift your awareness to experience me. Know that your Ego is a partner in your growth. Cherish it, for how it has led you to your learnings. Know that you are connected to All That Is. Know that you can grow through Joy and Acceptance and that the more you love, the more love surrounds you. Know that there is no right or wrong time to discover yourself: it is all beautifully unfolding just as it is.

S: Thank you for your warm embrace and your generous words of encouragement. I love You so much and send lightwaves of gratitude to all that You are.

Acknowledgement and Celebration of the Inspirational Artists who contributed to the First Edition of "Visitors at My Door"

Regina Argentin	www.argentinstudio.com
Willow Arlenea	www.designsbywillow.com
Coleman Barks	www.colemanbarks.com
Gina Brezini	www.ginnart.com
Beth Budesheim	www.paintedjourneys.com
Darren Cole	www.photoboxgallery.com/digiart
Angeline Damigos	www.anjlart.com
Mara Berendt Friedman	www.newmoonvisions.com
Noud Jan Gilissen	www.silvershadesofgrey.com
Francene Hart	www.francenehart.com
Beth Kingsley Hawkins	www.hummerlady.com
Daniel B. Holeman	www.awakenvisions.com
Christine Lebrasseur	http://ellesait.blogspot.com
Ober-Rae Starr Livingstone	www.newageart.com
Angela Minkova	www.artangela.com
Marina Petro	www.marinapetro.com
Padma Samchuk	www.padmapa.com

About the Author

It has always been Sabrina's heart desire to inspire others and guide them into the light of their own authenticity. She believes that we are all connected, and that the higher we soar into the light of our true selves, the more beautiful and loving this world will be.

Sabrina wrote this book and established a line of inspirational tank tops to share her message with the world.

Sabrina Fay Teiger currently lives in Los Angeles, California with her husband, three sons, three cats, and one dog. She earned her Master's Degree in Spiritual Psychology from the University of Santa Monica. Her life's work is facilitating people's connection to their heart centers, both one-on-one and in circles.

Sabrina would love to hear from you. Please contact her through her websites:

www.sabrinafayteiger.com and www.qual-i-tee.com

Praise for *Oreos and Dubonnet*

"Clear, witty writing and capable research make this whimsically titled book about Gov. Nelson Rockefeller one of the best about New York state government ... *Oreos and Dubonnet* is a superb book about an important time in New York politics and history."

— Schenectady *Sunday Gazette*

"The authors ... have pieced together a breezy, slender portrait that combines oral histories from fellow Albany alumni and other anecdotes they gathered about Rockefeller the governor, the vice-president, the campaigner and the man."

— *New York Times*

"*Oreos and Dubonnet* offers the reader fascinating insight into the era in New York State and national politics so dominated by Nelson Rockefeller. If one is interested in the fun that accompanies political shenanigans, this book will captivate you."

— Richard M. Rosenbaum, former
New York State Chairman and author of
No Room for Democracy:
The Triumph of Ego over Common Sense

OREOS
&
DUBONNET

OREOS
&
DUBONNET

REMEMBERING
GOVERNOR
NELSON A.
ROCKEFELLER

Joseph H. Boyd Jr.

and

Charles R. Holcomb

excelsior editions

Published by State University of New York Press, Albany

Publication of this book was made possible with the support of the New York State Archives Partnership Trust and Robert and Patricia Phillips.

 Archives Partnership Trust

Excelsior Editions is an imprint of State University of New York Press

For information, contact State University of New York Press, Albany, NY
www.sunypress.edu

Production by Ryan Morris
Marketing by Fran Keneston

Library of Congress Cataloging-in-Publication Data

Boyd, Joseph H.
    Oreos and Dubonnet : remembering Governor Nelson A. Rockefeller / Joseph H. Boyd Jr. and Charles R. Holcomb.
        p.   cm.
    Includes index.
    "Excelsior editions."
    ISBN 978-1-4384-4183-2 (hc : alk. paper)—978-1-4384-4184-9 (pb : alk. paper)
    1. Rockefeller, Nelson A. (Nelson Aldrich), 1908–1979. 2. United States—Politics and government—1974–1977. 3. New York (State)—Politics and government—1951–   4. Vice-Presidents—United States—Biography.
5. Governors—New York (State)—Biography. I. Holcomb, Charles R. II. Title.
    E748.R673.B69 2012
    973.925092—dc23
    [B]
                                                        2011022070

10 9 8 7 6 5 4 3 2 1

This book is dedicated to Joe Boyd's deceased wives—
Margaret Mayes Boyd (1943–1998) and Sara Gear Boyd (1941–2008)—
both of whom died of cancer, and to Joan Hamilton Holcomb,
whose patience and support despite illness have been indispensable
in her husband's completion of this work.

Contents

1

A Word of Introduction

Charles R. Holcomb

Nelson Aldrich Rockefeller had an enormous and long-lasting impact on New York State during his fifteen years as governor, and to some extent, on the country as well. He changed the lives of many, particularly those who worked closely with him over the years.

One such who was there to see it all was Joseph H. Boyd Jr., the initiator and coauthor of this book. He signed on with Rockefeller while still in college and served in various responsible capacities for nearly two decades, primarily during the gubernatorial years, which are the principal focus of the book.

A Long Shot Candidacy

Nelson A. Rockefeller began to consider the possibility of running for governor of New York several years before the 1958 election. He knew that if he ran, he would face very long odds. He had built an impressive record in Washington, serving three presidents, but he was not widely known in New York State. He had no political organization and no record or standing within the Republican Party in New York State. His knowledge of New York State politics and government was sketchy. In July, 1958, he would turn fifty, and he had never before run for any office, much less New York State's highest office. And it was far from certain that he could secure the Republican nomination for governor.

Even if he did get the nomination, he would then have to take on a wealthy and well-entrenched incumbent governor, Democrat W. Averell Harriman. And Harriman, while not the warmest public figure, was a hard worker generally viewed as running a reasonably competent, if dull, administration. Nationally, furthermore, 1958 was expected to be a year of Democratic gains in Congress and in state races all across the country.

Former governor Thomas E. Dewey, who had retired after twelve successful years as governor and two unsuccessful runs for president, was of the opinion that Rockefeller, whose name connoted such vast wealth and power, could not be elected dogcatcher in New York State. He nonetheless gave his former top aide and law partner, R. Burdell Bixby, his blessing to work as director of scheduling for the Rockefeller campaign.

But Rockefeller brought impressive strengths as well. Along with that famous name came formidable personal and family financial resources. He had boundless energy and drive, an electric personality, and unshakeable self-confidence. He also brought the skills, as well as the scars, of nearly two bruising decades of operating in the bureaucratic and political thickets of Washington, where he had held high-level appointive positions in the Roosevelt, Truman, and Eisenhower administrations.

Albany as Stepping Stone

It is fair to say that in seeking the governorship, Nelson Rockefeller didn't plan to make it the career it subsequently became. His goal was to become president of the United States, and Albany looked like the best available stepping stone.[1]

Like many before him, Rockefeller had chafed in appointed office. Washington was where the power was, but serving at the pleasure of the president—and even reporting to him directly—meant that power and independence were temporary at best, and often illusory. Even high-ranking cabinet or subcabinet appointees were vulnerable to legal, political, and budgetary roadblocks thrown up by special interest groups, by adversaries in Congress, and by other administration officials with competing agendas or policy views.

And so Rockefeller had concluded, as others had done, that he needed the credentials and the independence conferred by high elected office in order to have any chance of reaching the presidency. You had to show not only that you were capable, but that you were electable, and the governorship of a large state could provide the requisite platform for doing so.

In fact, Averell Harriman was trying to do the same thing, and for the same reason. Harriman had an impressive background as a businessman and diplomat. Heir to a railroad fortune, he had built his own business empire and served as chairman of the Illinois Central and Union Pacific railroads from 1932 to 1942. In 1942, Franklin Roosevelt sent his friend Harriman to negotiate the Lend-Lease program with Winston Churchill. But Harriman, too, had been an unknown commodity politically until he won the governorship in

1954 by a razor-thin eleven-thousand-vote margin. That ended twelve years of Republican rule, although the Republicans kept control of both houses of the legislature. Harriman lost out to Adlai Stevenson for the 1956 Democratic nomination for president. Reelection as governor in 1958 would put him in position to compete for the Democratic nomination for president in 1960, or for a high place in a Democratic administration.

Similarly, Rockefeller hoped to use the governorship to build a national reputation as a strong, visionary leader who could get things done, solve big problems, and win elections. New York City's position as the nation's financial and media capital meant that almost anything he did as governor would attract wide newspaper and television coverage. And so it did, although this would later turn out to be a double-edged sword.

Trojan Horse

In any case, Harriman himself had already given Rockefeller a huge, if inadvertent, boost in the summer of 1956 by agreeing to his appointment as chairman of the state's Temporary Commission on the Constitutional Convention. This crucial element in the buildup to Rockefeller's nomination was described by the late Cary Reich in his excellent book *The Life of Nelson A. Rockefeller: Worlds to Conquer*, the first volume of a planned two-volume biography.[2]

New York's constitution requires a referendum every twenty years on whether a constitutional convention should be held to revise the state's fundamental laws. Such a referendum was to be held in November, 1957, and following precedent, the legislature in 1956 created a temporary commission to study and report on possible constitutional changes. Five of the fifteen members were to be appointed by the governor, five by the senate majority leader, and five by the speaker of the assembly. As both houses had Republican majorities, the Republicans would control the commission, but the intention was to make it a bipartisan effort. Accordingly, the chairman was to be named jointly by the leaders of the two houses—Assembly Speaker Oswald Heck of Schenectady and Senate Majority Leader Walter J. Mahoney of Buffalo—and the governor. Thus the chairman would be a Republican, but someone acceptable to Governor Harriman.

Harriman rejected out of hand all the Republicans put forward for the chairmanship. At this point, the Republican state chairman, L. Judson Morehouse, who had already identified Rockefeller as a political comer who might be capable of regaining the governorship for the GOP, told Mahoney to offer up Nelson Rockefeller's name.

"Oh, Nelson," Harriman is reported to have said. "I know Nelson. That would be all right. I'd go for Nelson." Harriman, who had worked with Rockefeller in Washington in promoting President Truman's Point Four foreign aid initiative, seems to have viewed Rockefeller as a civic-minded, younger friend and fellow patrician—someone who had no political aspirations in New York State, and was thus no threat to his own reelection.

But the very prospect of Rockefeller as commission chairman alarmed Harriman's closest political advisors. Carmine De Sapio, boss of Tammany Hall and a kingmaker whose support had enabled Harriman to become governor in the first place, was aghast. He saw it as giving an ambitious, deep-pocketed potential rival a mandate to poke into every state agency and operation and to get to know—and become known in—every corner of New York State. Nevertheless, Harriman agreed to the appointment. It proved to be a huge mistake.

Meanwhile, some Rockefeller advisers had strong misgivings as well. Former GOP lieutenant governor Frank Moore argued that chairing the commission would be a lot of work with little opportunity for achievement, as a constitutional convention was neither necessary nor likely. More worrisome, a convention, if held, might enable the Democrats to raise the volatile issue of reapportionment and potentially undermine all-important Republican control of the legislature.

Rockefeller accepted the position anyway. Following a pattern he had already established in Washington, he hired a heavyweight staff and commissioned studies of every aspect of the state's government. His choice for chief of staff was Dr. William J. Ronan, the energetic and ambitious former dean of New York University's Graduate School of Public Administration, whose academic credentials were unimpeachable.

But his choice for counsel set off warning bells among Democrats. George A. Hinman was a prominent member of a politically connected Binghamton law firm founded by his father, Harvey Hinman, who had been a Republican state senator, lieutenant governor, and a longtime power in New York's Southern Tier. The appointment convinced Democrats there was more to Rockefeller's agenda than an objective, nonpartisan examination of the state constitution.

At Rockefeller's insistence, the commission maintained a neutral position on the issue of whether a convention should be held in 1959— the proposition on the ballot. He contended that the commission's role was only to explore and publicize the issues involved. Only after the election, in which the proposition was voted down, did the commission come out in favor of revising the constitution. Harriman, who favored the proposition, was furious at Rockefeller's delaying tactic.

In the meantime, the process had indeed provided Nelson Rockefeller with a crash course in state and municipal government, and given him considerable exposure around the state.

(Ronan and Hinman played prominent and continuing roles, not only in Rockefeller's subsequent campaign for governor, but throughout his fifteen years in that office. Ronan, as secretary to the governor, was chief of staff and, in effect, chief operating officer. Later he headed the powerful Metropolitan Transportation Authority, the umbrella agency that controls bridges, tunnels, subways, and commuter railroads in the New York metropolitan area. Hinman, who became Republican National Committeeman from New York, was Rockefeller's top political operative and liaison with the Republican Party nationally.)

In early 1958, moving closer toward a candidacy, Rockefeller sought the support of the Republican county chairman of his home county of Westchester. The chairman, Herbert Gerlach, told him that the organization would support longtime Yonkers assemblyman Malcolm Wilson if Wilson decided to run for governor. A meeting was arranged, at which Wilson said he would like to be governor some day, but would not run for governor in 1958. But, he said, if Rockefeller wanted to run, he, Wilson, knew how he could get the nomination.[3]

Weeks later, Rockefeller pursued the subject with Wilson. What Wilson suggested was that he and Rockefeller make an extended tour of the state by car—no entourage, just the two of them—during which Wilson would introduce Rockefeller to the GOP faithful, including potential convention delegates, in each of the state's sixty-two counties.

Thus began one of the most fruitful and long-lasting political partnerships in American political history, between two men who could hardly have been more different in their backgrounds, attributes, or attitudes. In contrast to Rockefeller's ebullience and dynamism, Wilson was cautious, conservative, precise, and lawyerly. Where Rockefeller was brought up a Baptist, Wilson was a devout Catholic. He also had an encyclopedic knowledge of state and local government in New York and of the politics and politicians in virtually every county in the state, and his memory for people's names, faces, and individual circumstances was already legendary.

Road Trips

On June 30, 1958, Rockefeller announced in New York City that he was a candidate for governor, and he and Wilson immediately drove north to Kinderhook, in rural, conservative Columbia County, to meet with the Republican county committee. The trip, in Wilson's Buick, was the first in a series that extended nearly eight weeks, leading up to the party's late-August nominating convention, and that took Rockefeller into every corner of the state.

In Kinderhook, a sleepy Hudson Valley village that had been the home of President Martin Van Buren, they were greeted by the Republican county chairman, Myrtie Tinklepaugh, and her county committee members. Rockefeller was charming, and soon after the dinner ended, the committee voted to endorse his candidacy—as Wilson intended—making Columbia the first county to do so. Mrs. Tinklepaugh, although a conservative, was well disposed toward Rockefeller in any event because, some years before, he had accepted her invitation to take part in a debate at Ichabod Crane High School in Valatie.[4]

She was less favorably inclined toward another principal contender for the nomination, Senate Majority Leader Walter J. Mahoney of Buffalo, whose views were surely closer to her own than were Rockefeller's. Her daughter, Mary Ann Tinklepaugh Fish, recalls that earlier her mother had represented the county at a Republican state committee meeting when the then-county chairman was wintering in Florida. When she explained the situation to Senator Mahoney, who was presiding at the meeting, he sneered, "So I suppose you think you're in charge!" Mrs. Tinklepaugh seethed, and never forgot the slight.

As the weeks passed, Rockefeller's charm and personal magnetism drew more and more upstate Republican organizations to his banner. His rivals for the nomination—Mahoney and former Republican national committee chairman Leonard Hall, a Long Islander—fumed that Rockefeller's liberal views were being kept under wraps. Selling the candidate on the basis of his dynamism and electability, rather than his philosophy, was in fact the strategy.

Seldom mentioned but clearly a factor in the minds of local party leaders was Rockefeller's ability to fund an aggressive election campaign against a wealthy incumbent in what was widely expected to be a Democratic year. (Nationally, it was—the Democrats added thirty Senate seats, forty-seven House seats, and four governorships.) A vigorous, well-financed campaign for the top of the ticket could stymie or reverse Democratic gains upstate and help the GOP maintain control of the legislature. In addition, polls showed Rockefeller would draw more votes from independents and Democrats than would his rivals.

In that era, statewide candidates were chosen by delegates to the state party convention, who were hand-picked by local party organizations. The GOP convention was scheduled for late August in Rochester, and as it drew near, Hall and Mahoney each concluded that they could not put together a majority of delegates. And so, almost on the eve of the convention, both dropped out of the race, enabling Rockefeller to arrive in Rochester triumphant, and to leave a few days later with impressive momentum and a united party behind him.

In the meantime, the statewide ticket had been put together. Rockefeller chose Wilson for his lieutenant governor, although this flew in the face of conventional wisdom, since they were both from Westchester County. But Wilson's knowledge of the state and its politics, and his clout among conservative upstate Republicans, plus his strong Catholicism, were acclaimed as crucial attributes. The other members of the ticket, meanwhile, provided both ethnic and geographic diversity. Attorney General Louis J. Lefkowitz of Manhattan, previously appointed to that post to fill out the unexpired term of Jacob K. Javits, who had been elected to the United States Senate, would run for a full term. James A. Lundy, former borough president of Queens, was nominated for comptroller, and Congressman Kenneth B. Keating of Rochester agreed, albeit reluctantly, to run for U.S. senator. All except Lundy would win in November.

In contrast to the harmony and jubilation of the Republican convention in Rochester, the Democrats' convention in Buffalo was a shambles. Weeks earlier, Harriman had waffled on the choice of a Senate candidate, but had flatly rejected Manhattan district attorney Frank Hogan, the candidate proposed by De Sapio and other New York City party leaders. At the convention, De Sapio proceeded to round up the votes to ram Hogan down Harriman's throat, along with the Erie County Democratic boss, Peter Crotty, for attorney general.

Harriman was thus publicly exposed as weaker than the party bosses. Not only was the party in disarray going into the two-month election campaign, but Harriman had handed Rockefeller and the Republicans a powerful issue: party bossism. Tammany Hall's De Sapio, with his trademark dark glasses, was a perfect target.

And so began the brief, intense election campaign that put Rockefeller in office by 558,000 votes and sparked the political career of Joseph H. Boyd Jr., then a junior at Colgate University, who would work for nearly two decades under the Rockefeller banner, primarily during the Albany years.

2

A Pivotal Encounter

Enlisting for the Duration

The circumstances of Joe Boyd's recruitment to the Rockefeller cause in 1958 illuminate not only Nelson Rockefeller's personal magnetism and political appeal, but also the free-wheeling, opportunistic nature of that first campaign for governor.

Joe grew up in suburban Montclair, New Jersey, the son of a stockbroker. By the time he got to Colgate University, in upstate Hamilton, New York, he already had a strong interest in politics and considered himself a Republican.

Here is Joe's account of his first, pivotal encounter with that emerging force of nature, candidate Nelson Rockefeller:

> Early one fall morning in 1958, I received a phone call from one of the Colgate University deans, asking me to come to his office. I was a junior at the university, political science major, and president of the Young Republicans Club.
>
> The dean had received a phone call from the Rockefeller campaign scheduling office, asking if Nelson Rockefeller, who was then the Republican candidate for governor, could speak to the students. The Colgate administration said yes, even though the president, Everett Case, was a big Democrat and friend of Governor Averell Harriman, Rockefeller's opponent.
>
> The speech was set for the 10 a.m. chapel period, so it would not interfere with classes and most of the students (1,300) would be able to attend. Rockefeller arrived the night before on the campaign bus from appearances in the Syracuse-Utica area. The Republican county chairman, several Young Republicans, and I met him when he arrived at the Colgate Inn for the overnight.
>
> I can visually remember Rockefeller walking into the hotel lobby to some stares, wearing a dirty tan raincoat and eating an apple. He seemed dog tired but spent ten minutes with me and my fellow students, asking us about concerns of college-age young people. This

was to be Rockefeller's first campaign appearance before a college audience.

The next morning, the campaign bus arrived at the chapel right on time to an overflow audience of students and faculty. I introduced him and Rockefeller spoke for twenty minutes, receiving many interruptions of applause. At the end of the speech, the students broke out with hoots and yells and rushed the stage to shake Rockefeller's hand. As he was to do so often, Rockefeller jumped into the middle of the outreached hands. The one TV station from Utica and the writing press recorded his reception by the students.

On the steps of the chapel, Rockefeller asked me to be the campaign chairman of "Students for Rockefeller." I, of course, was thrilled and said yes. He took me by the arm and told me to get on the campaign bus. I replied that I couldn't "cut" classes. He walked over to the dean and got me excused with the promise that I would write a paper on my experience and he would make sure I got back to Colgate safely.

Once on the bus, he introduced me to the press corps with my new title, and off we went to Norwich and Binghamton for campaign events. At each stop, Rockefeller introduced me and told the story of my recruitment at Colgate.

Joe may not have been totally surprised at the request that he travel with the Rockefeller campaign. John B. (Jack) Vandervort, sole advance man for the campaign, has a slightly different perspective on the events at Colgate. Vandervort had long been active with the Young Republicans and knew some of the Colgate YRs, including Joe, along with several others who had worked with him in President Eisenhower's reelection campaign two years before. On arriving at Colgate, Vandervort recalled, "After the last evening activity—putting the boss [Rockefeller] to bed—we all went down to have a cocktail at the Colgate Inn. And I asked Joe Boyd, who at the time was president of the Young Republicans, 'How do you sit the next couple of days? Why don't you travel with us?' And Joe did, and the rest, obviously, is history."

In any event, even before Joe's initial euphoria had dissipated, some of the lessons of life on the campaign trail had begun to sink in. One, you can't always be sure where you'll end the day, so, as the Boy Scout motto urges, Be Prepared. Two, reporters traveling with the campaign need to file a story every day, whether there's any real news or not. As Joe described it:

In Norwich I borrowed $20 from staff aide Carl Spad, bought a toothbrush, underwear, a clean shirt and some other basics. The AP [Associated Press] reporter followed me as I visited the drug and clothing stores and wrote a wire story on my selections.

We stayed in Binghamton, and the next day the Rockefeller campaign bus made ten stops on Route 7 on the way to Schenectady. I was introduced at each stop. Finally, we came to Route 20, a major east-west road that would get me back to Colgate.

The question was how, since Rockefeller was not governor and didn't have the use of the state police. The answer was the county sheriffs, who were mostly Republicans. I said goodbye to Rockefeller, who said he was counting on me, and off I went in the back seat of a sheriff's car, west along Route 20. At each county line (there were five), I changed sheriff's cars. Most used their bubble machine (light on top) as we drove through small hamlets. When we got to Madison County (where Colgate is located), we were met by the sheriff (Republican), a deputy, and two state troopers.

As we approached the village of Hamilton around noontime, we picked up the village police and Colgate University security, who led the four cars—university, village, county, and state police—down fraternity row. The university proctor in the front car had a microphone and urged the brothers on the row to come out of the houses and welcome me back. Realizing the importance of the event, I lowered the rear window in the back seat of the sheriff's car and waved. My political career with Rockefeller was off to a good start!

Indeed it was. Throughout that campaign, Joe recalled, the Rockefeller staff called him often from campaign headquarters, which was in the Roosevelt Hotel in Manhattan. Joe continued:

I set up seventeen "Students for Rockefeller" groups at such colleges as Syracuse, Cornell, Vassar, Skidmore, Brockport State, Rochester, NYU, Columbia, and Morrisville State, among others.

When Rockefeller took office in '59, his office called whenever they wanted input on student issues. Upon graduating in June '60, I went to work in Governor Rockefeller's State Capitol office in Albany.

In the gubernatorial campaigns of '62, '66, and '70, Rockefeller insisted that he speak to the students at Colgate and that I accompany him. Each year he told the story of the '58 visit and introduced me.

Life on the Inside

I first met Joe Boyd in 1964. In January of that year, I was sent by my newspaper, the Rochester *Times-Union*—then the flagship of the Gannett Newspapers—to Albany for the first time to cover the legislative session, supplementing the full-time staff of the Gannett News Service Albany bureau. We served the Gannett-owned newspapers throughout New York State—eighteen of them, including nine in the Westchester-Rockland group.

I remember Joe from that period as a tall, handsome young man, with wavy blond hair, wide blue eyes that seemed to take in everything around him, and an air of quiet competence.

He was indeed a keen observer, an attribute essential to performing well in the many governmental and campaign positions that he held in his long career with Nelson Rockefeller. For in almost all of his assignments, he had to operate in close contact with the governor. To do so successfully required constant awareness and understanding of the governor's likes, dislikes, moods, needs, habits, and methods of operating.

Such methods included, for example, the processes for following through on commitments made in conversations or meetings with legislators, officials, and other visitors to his office in Albany. Joe described the office setup as it operated during his days as a special assistant to the governor.

At the State Capitol the governor's office was located on the second floor. It consisted of the governor's inner office and the offices of secretary, counsel, communications and appointments (patronage), plus the Red Room that was used as the governor's ceremonial office and for press conferences.

An adjoining larger room was occupied by Governor Rockefeller's personal secretary, Ann Whitman, another secretary, and me. There was also a chart/video conference room and a larger conference room with a long table, which could seat fifteen people for staff luncheons on Mondays and Tuesdays during the legislative session.

The governor did not record conversations or meetings, but he did have a phone listening device under the three outer office desks. Mrs. Whitman usually kept track of his phone commitments, but if the subject was political or involved the legislature, I was asked to pick up. For meetings in his small office with outside people [non-staff] and some [governmental] commissions, I was invited by the governor to sit in and record on a yellow pad any commitments he made.

Then I would notify in writing the secretary, counsel and, if it warranted, the press office and appointments office. In addition, I would plug into the governor's position a time for a reply to the governor. I would keep him informed weekly of the status of each issue. When a decision was made, the governor, Ann Whitman, or I would get back to the appropriate person.

The one meeting that left the most long-lasting impression (on me) was with the head of the New York City Waterfront Commission, who discussed the role of the Mafia and its relationship with the International Longshoremen's Union.

The note-taking system was thus both effective for the governor and educational for Joe.

Oreos and Dubonnet

During his years with Rockefeller, Joe held more positions in state government than almost any other state employee—not because he couldn't keep a job, but because his abilities and experience made him such a valuable commodity in an election campaign. And there was an election campaign every other year—successful gubernatorial reelections in 1962, 1966, and 1970, and unsuccessful efforts to win the Republican presidential nomination in 1960, 1964, and 1968. There were also some major efforts in between, such as Rockefeller's four goodwill trips to his old stomping grounds in Latin America in 1969 at the behest of his former rival, President Richard Nixon. So Joe was constantly on and off the state payroll, and when he returned to the Executive Chamber he often wound up with a new and more challenging job.

But much of his work on the campaign trail, and a fair amount as a state employee, involved advance work. When Rockefeller traveled, one or more advance-men went ahead, working out arrangements with the local people involved, and making sure each event, appearance, or meeting went smoothly and, if possible, on time.

Of course, the governor had strong personal preferences, among them Dubonnet red wine, for an occasional drink at the end of a long day, and Oreo cookies—hence the title of this book. These preferences, as a matter of routine, were accommodated at every stop, and Rockefeller took them for granted.[1]

In recounting an incident in 1968, Joe described an amusing variation in the pattern that revealed the governor's seldom-seen frugal side:

Rockefeller was campaigning in South Carolina and Happy [Mrs. Rockefeller] was with him. Normally before dinner the governor took an hour break when he could make phone calls, review issues with his staff, or put his feet up and rest. The suites he used during this period were usually a local hotel's "Presidential Suite," which the advance-man was required to equip with a private outside phone line, Dubonnet red wine, milk, and Oreo cookies.

On this particular day, I was summoned to the suite during the break by New York State Police Major Edward Galvin, his upstate and traveling bodyguard. The governor and Happy were lying down on twin beds. Happy made room for me at the end of her bed as the governor asked me to sit down. He told me he was very pleased with the advance team and that I had recruited a fine group of young people.

However, there was one item that bothered him and that was the fresh supply of Oreo cookies at every stop. He felt the campaign was spending too much money on "cookies." And with that statement, he took a full but opened bag of Oreos and gave them to me, asking if an advance-man could take them back to the store and maybe get a refund. I said it was not likely, but I would take the opened bag with us so they were available to the traveling staff.[2]

Moving the Governor

Joe Boyd's professional skills, along with his solid personal relationship with the governor, were the envy of the advance team and others who worked for Joe in the Executive Chamber or on the many Rockefeller campaigns.

One of his advance-men, Bert Levine, described an incident during Rockefeller's 1968 pursuit of the GOP presidential nomination that demonstrated how critical Joe's particular skills could be.

Recalled Levine:

The event that night (at a hotel in Portland, Oregon) would not be "heavy lifting" for an experienced advance team—a private airport arrival, a small motorcade, a hotel arrival, the usual Dubonnet and Oreos for the governor's room, a cocktail party, a dinner, and that was about it. Pretty routine stuff—routine, that is, until Joe Boyd threw me a curveball.

Joe was the head of advance—my boss. He was also the governor's "shoulder man." That was the guy who accompanied the governor at campaign stops and told him what he needed to know about each event: "You are going to be greeted by Mayor X. We have to get out of here in fourteen minutes."

Among the advance team he was known as the one person who could "move the governor." As it came time for an event to end, Joe would position himself in front of the governor, about ten feet away, make eye contact, and through some signaling system that would make a major league third-base coach envious of its subtlety, would get the governor to move on. The staff joke was that Joe was the only person the governor feared. Certainly an overstatement, but the fact remained, when Joe did whatever he did, the governor moved.

So now the curveball. Joe, shoulder man extraordinaire, was not planning to be at his usual post during the cocktail party. The only man that could "move the governor" was going to be several floors away schmoozing some GOP delegates who would have been assembled for a very private (off-schedule) reception just before the main dinner. In other words, everything else was fluff: what really mattered, the real reason for being in Portland, was the meeting with these delegates. It was left to me, the one who had been taking a "crim" law exam in Brooklyn twenty-four hours earlier, to deliver him upstairs on time. I was flattered and scared, but more scared than flattered.

That evening, before the cocktail party, Joe and I positioned ourselves just outside of the governor's hotel room. When he came out, Joe reintroduced me to the man for whom I had already done several hundred advances. "You remember Bert Levine. He advanced for you in '66 and then worked in the Executive Chamber last year." The governor was cordial. "Sure, Brett, how are you?" He had no idea who the hell I was.

Going down in the elevator, Joe went over the schedule for the evening. He told the governor that it was "absolutely critical" that he should be at the upstairs reception on time, that I would be at the downstairs cocktail party with him and would signal to him when we should head upstairs. The governor looked at me and nodded, "Okay, Bart." I could tell this was going to be a "best laid plans" deal.

The cocktail party was a typical "Parlor A and B" event. The folding wall had been collapsed and both parlors were filled with local party stalwarts.

As always, the governor worked the crowd deftly. With each passing minute he seemed to get more and more "into it." He actually seemed to be enjoying himself. Given Joe's last words to me—"Remember, Bert, 7:30 on the button"—this was not a welcome turn. Restless candidates are easier to move than those who are content with what they are doing at the moment.

I made an executive decision: earlier would be better than later. At 7:15, I positioned myself about ten feet in front of the governor. I figured if we were moving by 7:17 that would be perfect. The governor and I made eye contact—at least I thought so. I gave a discreet nod, hoping the governor would wrap up his conversation, move toward me, and then to the waiting elevator. No such luck! The governor did end his conversation, but immediately began another one with another drink-in-hand enthusiast.

Not time to panic, not yet! I held my position, once more caught the governor's eye, once more nodded, once more didn't make a dent. A third try: Position, Nod, Nothing!

Now it WAS time to panic. I found myself doing the Joe Boyd impersonations. Joe had a unique way of stretching his neck, as if his collar was too tight. So I began to stretch—profusely. Nothing! I took out some white cards and held them in my hand as I not-so-subtly pointed to my watch. Response: blank stare, more conversation, no movement.

By 7:27, the crisp suit I had started the evening with was a limp rag. I wasn't perspiring—it was more like a hemorrhage. Even if the governor left now, he would be about five minutes late getting to the private reception. Oregon was a state the governor could win. These were delegates he could get. But not if he snubbed them. And thanks to my incompetence, that was what he was about to do.

I was left with no choice. I did the unthinkable—at least for me. I broke into the governor's conversation and with a none-too-firm voice announced that we really had to go upstairs. Going back to the third-base coach analogy, this was the advance-man's equivalent of yelling, "BUNT! NOW!"

Nothing subtle about it. Where Boyd impersonations had failed, rudeness succeeded. The governor, now already a few minutes late, began walking toward the elevator. When the door closed I gave him the card that Joe had prepared with some key names of people he was about to meet at the reception. He studied it until we arrived at the "Rooftop Something-or-Other."

Joe met us at the elevator. I knew it was Joe because I recognized his suit pants and loafers. I had no intention of getting any closer to eye contact than that. I never even got off the elevator. But as the doors began to close again, the governor, gracious as ever, thanked me for my efforts: "You did a good job, Ben."

Levine's trepidation about interrupting Rockefeller is quite understandable. The governor did not like to be interrupted, and staffers who broke his unwritten rules of behavior, for whatever reason, might find themselves temporarily in purgatory, given the cold shoulder at meetings, or even banished from the Executive Chamber altogether, although seldom actually fired or transferred.

Even Joe Boyd trod cautiously. But with Rockefeller, there were always surprises, as Joe recalled in the following account:

> Rockefeller had a tendency to run late for appointments, but Ann Whitman, his personal secretary and controller of his schedule, ran a tight ship. One day when he was still in a meeting in the seventh-floor conference room at his Fifty-Fifth Street office in Manhattan, she sent me up to tell him his next appointment was waiting and he needed to come now or the man would leave.
>
> I started to knock on the door but heard loud screaming between two men in German. I retreated to Ann's office, only to be sent back with instructions to enter the room and break up the meeting.
>
> With great temerity I knocked and entered the room with the still-screaming Germans. There sat Nelson Rockefeller listening patiently to Henry Kissinger and Edward Teller.[3]

Commuting to Albany

While Albany was and is New York's capital, New York City was much more the center of Nelson Rockefeller's expansive (and expensive) universe. He was well supplied with offices and residences in both places, including the executive mansion in Albany, a half mile from the Capitol; his large and art-filled Manhattan apartment at 812 Fifth Avenue; the office in his townhouse at 22 West Fifty-Fifth Street; and thirty miles up the Hudson River, Kykuit, the grand house on the sprawling Hudson River estate built by his grandfather, John D. Rockefeller.

Getting back and forth to Albany, 140 miles up the Hudson, was a continuing challenge for staff members who lived in the New York metropolitan area but needed to be in Albany much or most of the time. But it was no problem for the governor. He had the family's air fleet at his beck and call, and most Monday mornings, particularly when the legislature was in session, he would fly to Albany from Westchester County Airport with a select group of passengers. Joe Boyd was often included.

Joe recalled how the system worked during the administration's later years, when he was serving as appointments officer and legislative liaison:

> I would fly to Albany Monday mornings with Governor Rockefeller, Attorney General Louie Lefkowitz, Ann Whitman, and other key New York City staff. We would travel on the Governor's F-27, a prop plane which was configured with four swivel chairs, two four-person conference tables, one of which converted into a bed, a five-person couch, which also could become a bed, plus a galley kitchen and small bar.
>
> On the way, I was usually invited to stay at the governor's mansion. This, of course, meant canceling the reserved motel room and rearranging one's plans.
>
> I was assigned to the Princess Beatrix Room on the second floor, front.[4] Louie Lefkowitz was in the next room. Ann Whitman and the lieutenant governor, Malcolm Wilson, had rooms on the third floor.
>
> The Princess Beatrix Room, named after the royal from the Netherlands who had stayed there, contained a queen-sized, four-poster bed with an assortment of reading chairs. A bath was attached.
>
> When I retired at night, I told Robert, the master butler, what time I wanted to be woken up and my preference for breakfast. At the appointed hour he would knock and arrive with the morning papers and my breakfast on a tray. He would return in twenty minutes to draw my shower to the temperature of my choice. Being in my early thirties, I thought I'd gone to heaven and reached the promised land.

But Albany, like most state capitals, is a town where, especially during the annual legislative session, a fair amount of business is transacted after hours. And as Joe found out, staying at the mansion, despite all its amenities and the relatively easy access to the governor it provided, also had its limitations and its rules—Nelson Rockefeller's rules.

"After awhile," Joe wrote, "I found the mansion quite confining, since the door was locked by 9 p.m. If you wanted to stay out later, you had to ask the governor for the one extra key."

3

Getting the Governor's Ear, and Other Necessities

Time was always in short supply for Nelson Rockefeller. His energy, like his ambition, was prodigious, but so, too, was the range of interests, projects, and goals to which he applied it. By the time he became governor, at the age of fifty, he had spent almost three decades as a senior executive, managing large projects, programs, and initiatives in New York and Washington, starting with overseeing the building of Rockefeller Center while in his early twenties.

Not surprisingly, especially given his background as a Rockefeller, by the time he reached Albany he was already adept at assembling and using staffs to extend his reach and effectiveness. He had also developed numerous skills and techniques for increasing his influence or asserting his dominance in all kinds of circumstances.

Managing Access

Like most busy executives, Rockefeller as governor had a gatekeeper to help manage his schedule, screening and limiting the numbers of people who got in to see him on a given day at the Capitol, or at his New York City office. Mrs. Ann Whitman, his executive assistant and personal secretary, was a gracious, highly organized, tough-minded woman who, among other things, had spent eight years in the White House as personal secretary to President Dwight D. Eisenhower. She was no pushover.

Executive chamber staff, state agency heads, legislative leaders, and others who wanted some of the governor's time soon learned to work with her rather than trying to get around her. They also learned that when the governor wanted to see them, the invitation— sometimes a politely expressed command—usually came via a telephone call from Ann Whitman.

In certain staff positions, of course, being able to get the ear of a busy boss in a timely fashion can be critically important, particularly when decisions must be made. Joe Boyd recalled a period when he was both legislative liaison and appointments officer, and also in charge of external travel and the advance team. He needed daily access to the governor and could see that trying to wedge himself into the governor's crowded daily appointment schedule was a ticket to frustration. As he told it:

> I quickly discovered that one way I could get a decision by the governor was to ride with him to the Capitol from the mansion. Each morning I would arrive at the front door by 9 A.M. with a folder full of memos concerning appointments, individual problems of legislators, and a schedule of possible events, all with "yes," "no," and "let's discuss further" boxes at the bottom of each memo. By 9:30 I had the decisions.

Joe, of course, had no trouble getting to the front door on time because, as noted, much of the time he was actually staying at the mansion.

While some governors have made the mansion their real home while in office, most have kept their homes elsewhere and used the mansion primarily when state business required them to be in Albany. Rockefeller, of course, was not in need of another place to live. In addition to Kykuit and his Fifth Avenue apartment, he had a house in Washington, another in Seal Harbor, Maine, plus a ranch in Venezuela. Besides the Fifty-Fifth Street townhouse that included his New York office, he owned a townhouse on Fifty-Fourth Street that backed up to it.

At any rate, Rockefeller used the mansion as a luxury hotel for friends and important visitors, such as GOP National Committeeman George Hinman, and as something of a boarding house for a few key staff members and such high-ranking team members as Lieutenant Governor Wilson and Attorney General Lefkowitz.[1]

Methods, Meetings, and the Pecking Order

Two of Nelson Rockefeller's basic characteristics, among others, significantly affected the way he operated as governor. One factor—perhaps reflecting his ebullient personality, great wealth, and upbringing—was his enormous self-confidence. As a result of it, he was perfectly comfortable surrounding himself with people brighter than he. Some were senior staff members. Others were experts whom he brought in to consult or help solve specific problems. Still others were brilliant people he knew from the high-level social, governmental, political, and artistic circles in which he traveled.

The other factor was his dyslexia, which made reading uncomfortable for him. He did read, of course, but staffers soon learned that any memos they wrote for him had to be short, usually no more than a page.

Because of this condition, his principal method of gaining information was through listening, not reading. He wanted to hear and question the experts directly, rather than plowing through their published papers or long-winded memos. He also wanted the considered opinions of his senior staff, but only if the subject was within their particular area of expertise.

Michael Whiteman, who was hired as an assistant counsel in 1963 after Harvard Law School and was counsel to the governor in Rockefeller's last three years in office, described his own experience with the governor's insistence on expert opinion. At the time, funding the state's unemployment insurance program had become a problem, and the administration faced conflicting pressures from employers and advocates for the jobless. Rockefeller asked Whiteman to bring in an expert to discuss the issue.

"So I brought in Fred [Alfred L.] Green, who was head of the unemployment insurance program and was nationally recognized as an expert in the field," Whiteman said. "And Fred was explaining something to the governor and I perceived, rightly or wrongly, that the governor was not following what Fred was saying. So I interrupted, and started to give my own explanation, which I thought would be in plainer English. The governor punched me on the arm and said, 'I don't want to hear from you—he's the expert. Let him talk.'" Others had similar experiences over the years.

In part because of this emphasis on expert opinion, staff meetings developed a distinctive character. Recalled Whiteman:

We used to say there was a pecking order around the lunch table where you had senior staff sitting. It was a long, narrow table. The governor would sit here [at the head of the table], and Malcolm [Lieutenant Governor Wilson] would sit here [on the governor's left], and Louie [Attorney General Lefkowitz] would sit there [next to Wilson], and Bob [Counsel Robert R. Douglass] would sit over there [on the governor's right], and I would sit here [next to Douglass], and then you'd go down the table from there. And once you'd got past the first two or three on each side, the next person might have been somebody who was there specially to talk about something. But once you got past that, you got into some sort of pecking order, which could vary from time to time, depending on whether you were in good standing or not.

Staff members who had committed some blunder or otherwise annoyed the governor were sent to the far end of the table, or simply not invited at all for awhile. Joe Boyd recalled those Albany staff meetings, which he first began attending in 1966.

They were held Mondays and Tuesdays in the conference room on the second floor of the Capitol, where the governor's office and other Executive Chamber offices were located.

The room was easily accessed from the governor's inner office via Ann Whitman's office, where my desk was first located, and from the secretary to the governor's office, or by a door that opened to a corridor opposite the desk where a New York state trooper sat. Invitations were good only one day at a time. A secretary would call at 11 A.M. on the day of the luncheons. Sometimes you were invited one day but not the next, according to your behavior the first day.

Joe's description of the typical lunch meeting was similar to Whiteman's, but he elaborated on who was likely to be in attendance. In addition to the secretary to the governor, Alton G. Marshall (in effect, the government's chief operating officer) and the budget director, T. Norman Hurd, there were such others as the appointments officer, the press secretary, the director of communications, various special assistants, Ann Whitman, often the current Republican state chairman, and different commissioners, depending on the issues to be discussed. In Joe's words:

We all gathered at 1 P.M. for ONE glass of Dubonnet red wine or Harvey's Bristol Cream sherry, followed by a hot lunch catered by Joe's Restaurant of Madison Avenue [Albany] and served by Julio.

Usually the governor would bounce in from his last morning appointment, followed by Ann with a stack of folders containing memos from staff, commissioners' weekly reports, Legislative Program bills, and mail from friends, party leaders, and constituents. The governor would get his Dubonnet and then assign seats according to "rank" on that particular day. For example, if you had gotten into a difference of opinion with the governor on Monday, he might tell you to move down two seats toward the corridor door on Tuesday.

Since I was thirty years younger than the governor and most of the staff, I was always seated at that end of the room, but happy just to be included in the inner circle.[2]

As we started lunch, the governor would begin at the top of his pile. He expected each participant to listen to every issue and subject discussed.

The governor ran his meetings like a strict schoolmaster, Joe explained.

If he thought your attention was elsewhere he would ask you a question about the issue at hand. You could only take one strike a month in this ballgame. On administrative or legislative issues the governor would many times call the [relevant] commissioner on the phone next to his place at the head of the table. Occasionally a commissioner would have a time when he was to appear before the whole group and explain a memo. On some issues, he would just be summoned.

Commissioners learned that on the days Rockefeller was in Albany, it was prudent to have their lunch in their office, stay by the phone, and wear a suit.

Commissioners who had outside appointments would let Ann Whitman's office know when and where they could be reached. Added Joe:

These sessions focused on the problems of running New York State's government, whether it was the size and water capacity of toilets required on boats or how more money could be found to expand some social program. The governor's legislative program was normally reviewed each Monday, since he wanted to be prepared for the regular Tuesday morning breakfast at the mansion with the legislative leaders.

The staff luncheon meeting would continue many days until 4 p.m., with the governor sliding out of his office for quick, five-minute meetings with outside people.

Joe said that staff would continue the discussion, often presenting the governor with a recommendation when he returned.

Thus were the grand programs and gritty minutiae of government hashed over and dealt with, and the entire administration team kept informed and focused and moving in the direction of the governor's goals.

That is not to say there weren't lighter moments amid the daily grind of decision-making. Joe described one such occasion in his letter of condolence to Malcolm Wilson's daughter Katherine after her father's death in 2000 at the age of eighty-six.

My favorite memory was the time in the early '60s when Malcolm, Louie, and senior staff would gather Sunday evenings at the mansion in Albany. We met in the living room and your father had his papers arranged by subject in his open briefcase on the floor. His glass of orange juice was next to the briefcase. We were ready to adjourn from dinner and continue our discussion of various issues when Carl Spad, then appointments officer, in getting up knocked over the orange juice into the briefcase and all over the papers.

Malcolm didn't say a word to Spad. Rockefeller was beside himself trying to contain his laughter. Malcolm took out his handkerchief and started to wipe off each paper. He turned to Nelson and said, "It would be injudicious to continue our discussion and make decisions before I am able to dry off my notes."[3]

Leadership and Accountability

In running the state, Rockefeller managed to avoid getting bogged down in all the nuts and bolts.

"He liked the governing process," recalled Whiteman. "I wouldn't have described it as attention to detail. He was interested in how things worked and how things were built. But I think more characteristic of his executive style was to find people in whom he had confidence as knowledgeable in their field, an Alan Miller [Dr. Alan D. Miller, Commissioner of Mental Hygiene], for example, and to give them their head."

As a prime example of the impact and success of this approach, Whiteman cited the case of the Public Service Commission, a bipartisan board that regulates utility rates in New York State. After he took office, Rockefeller had not reorganized or revamped the PSC, unlike most other state agencies. Now he was getting complaints about the commission, whose members were not very experienced, and it had become an embarrassment. A strong hand was needed.

Rockefeller directed Harry W. Albright Jr., the appointments officer at the time, to compile a list of potential candidates to chair the commission. The top name on Albright's list was that of Joseph C. Swidler, a tough, Democratic lawyer, early New Dealer, and public power expert who had headed the federal government's Tennessee Valley Authority.

"There were several things about the appointment of Joe Swidler that impressed me," recalled Whiteman. He continued,

> The first was, Swidler came in and said to the governor, "I need to know that I have your backing." And the governor's response was, "If you're named the chairman, it's your responsibility to carry out the mission and straighten the place out, and I just want results. I'm not going to interfere—you're the one who knows how to do it." That was very explicit on both sides.
>
> The second thing was that he [the governor] called in the heads of the utilities. You asked how did he get things done, how did he persuade people, and it was the sort of crowding them, getting his arm around them, "How are ya, how are ya, fella," look you in the eye and remind you, with all kinds of body language, that you were the only person in the room. He called them in and said, "Guess what we're going to do!"
>
> And the response was, essentially, well, he wouldn't have been our choice, but he's a good man, we can trust him. And we know you'll make sure that he carries out the mission, gets it done. And they swallowed that because they knew that he had the governor's backing, that he wouldn't be wishy-washy, and that whatever he said would stick, because there wouldn't be a lot of pushing and pulling and changing overnight as had been the case with his predecessor. But nobody had paid much attention to the Public Service Commission, and they saw, by appointing Swidler, that he [the governor] was paying attention.
>
> And the third thing that impressed me is that Joe did one hell of a job turning that place around, professionalizing the staff, getting the commission to function as a commission. He was a superb cabinet member.

Fixing Mistakes

"The chief executive's job," Whiteman noted, "is to set the mission, assign it to people and then demand accountability. And as much as he might have been interested in detail, he was not a micromanager. If you had a job to do, go do the job and bring back the result. If you made a mistake along the way (and we all had this experience of having to go and tell him, well, we did thus and so and it didn't work out or made somebody mad), he didn't dwell on that. His focus always was, okay, how are we going to fix it, or where are we going to go from here, because we still want to get something done. So let's figure out what we'll do to fix it."

A classic example of this way of dealing with subordinates' errors was recounted by Robert D. Stone, a lawyer from Binghamton who held various positions in the Rockefeller administration, and whom the governor tapped in 1967 as his appointments officer.

Stone recalled that during the 1967 legislative session, the legislature created the Niagara Frontier Transportation Authority, and that it had fallen to him, as appointments officer, to recommend to the governor the people to be appointed as members of the authority. One of his recommendations, championed by the Erie County Republican organization, was the then editor of the Buffalo *Evening News*.

> The governor accepted the recommendations, and a press release was duly issued. That very evening, while my family and I were at dinner, the phone rang and one of my daughters answered. A moment later, she returned breathlessly to the dining room, saying, "Dad, the governor's on the phone!"
>
> This was not an everyday occurrence at our house, and I grabbed the phone equally breathlessly. "Yessir!"
>
> "Robert," the governor said calmly, "I have just had a long and unpleasant conversation with the publisher of the Buffalo *Courier Express* (a formidable lady of the same ilk as the former publisher of the *Washington Post*, Katharine Graham, and an important Republican contributor), who wants to know how in hell I could appoint her competitor to anything. What are we going to do about it?"
>
> I responded, with what I thought in retrospect was admirable alacrity, "We're going to appoint her to something else."
>
> "Right,' said the governor. "Let me know by 9 A.M. tomorrow what it is." In my years on or near the second floor [the floor of the Capitol housing the Executive Chamber], I never saw Nelson Rockefeller lose his cool, even when his staff goofed.

Rockefeller expected his commissioners and their staffs to carry out their duties rigorously and impartially, although in doing so they might step on the toes of people in high places. John Hanna Jr. recalled an experience at the newly created Department of Environmental Conservation (DEC) that illustrates the governor's effective management technique in such situations.

I was general counsel and had approved the drafting and promulgation of regulations forbidding the construction of jetties along beaches on the South Shore of Suffolk County, Long Island. These were being constructed by wealthy shorefront property owners to collect sand for their beaches.

Trapping the sand meant depriving their neighboring beach of sand and also damaged the ecology of the east-to-west sand renewal of the Long Island South Shore. Juan Trippe, the flamboyant founder and longtime head of Pan American World Airways, was such a property owner.[4] Trippe was assertive about what he wanted. He was furious with DEC and especially me.

I called Michael Whiteman, counsel to the governor, to alert him that Trippe might be calling. I said the regulation was greatly needed and that if an exception was to be made for Trippe then the regulation should be scrapped. I wasn't asking for permission, just giving a heads-up. Nothing, so far as I heard, ever happened. Several years later when Michael and I had been law partners for a couple of years, I asked him if anything had happened. "Oh, yes," said Michael, "Juan called the governor and demanded that you be fired." In other words, I was told nothing because even the knowledge that Trippe had involved the governor might dampen my willingness in the future to do what was right. I hope not, but I endorse the management technique.

Lugheads Need Not Apply

Rockefeller's habit of ignoring party affiliations in the hiring process was an aspect of his management style that contributed greatly to the competence of his administration but posed an ongoing challenge to his appointments officers.

One such was the previously mentioned Robert Stone, a combat veteran of World War II and graduate of Hamilton College and Columbia Law School. He was one of the administration's principal utility infielders—able to handle any position capably. Appointed deputy secretary of state when Rockefeller took office in 1959, he became deputy commissioner of the Office of General Services in 1960, serving until Rockefeller asked him to be appointments officer in 1967.

NAR's invitation to me to become his appointments officer was issued—typically, as I was to learn, in the back seat of the Albany limousine en route to the airport. I said yes, of course; and then the governor said, "I want to be sure you understand the job. I want you to keep the county chairmen happy, but I don't want any lugheads."

Although just a country boy from Broome County, I recognized an oxymoron when I heard one. After a minimum of reflection, I made the decision—no lugheads—that had Charlie Schoeneck and Jack Vandervort, the chairman and executive director of the Republican state committee, gnashing their teeth during most of 1967.[5]

NAR didn't abide lugheads, and richly deserved his reputation of attracting top people to government.

Stone also recounted a story that reflected another facet of Rockefeller's particular style of running things—his willingness to ignore established lines of authority in the interest of achieving a specific goal.

"Also in 1967," said Stone, "the November ballot included a proposition that would authorize a transportation bond issue." The $2.5 billion bond issue was controversial, not only because of its unprecedented size but because voters were beginning to sense Rockefeller's proclivity for borrowing to finance programs the state couldn't otherwise afford. As Stone recalled it:

The pitch for voter support was carefully crafted to include funds for subways, buses, rail, and highways. In September, 1967, the governor perceived that the campaign for voter approval wasn't going well. Ann Whitman summoned me to the governor's office, where NAR said: "Robert, I don't like the way the bond issue campaign is going. Turn the appointments office over to Hi Sheffer [Hiram F. Sheffer Jr., then assistant appointments officer], move to the Flag Room, and take control of the bond issue campaign."

Having done that, I traveled to Manhattan to take a look at a bunch of TV ads that were being developed by the ad agency we were using. They were good. But when I asked which would be shown where, the ad people said, "Well, they'll all be shown in all markets."

Without pausing to think about the fairly heady company I was in, I blurted out: "You mean you're going show subway ads in Watertown?" The ad campaign was retargeted with a more local focus.

When I later recounted the story to the governor, he fairly beamed. And the bond issue was approved by the people. Moral: When it came to accomplishing what he wanted, NAR didn't worry about organizational lines, or indeed about disrupting the hell out of someone's office.[6]

The Recruiter

Throughout his career, Rockefeller staffed his operations with the most capable people he could find, and he was a skillful and persuasive recruiter. Party affiliation didn't matter, as Stephen Berger learned personally in 1971.

"The governor had established the Scott Commission to investigate the city of New York," Berger recalled, "and I received a call one day from Ann Whitman, who said the governor wanted to meet me and discuss my becoming executive director."

Ann said he'd like to see me that day and she'd send a car for me. Since I lived on Seventy-Fifth Street and his office was on Fifty-Fifth Street, I offered to get there on my own. She said he wanted to see me in Albany. Fifteen minutes later a car was there and in a couple of hours I was in his office in Albany.

I had never met him before, was a very active Democrat, and my candidacy was strongly opposed by Malcolm Wilson. The governor knew that I had recently run [former Bronx borough president] Herman Badillo's campaign for mayor and Badillo had been one of the members of the Attica negotiating team. He began the conversation by asking about Herman and describing Herman's role at Attica. I told him that I frankly thought that Herman had been right in proposing delay, and expected that that would be the end of the interview and I would be back in the car in ten minutes.

Instead, the governor seriously and calmly laid out the reasons he made the decisions he did and we talked about it for almost an hour. At the end of the hour, and he was just warming up, he said we should continue at dinner, which went late into the night.

What I saw that night was not only the charm, persuasiveness, and seductiveness of Nelson Rockefeller, but also his sense of total command. Most impressive was the quality totally unique among political leaders: his lack of defensiveness and the incredible willingness to talk extraordinarily frankly with someone who saw things very differently, and the ability to find common ground to move forward. It was the same force of personality that enabled him to reach labor leaders, rural politicians, bankers, academics, intellectuals, and people across all political spectrums that I saw in the first hour I met him and continued to see in the years ahead. Of course, I went to work for him.

Dr. Abe Lavine, in his own very first substantive conversation with Rockefeller, saw how that vibrant, outgoing personality helped the governor in his work. Lavine, deputy director of the state Labor Department's Division of Employment, was being interviewed—on a plane ride from Albany to New York, not surprisingly—for the newly established position of director of the Office of Employee Relations.

What was most evident was Governor Rockefeller's high respect for unions. The point that he stressed particularly was the importance of personal relationships with union representatives, a view reflected in his own strong and friendly relations with state and national labor leaders.

This view was evident again when on the occasion of a social event at the mansion, I mentioned to Governor Rockefeller my first meeting with the then-AFSCME president, Jerry Wurf. [The American Federation of State, County and Municipal Employees represented mental health employees and prison guards, among others.]

I related to the governor some of the nasty, insulting language that Wurf had used in an obvious attempt to intimidate a newcomer to the scene. We both laughed about it. Sometime later, the governor told me how incensed he was, and how he told his friend, George Meany [then president of the AFL-CIO], to calm down this fellow, Wurf.

One key member of the Rockefeller inner circle who joined the team by a different route was Harry Albright, an Albany lawyer who frequently represented clients before the legislature or the governor's office.

"I wouldn't call him a lobbyist, but he was a very persuasive fellow who could get anything through the legislature, and often did, except for this one incident," recalled Robert Douglass, speaking at a memorial tribute to Albright in early 2009. The incident occurred in 1967, when Rockefeller announced that he was going to sign a special bill he had promoted involving public health care.

So everybody thought it was a great bill, especially the governor. But the Medical Society [of the state of New York, Albright's client] didn't particularly like it. They had several objections to it. So Harry came in and he worked with me and he talked with the governor and we ironed out some of the differences, and finally the bill was shaped up and was passed by the legislature. The bill-signing was to take place in the Red Room [the Governor's formal office in the Capitol].

Everybody came—the press came, the public came, public officials came, the Medical Society people were there—they didn't get all that they wanted, but they got a lot of it. And I thought, "I think I'd better write the governor a note here," because Harry did not want to be singled out, especially since he had helped his client with the bill, but not all of the bill, and he didn't want any of the credit or any of the attention. So I wrote a note to the governor, and I said, "Governor, whatever you do, do NOT mention Harry's name in front of his client."

Well, the governor was dyslexic, and the "not" looked like, well, I don't know what. Anyway, he launched into this great accolade about Harry Albright—if it hadn't been for him the bill would never have passed—and Harry kept sinking down in one of those big leather chairs. Afterward, he came up to me and he said, "I have to resign." And I said, "Why?" He said, "It's a matter of honor." I said, "What's the matter of honor? The Medical Society got almost everything they wanted." He said, "No, I really shouldn't have played such an active role." I said, "Harry, go home and forget it."

One week later, Harry was in my office, with his tail still dragging, and he said, "You know what? I want to join the Rockefeller administration." And I said, "Harry, we welcome you."

Albright was appointed a deputy secretary to the governor and later given the added job of appointments officer. Still later he became superintendent of banks.

Douglass noted that Albright brought many unusual talents to the job of appointments officer, but one useful talent he didn't bring—he couldn't remember people's names. "And when you're the appointments officer, you're supposed to make hundreds and hundreds of appointments, and you've got to remember people's names."

One day, Douglass recalled, he was reminding Albright that the governor was anxious to appoint a new chairman for the Ogdensburg Bridge Authority.

I said, "It's been on your desk for two months." Maybe it was in the trunk of his car—he kept his whole life in the trunk of the car. He had skis and boots and tennis racquets in there all season long. And he said, "Yeah, yeah, I'm sorry. It's on my desk somewhere—what's the guy's name?" I said, "I don't know, you're the appointments officer." "Oh, yeah," he said, "he's a banker up in Ogdensburg, a guy with white hair who wears blue suits a lot, and he wears neat ties. That's the guy," Harry said. "Well, I'll figure it out and we'll get him appointed."

As de facto leader of the Republican Party in New York State, Governor Rockefeller frequently sought to persuade capable people to run for office. Roy M. Goodman, who was finance administrator for the city of New York during the first two years of John Lindsay's first term as mayor, told this story:

The place was the Dorado Beach Hotel in Puerto Rico, the year, 1968. My wife, Barbara, and I and our five-year-old son went to the beach and encountered Nelson and Happy Rockefeller and their five-year-old son, Nelson Jr. While our two little boys played in the sand, the governor and I were discussing politics. My wife emerged from our beachside suite to announce that I had a phone call from state senator Mike Seymour [Whitney North Seymour] and Republican county chairman Vincent Albano.

The two of them urged me in that phone call to come back to New York to run for the state senate seat being vacated by Seymour, who planned to run against Ed Koch for the 17th congressional district seat in the House of Representatives. I told them I would have to consult with my political adviser, who was with me at the time (not mentioning the governor by name).

I came out to the beach and said to the governor: "You'll never guess what just happened, speak of crazy coincidences, just as you and I were discussing the politics of it, my state senator and county chairman called to offer me the opportunity to enter a contest for the state senate seat from the 26th senate district. What is your advice?" I asked the governor.

His reply was an enthusiastic, "Go for it!" After a hurried conversation with my wife, who had heard the governor's urgings, I returned to the telephone and accepted the bid to run for the state senate. Little did I imagine at that time that Governor Nelson Rockefeller had persuaded me to embark on a course of action that was to last thirty-three years in the state senate.

The governor did not always succeed in his persuasive efforts, however. He tried repeatedly with a promising young lawyer named Harold Tyler, with only brief success. Tyler recalled that on his return to New York in 1961 after several years as an assistant U.S. attorney general in the Eisenhower administration, Rockefeller asked him to run for Congress from the 26th congressional district, essentially the eastern half of Westchester County. Tyler said no, despite offers of financial help.

"At the conclusion," Tyler said, "he said to me that he would catch up with me with another job for the state of New York in the near future. True to his word, later that year he persuaded me to be the New York State commissioner of the [bi-state] Waterfront Commission of New York Harbor."

But in 1962, Tyler wrote Rockefeller that he had been nominated for a federal judgeship by President Kennedy and would have to resign as waterfront commissioner. That summer, Tyler attended the swearing-in ceremony of his successor at the governor's Fifty-Fifth Street office, "whereupon Nelson Rockefeller congratulated me for becoming the new Waterfront Commissioner! I believe that we all had a good laugh about that mistake." Some years later, Tyler said, Malcolm Wilson called him on the governor's behalf to ask if he would consent to be appointed to a vacancy on the court of appeals, the state's highest court. That would require him subsequently to run for election later that year.

"As I told Malcolm, I did not want to leave my position as a trial judge in the federal system. A day or two later, a familiar voice called me directly. It was Nelson Rockefeller. He said, 'I don't know what is wrong with you—or me—but I certainly have a very difficult time persuading you to take some very good positions.'"

One officeholder who was not recruited by Rockefeller became a huge fan of the governor during the 1966 campaign and has remained one ever since.

"When I was in the Senate," said former Long Island Republican senator John Dunne, "my feeling about Nelson Rockefeller was the same as it is today. I'm not ashamed to say that he was one of my heroes."

Dunne, who now practices law in Albany, recalled that in the summer of 1966, he was finishing his first term as a senator, and the Republican organization asked him to come to the capital district to campaign for a new candidate for the Senate seat in that area. In their travels around the district that hot summer day, they crossed paths with the Rockefeller reelection campaign, and Dunne was offered a ride back to the metropolitan area on the governor's plane. On the plane, he happened to sit across from the governor.

"I was exhausted and he looked pretty spent," Dunne remembered, "but he spent half an hour talking with me." He continued,

You know, I was a freshman senator, and that doesn't amount to much, but he talked about politics and life in general. And I asked him, straight out, how is it that you became a Republican? And he kind of smiled and said, "Well, I'll tell you. There was one point, down there [in Washington], I didn't know which way I'd go. And I said if I became a Democrat, I'd probably have to spend a lot of energy holding back people in the Democratic Party from engaging in certain programs or activities. Whereas, I think I can spend my energy more effectively in the Republican Party by leading and drawing them in the right direction and toward some of the programs and policies that I believe in."

I've never forgotten that—not only his generosity in taking time to speak to a freshman senator, but also his interest in people and his character, in speaking out so frankly, and I believe, honestly, because his record certainly demonstrates the great leadership ability that he had.

A Thoughtful Boss

Rockefeller's interest in people was reflected in many ways, including his thoughtfulness and concern for the members of his staff and their families.

Melvin Osterman recalled that during a period when he was an assistant counsel to the governor, his then wife broke her leg, and they subsequently attended a reception at the mansion. His wife was on crutches, her leg in a cast.

"Several months later," he said, "we had occasion to be at another reception. By this time, my wife had shed her cast and crutches. When we reached the governor on the receiving line, he commented about the fact that my wife seemed to be recovering. That kind of attention to detail inspired incredible loyalty."

Mike Whiteman observed that Rockefeller was warmer and more open with old friends, such as several from his college days, than with his staff. "The nature of the relationship was different," he said. "He was friendly with the rest of us. He was warm, to a degree, he was thoughtful, he would ask about family. If it was a party, he would always come up to the spouse and say something nice. He always said something nice to Margery about me, always thanked her for her sacrifices. And I remember I said to Margery once, 'I bet he says that to everybody.' And she said, "Yes, but he thought enough to say it.'"

Rockefeller worked extremely hard and expected his staff to do the same. But he knew when to lighten up.

Osterman, who later served as director of the Office of Employee Relations, again harked back to his assistant counsel days with this story about the annual scramble at the end of the legislative session, the so-called thirty-day bill period. This is the period after the legislature adjourns when the governor signs or vetoes every one of the thousand or so bills the departing lawmakers dump on his desk. The counsel's office has to prepare a detailed memo and recommendation on every bill. Osterman reflected,

The thirty-day bill period in those days was a horrendous experience. It is my recollection that the first week we were there every night until about eleven, the second until midnight, the third until two or three in the morning, and the final week virtually all night. At some point in the process, at about eleven at night, I put my feet up on my desk and started to read the *New York Times* to take a break from dealing with the hundreds of bills before us. The governor picked that moment to come down the corridor, passing my office on the way to the office of Sol Corbin, then counsel to the governor.

The same thing happened a week later. At this point, however, the governor stopped and came into my office. I was, of course, mortified. To be caught twice in two weeks "goofing off" seemed to me a terrible offense. The governor, however, grinned broadly and commented, in substance, "I really enjoy seeing you like this, Mel. It tells me that all's not quite crazy in this world."

Thus we see a governor who knows what he wants and is accustomed to getting it. He is energetic, ambitious, and self-confident. He understands leadership, likes the process of governing, and has his own techniques for gathering information and arriving at decisions. He does not hesitate to shake up his organization in pursuit of a specific goal or result.

He likes people, attracts talented individuals to his service, and is skilled at getting their best out of them. He is masterful at gaining their loyalty.

Nor is he reluctant, as we shall see, to use other tools in his kit—his personal charm, his wealth, and his family's reach and influence—that contribute to his success and to his unique place in the political and governmental life of his time.

4

Governing New York

Governing in a democracy is a messy process, and governing a state as large, complex, and populous as New York is even messier. The process is untidier still when the governor is an energetic visionary who views large public projects and far-reaching programs as not only important progress for the state and its populace but as demonstrable evidence of his own fitness for higher office.

Bold Visions, Gritty Realities

Major projects and programs seemed to flow like a bubbling stream from the fertile mind of Nelson Rockefeller, constrained mainly by the need to obtain the resources and legal authority to carry them out.

Not surprisingly, opposition began to develop early on as voters and lawmakers came to perceive and fret about the scope and cost of Rockefeller's ambitions. Republican Party officials worried about losing their longtime but narrowing margins of control in the legislature.

That Governor Rockefeller was able to accomplish as much as he did, while winning election four times, is a reminder of his skill as a politician and his forcefulness as a leader. Stories relating to some of his major legislative and construction accomplishments offer some insights as to how he was able to work his will on so many for so long.

Although the vast expansion of the state university is probably his biggest undertaking overall, Governor Rockefeller's largest and most dramatic single construction effort was known, at the time, simply as the South Mall.

Brasilia on the Hudson

The capital city that Rockefeller found when he took office in January 1959 was quirky, somewhat down-at-heel, and tightly controlled by the entrenched O'Connell machine.

Daniel P. O'Connell was elected city assessor on a reform ticket in 1919, and two years later, as Democratic county chairman, engineered the ouster of the corrupt Republican Barnes machine. Remaining largely behind the scenes, "Uncle Dan," as he was widely known, ran the city and later the surrounding (and more Republican) county with an iron fist for five and a half decades, until his death in 1977, and his political heirs run the city today. So dominant was the Democratic vote in the city of Albany that in 1948 President Harry Truman, running for a full term but considered certain to lose to New York governor Thomas E. Dewey, made a courtesy call on Uncle Dan to ask for support.[1] He got it. In the city of Albany, with a population of 135,000, the machine gave Truman a huge majority, enough to overcome Republican strength in the surrounding suburban and rural parts of Albany County by 16,000 votes. Running against Dewey, who was in the middle of the second of his three terms as governor, Truman came extremely close to capturing New York State, with its huge block of forty-seven electoral votes. Truman lost by only about 61,000 votes out of almost 6.2 million cast, a margin of less than 1 percent.

Dewey, who had made his name as the racket-busting Manhattan district attorney, had no use for the O'Connell machine, but had no success in driving it from power, either, despite several corruption investigations. When Rockefeller became governor in 1959, he took a different approach: as it turned out, he did have a use for the O'Connell machine.

Princess Beatrix of the Netherlands visited Albany in September 1959 to commemorate the 350th anniversary of Henry Hudson's historic exploration of the Hudson River in 1609 and his voyage up the river to what is now Albany, which was founded as a trading post later that year.

Rockefeller was reportedly distressed that the she had to travel through a slummy section of town to reach the mansion. Supposedly he decided right then and there that something had to be done to spruce up and modernize the city. The gigantic South Mall project—now called the Nelson A. Rockefeller Empire State Plaza—was the result, and all because of Princess (now Queen) Beatrix's visit.

John Egan, who at this writing is commissioner of the Office of General Services, has a slightly different take on the story. In 1959 he was part of a core group established as a nucleus for the newly created OGS, which consolidated all the buildings-and-grounds and state office construction and maintenance functions of the many state departments.

Recalled Egan:

Everybody knows the story of him bringing Princess Beatrix up from the railroad station. Some people think it was from the river. There are two schools of thought on that, that she came by boat and he brought her to the mansion. But to do that, he had to go through this seedy part of downtown Albany. That's part of the folklore—I think it's probably right.

But a lot of us that were here knew that he had something in mind for Albany, and that it was an excuse that Princess Beatrix was here and saw how distressed downtown Albany was. So the announcement (of the formation of the Commission on the Capital City) came out, under the head of (Lieutenant Governor) Malcolm Wilson. She had gone. And in nineteen days after the announcement of the commission, Malcolm Wilson came out with a report that we should have a new seat of state government called the South Mall, and the legislature appropriated $20 million for it.

Those of us who were here in OGS were given major responsibilities for it. My commissioner was Gen. Cortlandt van Rensselaer Schuyler. He could strut sitting down. He was very friendly with Governor Rockefeller. Rockefeller was big on bringing ex-Army generals into state government.[2]

So that's how it all began. We started the project. The design of it was very difficult. We were pretty much told what to do by Governor Rockefeller, because he knew exactly what he wanted to do. And we'd learned that when Governor Rockefeller said something "would be nice," well, that was marching orders.

Sometimes we questioned it privately. When he announced that we were going to clean up the water and the air and the earth and started the new Department of Environmental Conservation, we kind of laughed, because we knew the Hudson River was never going to be cleaned up—but it is.

So whenever he said something, it was an order. So it was with the South Mall. I was assigned down here at the time with the design and construction unit. Almost every Friday, General Schuyler would go to New York City to meet with the governor, the architect, and the engineering firm. John Hennessy was the lead engineer, and Wally [Wallace] Harrison was the architect. But the real architect was Nelson Rockefeller. Conceptually, every bit of this project was his idea, I'm convinced of that. When our fellows came back from New York, we held our breath, because we knew there was going to be something new, there'd be something dramatic, something was going to change. And we didn't question it, because that was what

the governor wanted. And so the project was built. It started out to
be an estimated $250 million, and at the end, it was $985 million.

Design changes and the resulting construction delays were major
contributors to the soaring cost. One such change involved designing
and building a six-story Cultural Education Center to house the
State Museum, State Library, and State Archives, which had all been
squeezed into the State Education Building. The governor thought it
would more effectively anchor the south end of the project than the
triumphal "Freedom Arch" originally planned. And it did, but at a cost
of $250 million, which included the cost of building a bridge over the
highway. Costs also escalated because of the difficult, hilly terrain, the
sheer size of the project, and the impossibility of keeping the various
contractors from getting in each other's way.

Today the Mall—that is, the Nelson A. Rockefeller Empire State
Plaza—is a an open but landscaped stone platform almost a half mile
long, extending from the Capitol to the Cultural Education Center,
which is near the mansion. That platform is flanked on one side by an
office building, a performing arts center ("the Egg"), and a forty-four-
story office tower, and on the other by a legislative office building and
four state office buildings. But it is not just a platform: it is the roof
of a gigantic six-story building that contains underground parking,
meeting rooms, restaurants, offices, and a central corridor enabling
people to get from the Capitol to any of the buildings without having
to cope with the wind, cold, and snow of Albany's bitter winters.

Early in the construction process, Rockefeller had the state begin
buying the massive artworks that many years later would line that long
central corridor—ninety-two pieces. This was done via a committee
whose carefully chosen members knew Rockefeller's tastes.

"So everybody understood what the artists were going to be
providing," explained Egan, "and the rest is history. So we went
through the project, and the changes, but he was involved in every
major aspect of it. You know the story of the Egg, with the grapefruit
at the breakfast table—I believe that's true."

The story is that Rockefeller, in trying to demonstrate what he
wanted the performing arts center to look like, took a water glass and
perched a half grapefruit (his regular breakfast) on top, at an angle.
And that is just what the building looks like, although some at the time
likened it to a deviled egg on a pedestal, and the egg nickname stuck.

Of course, there were many potholes in the road to completion.
An early one came soon after the first renderings were made public.
Robert Stone, deputy commissioner of OGS at the time, recalled a

panicked call from the architect, Wallace Harrison. The Federal Aviation Agency, Harrison said, had just called and said the planned tower was too tall and would pose a navigation hazard for planes flying in or out of Albany Airport. As Stone described the incident:

In my naivete, I said, "Well, we'll just have to make the tower shorter, right?"

"Wrong," said Wally. "Nelson wants it just the way it is." We quickly decided that we had better lay on a meeting with the F.A.A. to see what we could work out.

We met in the OGS offices in Albany, almost across Washington Avenue from the Alfred E. Smith State Office Building. They brought with them a twenty-foot-long map of the glide paths in that part of the county that was implicated by the airport, identifying most of the major structures in downtown Albany.

After struggling for several minutes to understand the map, I asked, "Where's the Alfred E. Smith Building on this map?" The Governor Alfred E. Smith State Office Building, at 388 feet and thirty-four stories tall, was Albany's tallest building at that point.

The chief of party for the F.A.A. responded, "What Alfred E. Smith building?" I pointed out our front window, raising my index finger at about an 80 degree up angle, and said, "That Alfred E. Smith building." After peering out the window for a few moments with a strange look on his face, the chief of party said, "When was that built?" "It was finished in 1932," I responded. He quickly called a caucus of his people in the hall.

When they returned, the chief said, "Mr. Stone, would you people be willing to put a strobe light on top of the tower?"

That solved the problem, and the strobe light can be seen from hilltops at least twenty-five miles away. The Alfred E. Smith Building remains unlit.

OGS commissioner Egan summed up the Mall experience this way: "I've said it was like being on a rocket about every week. It wasn't a rollercoaster, it wasn't up and down, it was always up, with a tremendous surge of excitement."

In short, the Mall was a project at least equal in scope and complexity to Rockefeller Center, where young Nelson cut his teeth in dealing with the construction industry in the 1930s. And some have likened it to Brasilia, the striking new federal capital city that Brazil created in the wilderness, completing it in 1960—a city that Rockefeller would visit in 1969.

Man and Machine

Whereas Governor Dewey sought to indict Uncle Dan O'Connell and his organization, Rockefeller co-opted them for purposes of his own. The state government could not borrow the sums needed to build the Mall without a statewide referendum, which would almost surely fail. But Albany County could do so, with payments from the state to support the bonds.

So began a careful courtship dance between Nelson Rockefeller and Erastus Corning II, the longtime mayor of Albany and elegant front man for Uncle Dan. Corning was named for his great-grandfather, founder of the New York Central Railroad and mayor of Albany from 1834 to 1837. Corning's father, Edwin, was lieutenant governor in Governor Alfred E. Smith's last term (1927–1928). Erastus II was tall, urbane, and well educated (Groton and Yale). A year younger than Rockefeller, he served in the state assembly and then the state senate, and was elected mayor in 1941. He was drafted into the army in 1942, served throughout the war as a private, and was reelected in absentia. He was in the midst of his eleventh four-year term at his death in 1983.

Corning was undaunted by the Rockefeller wealth and position, having grown up in similar social circles. He had known the Rockefeller family at least somewhat since boyhood, and once recalled for reporters that in his youth, he was sometimes required by his family to participate in summertime calls at the straitlaced Rockefeller household at Seal Harbor, Maine. He disliked going, he said, because "you could never get a drink."

The upshot of Rockefeller's pas de deux with Corning was an ingenious agreement under which Albany County would borrow to finance the Mall, which the state would build and then lease from the county. The lease payments would cover the costs of paying off the bonds, and the voters need not be consulted. Rockefeller was happy to give Mayor Corning all the credit for figuring out how to do the deal, although it is almost certain that Rockefeller's financial wizards put it together. (Many years later, the plaza was named for Rockefeller, its tower for Corning.)

This arrangement had benefits for both Rockefeller and the O'Connell organization. It meant that any serious effort to investigate and prosecute the machine's leaders for corruption was unlikely during Rockefeller's tenure. Vast numbers of local construction jobs would be involved, providing a golden opportunity for the local Democratic Party.

Rockefeller needed the machine's cooperation as well. The run-down area he planned to raze for the project—known as "the Gut"—was a heavily Democratic neighborhood whose concentrated votes Uncle Dan might otherwise be reluctant to see dispersed. A hostile city government could have made things hard and expensive for Mall contractors and their employees. Myriad local issues and projects, not all involving the Mall, would be easier to resolve with a slightly more cooperative relationship between local and state authorities.

The Rockefeller administration not only worked hard to assure labor peace in that complicated, multi-union, multiple-contractor working environment, but to keep the workers contented and productive. There was less thievery than on most projects, Egan noted.

"One of the things we did have was that you could always get a bet placed, a wager, at one of the coffee shops—they called them roach shacks. Nobody really got excited about it (although bookmaking was illegal) because construction workers, well, they like to get a bet in now and then. We tolerated it because it kept things calm." (Joe Boyd said the governor would occasionally disappear for an hour, and Ann Whitman would send him—Joe—to look for him. Joe said he usually found Rockefeller chatting with workers somewhere in the vast construction site.)

And where was the legislature while all this was going on? Why weren't they howling about the size and swelling cost of the project?

Many of them did complain each time a new cost estimate came out, but Rockefeller had carefully co-opted both the legislative leaders and the rank and file early in the process. The carrot he offered them was something every legislator wanted: office space, and by implication, staff and therefore, influence and stature. The Mall would have an entire building specifically for legislative offices.[3]

It is easy to see why this would have been so enticing to the legislators. Even a newly seated back-bencher in the minority party would have a separate office and a full-time staff. Compare that with what had existed before, when the office of even a majority assemblyman, if he wasn't a committee chairman, might consist of a lockable rolltop desk tucked under the eaves on the fifth floor of the Capitol, with one secretary shared with four other members. For the legislative leaders, it meant larger staffs, much more of a year-round operation, and increased resources that would help them hold their own against the power of a governor.

Even so, there were times when the leaders of the legislature balked at approving more money for the Mall, and the governor had to find other means of persuasion. Richard C. Dunham, Rockefeller's director of the budget at the time, recalled an issue with Perry B. Duryea Jr., then the Republican speaker of the assembly, who was refusing to sign off on a $124 million appropriation for the Mall's proposed Cultural Education Center, future home of the state's museum, library, and archives.

> The governor told me, "Dick, you've got to get it approved." It was about 7 p.m. and I walked up the [so-called] Million-Dollar Staircase to the third floor, and saw Duryea talking with Al Marshall (secretary to the governor). So I brought up the Museum Building appropriation and Duryea said, "You're not getting a cent!"
>
> When I told the governor, he said, "Put together a list of the unresolved items that Duryea wants and that Anderson (Republican Senate Majority Leader Warren M. Anderson) wants." Then the governor convened a meeting: Perry, Andy, Rockefeller, and me and my little list. We went over all the items on the list, and the governor agreed to almost everything the leaders wanted. Then we came to the funding for the Museum Building. Not only did both Anderson and Duryea agree to it, but Duryea said, "Are you sure that's enough money?" I don't know what happened between my conversation with Perry and the meeting with the governor a little later, but there must have been a very pointed phone call or two.

Work on the Mall extended virtually throughout Rockefeller's fifteen years in office, and was not yet complete when he resigned at the end of 1973. But all the buildings were either finished or under way by then. Recalled OGS commissioner Egan:

> When he knew he was going to be leaving government, he wanted all of the projects totally under contract. So we had drawings with huge bubbles on them, where it said "to be decided in the field, by field direction."
>
> Anyway, the Egg was the last major building complete. We were working on it and doing the outside to create the shape, and it was very difficult because no one had ever built a building like that, except for one in Poland. One morning the word came down that Nelson wanted to have two theaters inside. So we had to stop everything and regroup, redesign it, to put those two theaters in that are there now. We finished in 1976 or 1977.

Meanwhile, in 1974, according to Joe Boyd, OGS planned to remove the scaffolding from around the Egg, and asked Governor

Wilson if he wanted to use the occasion to dedicate the building as part of his election campaign. Wilson said no because he feared that the Egg would collapse when the scaffolding was taken down.

Putting Muscle behind Urban Development

One of Rockefeller's most controversial initiatives was the 1968 legislation creating the Urban Development Corporation. Not only was the legislation itself potentially explosive, but the way it was passed foreshadowed battles to come. The struggle to pass it pitted the power of a forceful governor, determined to get things built, against the caution of a legislature that tended to reflect constituents' fears for the sanctity of local zoning and about unchecked state power to override it.

Three people who were instrumental in developing the legislation were Charles J. Urstadt, deputy commissioner for operations in the Division of Housing and Community Renewal; Stephen J. Lefkowitz, a lawyer for the agency and son of the attorney general; and Lee Goodwin, assistant director of the State Housing Finance Agency.

Urstadt, whose family had long been in commercial real estate and who had worked for the flamboyant developer William Zeckendorf, was recruited for the housing post in 1967 by Robert Douglass, counsel to the governor. Urstadt said the governor told him there were three housing-related things he wanted to accomplish: to get low-income housing built in urban renewal areas, to build middle-income housing, and to build Battery Park City on the Manhattan site created along the Hudson riverbank in part by fill taken from the World Trade Center project.

During 1967, Urstadt worked on developing the legislation to create the Urban Development Corporation. "The concept was to have the government take over the property and hold it until construction was ready to start," Urstadt explained. What typically happened in government-funded urban renewal projects was that the property was turned over to the developer too soon, before the necessary commitments, financing, and permits were all in place. Many projects foundered when government snags or battles with local opponents led to long delays and ballooning costs. Urstadt's concept was to have the government assume this risk by not releasing the property until all such issues were resolved. In a late 1967 speech, he unveiled a proposal for a quasi-public benefit corporation that would undertake an initial four urban renewal projects in Manhattan, the Bronx, Brooklyn, and Syracuse. Payments received from the developers for the site would be recycled into additional projects.

"But that was never done," Urstadt said. Along the way, the concept changed.

Lefkowitz picked up the narrative:

> The governor wanted a state instrument that could do what cities had been unable to do—build low and moderate income housing, create jobs, and stimulate economic development, and rebuild inner cities that had been depopulated by "white flight" and scarred by unfinished urban renewal projects.
>
> He set out only the broadest outlines of this venture. Bob Douglass and Al Marshall provided some guidelines and parameters. But it was left mostly to Lee Goodwin and me to figure out what this innovative and powerful public agency should look like, how it should operate, and so on.

The governor, said Lefkowitz, "seemed content to paint a broad vision and let us get on with it." He continued,

> Sometime during the winter of 1967–68, I was asked to send a copy of the draft UDC legislation to Ed [Edward] Logue, known for his rebuilding efforts in New Haven and Boston and the author of a study commissioned by Mayor John Lindsay on reorganizing New York City's housing and redevelopment efforts.
>
> One winter morning, I attended a meeting at Fifty-Fifth Street with the governor, Bob Douglass, Harry Albright [appointments officer], and Ed Logue, who had come down from Boston at the request of the governor. The purpose of the meeting was to get Logue's reaction to the proposed corporation (and, I later realized, to allow the governor to meet Logue, whom he would appoint to run UDC). The governor was characteristically charming: "I hear you're quite a guy, Ed."
>
> Logue was characteristically blunt: "This won't work, Governor. The cities and towns will block the Corporation's projects. If it's going to work, it can't be bound by local zoning and other approvals."
>
> If the rest of us were apprehensive, the governor was delighted. This was a man after his own heart: if someone gets in the way, knock him down. And so, in one of the rare instances I can remember the governor giving a specific direction, he told us to do as Logue had suggested. Thus was one of the most controversial and important features of UDC established. The governor seemed unconcerned about the storm that would follow.
>
> The legislation was introduced during the 1968 session, where it was received unenthusiastically. As is the custom in Albany, it

sat quietly until political understandings and other arrangements were sufficiently refined so as to provide an atmosphere conducive to legislative deliberation. I do recall the governor briefing the press and legislative leaders [separately] on the proposal. What I found remarkable was his very quick grasp of a fairly complex piece of legislation based on hurried briefings by Bob Douglass. I do not think he ever read the legislation.

Deputy Housing Commissioner Urstadt was personally opposed to including the power to condemn in the bill. "I thought it was like the atomic bomb—you had it, but you didn't want to use it," he said. But it was now in the bill, and Urstadt, the good soldier, was assigned to explain the legislation to the assembly's Republican caucus. "A Westchester guy said, 'You mean this corporation can go into Scarsdale and condemn property and then build a twenty-story building, ignoring the local property code?' 'Yes,' I said."

Lefkowitz continued the story:

Somewhere between introduction and passage of the UDC legislation, I do remember a strategy meeting on the subject: the governor, Bob Douglass, Al Marshall, and Harry Albright. Perry Duryea's opposition to the bill was reported to the governor; I believe Duryea, the Republican leader in the assembly and owner of a family lobstering business in Suffolk County, was considering running for the U.S. Senate. The governor thought about Duryea opposing his initiative, narrowed his eyes, and said: "Perry's going to need to sell a lot of lobsters to run a statewide campaign." As is well known, the governor had many means of persuasion at his disposal.

Lefkowitz noted that the impetus for passage of the UDC bill was the assassination of Dr. Martin Luther King, on April 4, 1968. With assurances in hand from the legislative leaders that the UDC legislation would pass, Rockefeller, a longtime civil rights supporter, loaded a plane with legislators, civil rights leaders, and others and flew to Atlanta, Georgia, where the funeral was to be held in the Ebenezer Baptist Church. The governor sent word back to Albany that now was the time to move the legislation.[4] Said Lefkowitz:

I recall that it passed in the senate but failed in the assembly, mostly due to opposition by suburban Republicans. The governor was notified. Bill Pfeiffer, Republican state chairman, was produced.

Recalcitrant Republican assemblymen were summoned one by one to speak with Pfeiffer. The bill went back to the assembly later that night, and this time, it passed.

The dramatic turnabout was a major news story statewide next day, but left the *New York Times* with egg on its face. The newspaper's early editions ran with a story, based on the assembly's initial rejection of the bill, that the UDC legislation was dead—as indeed, virtually everyone in Albany believed—a big defeat for Rockefeller at the hands of assemblymen of his own party. There seemed no prospect whatever that the bill would be resurrected. Thus there was considerable chagrin at the newspaper on finding out that the bill had been resuscitated and passed in the wee hours of the morning.

Lefkowitz's description of the administration efforts that brought that about greatly underplays the pressure put on the assemblymen who balked at the UDC bill, and on their county chairmen. It was intense. The governor, informed about the defeat while en route back from the King funeral, was livid about it and pulled out all stops to get it reversed. In addition to Pfeiffer, Al Marshall, and Bob Douglass, and Urstadt, among others, were deployed to wield both carrot and stick to change votes. Their stock-in-trade: knowing what each legislator wanted, what he needed to get reelected, and what he feared.

The governor himself made calls, including one to Putnam Republican assemblyman Willis Stephens, chairman of the Assembly Ways and Means Committee, whom he threatened with a primary if he didn't change his vote. Like others, Stephens saw the light.

Douglass recalled rousting the Schenectady County GOP chairman, who was at a movie with his wife, and telling him he'd better get his legislators in line if he wanted to continue being county chairman.

The day after the vote, Rockefeller asked Urstadt to be president and chief operating officer of UDC, of which Logue would be chairman and chief executive officer. "I knew I couldn't work with Ed Logue," Urstadt said, "because Ed Logue was all government and I was all real estate. So I politely declined—the only time I ever turned him down. He made me Commissioner of Housing, Chairman of the Housing Finance Agency, and Chairman of the Battery Park City Authority."

Urstadt was a firm believer that projects had to be economically viable in themselves and not rely on government subsidies. "The bill as passed provided that the Commissioner of Housing had to approve each UDC project. I fought for two years to get the Department of Housing divorced from UDC because I didn't want to have to approve projects that were uneconomic."

The UDC, arguably the most powerful urban redevelopment vehicle in the country, was thus established under the visionary, activist Logue, a man unafraid to ruffle feathers. But the battle did not end there, as Lefkowitz went on to explain:

> The suburban Republicans never forgot how they had been pressured into voting for UDC, and in subsequent years, they made repeated efforts to curtail its wide power. The governor successfully resisted these efforts, promising to veto any legislation that would diminish UDC. (I was very aware of this phase since, after Harry Albright [appointments officer] told me the governor wanted me to "keep an eye" on Logue, I had gone to work for Ed as UDC's principal Albany operative until 1974.) The governor was very supportive of Logue and gave him a free hand with UDC.
>
> However, Logue, a self-described "old-fashioned liberal," finally pushed the envelope too far. With the governor's approval—I was with him when he asked for and received it—Logue initiated efforts to build low-income housing in nine Westchester towns and in Nassau County. We had several murderous public hearings on the projects, with the police called out to prevent a riot. Ultimately, the suburban Republican legislators forced the governor to accede to a UDC amendment which permitted towns and villages to veto UDC projects. As I recall, the governor was completely pragmatic about it; he had to run for reelection just like everyone else.

Nevertheless, Bob Douglass, for one, considers the creation of UDC, with its powers to override local zoning and the ability to issue bonds to finance housing, retail, or commercial developments, "a legislative triumph," even if its powers were later curtailed.

"Look at Roosevelt Island today, and it is occupied almost from one end to the other, and it was nothing but a couple of hospitals," Douglass said. Roosevelt Island, a mile-and-a-half-long sliver of land in the East River, is connected to Queens on one side by a bridge, to midtown Manhattan on the other side by a high cable car, and to both Manhattan and Queens by subway.[5]

"That was Ed Logue," said Douglass. "And Ed Logue had good ideas but he never worried about how to finance them. Ed had a wonderful attitude, which was, 'Look, we're building this stuff that's absolutely necessary, the state should be funding this, not a development corporation. My job is to get it built, their job is to figure out how to pay for it.'"

House of Cards

The principal way the Rockefeller administration paid for construction programs it couldn't otherwise afford or finance was the so-called moral obligation bond, devised for the administration by a clever municipal bond lawyer named John N. Mitchell.[6] New York's constitution forbids the state from borrowing without a referendum, hence the need for the Pure Waters Bond issue. Mitchell's innovation was to have revenue bonds issued by public benefit corporations, in effect, state agencies. They were not backed by the full faith and credit of the state, but were marketable anyway because the state had expressed its intention, the "moral obligation," to support them if necessary. The bonds successfully skirted the constitutional restrictions, being deemed legal by bond counsel, and soon there were billions of dollars in such bonds financing everything from middle-income housing, urban renewal projects, state university buildings, and other facilities.

Lewis Bart Stone, who served as an assistant counsel to the governor and later as special assistant to the secretary to the governor (Bob Douglass), recalled how the administration dealt with a potential threat to this crucial but fragile financial structure from an unexpected quarter.

"In 1970 or '71," Stone said, "mortgage money was drying up because of inflation. Mortgage lending was limited to [a maximum of] 6 percent interest, so banks were uninterested in lending. There was pressure to do something.

"Two senior staff members on Senator (Senate Majority Leader Earl W.) Brydges' staff, Thornton Edwards and Robert Amdursky, came up with the idea for a State of New York Mortgage Agency—SONYMA [pronounced Sunny May]. It would issue bonds backed by the moral authority of the state." The money would be lent out for home mortgages.

"The Rockefeller administration was lukewarm about it," Stone said, "because the state had so many other agencies borrowing in the municipal bond market. There were limits to what the market could bear, too many kinds of bonds.

"The governor signed the bill, but to activate it, it needed an opinion of bond counsel to say that it did not violate the law or the [state] Constitution, in this case, especially the gifts and loans provision." This provision bars the state from giving away its assets or allowing its credit to be used for private purposes.

SONYMA's bond lawyer, from a prominent Wall Street law firm, was reluctant to issue an opinion without further support, so he suggested a test case be brought by the agency, of which Edwards and Amdursky were now the executive director and assistant executive director.

"The administration," Stone said, "was worried that a test case, if the court decided it the wrong way, might cause the whole house of cards—UDC, HFA [Housing Finance Agency], SUCF (State University Construction Fund)—to collapse. So the decision was made to slow down Edwards and Amdursky. It was suggested to them that they talk with a senior wise man on such things, former governor Thomas E. Dewey, at the law firm of Dewey, Ballantine [at the time, Dewey, Ballantine, Bushby, Palmer & Wood]."

So a meeting was set up, and Stone and Harry Albright, the appointments officer and also a lawyer, were to attend the meeting with Governor Dewey, Edwards and Amdursky, and the bond counsel. An hour before the meeting, however, Stone and Albright sat down with Dewey privately, briefing him on the issues and explaining where the state needed to come out.

"During the meeting," said Stone, "Dewey raised questions and suggested that they not file a lawsuit." As a result, no suit was filed. "So SONYMA does operate, but based, like all the others, on opinion of bond counsel."

Plugging the Budget Gap

During his first two terms in office, Governor Rockefeller had repeatedly raised taxes, borrowed via referendum and subsequently through moral obligation bonds, and tapped various "rainy day" funds that state budget officials assiduously squirreled away for hard times.

The governor is required to present a balanced budget each year for the legislature to act on, and balancing it without boosting taxes was an annual challenge. Richard Dunham recalled that when he became budget director, there was no way to get the governor's proposed budget to balance. There was a deficit of twenty-one million dollars. The governor and his staff worried about how this would be reported when the press discovered it, as they surely would in the governor's annual budget briefing next day. The headlines would emphasize the unbalanced budget, rather than the positive programs the governor was proposing. Various suggested answers to possible questions were tried out and rejected.

Then came the briefing on the budget, a book three inches thick. Sure enough, Emmet O'Brien, Albany bureau chief for the Gannett newspapers and dean of the Capitol press corps, spotted the deficit immediately and asked Rockefeller why the budget was not in balance.

"Well, it's Dick's first year," the governor said, nodding at Dunham. "He'll do better next year." Staff and reporters alike howled with laughter, and the moment passed. The governor, said Dunham, had completely defused the issue.

Robert Douglass recalled a year with an even bigger deficit problem that called for bold action.

> One year there was no way he could cobble up enough money to have a balanced budget, and so he decided to plug the hole in the budget with "revenue sharing." The only trouble was that nobody had effectively come up with a revenue sharing program that would allow him to plug the budget gap. For some time, Rockefeller had advocated federal revenue sharing as an equitable means of funding state and municipal services. The federal government is an efficient collector of taxes, and efficient, as well, at sending out checks. But there was no federal revenue sharing program, and little evident support for one.
>
> Well, that didn't stop him at all. He went down [to Washington] and talked Wilbur Mills (an Arkansas Democrat and chairman of the powerful House Ways and Means Committee) into coming up to Albany for a hearing before the legislature, and committing that he would use his best efforts and would deliver a form of revenue sharing to make states like New York fiscally sound.

Mills did deliver, and New York and the other states received funding for numerous state and municipal projects and programs for several years before revenue sharing was dropped.

While revenue and expense estimates and proposed appropriations are generally listed in the annual state budget as precise figures, the numbers do cloak a certain amount of wiggle room. John Hanna, then a young lawyer with the state's Office of Employee Relations, part of the Executive Chamber, recalled a meeting in which Governor Rockefeller asked Budget Director Dunham if it would be possible to find two hundred thousand dollars in that year's tight budget for a particular project he had agreed to fund.

"I think we can, Governor," Dunham said. Then, walking back to his office after the meeting, Dunham remarked to Hanna with a chuckle: "Hell, the budget isn't even accurate within two hundred million!"

A Passionate Relationship

Lewis Stone, now a State Supreme Court Justice from Manhattan, refers to the landlord-tenant relationship as "the second most passionate relationship known to man." Just as the issue of Social Security is considered "the third rail" of national politics—potentially fatal to all who touch it—so, too, in his opinion, is rent control in New York City.

But in 1971, Stone said, Governor Rockefeller decided to take on the issue of rent control, and Stone was assigned to work on the problem.

Federal rent controls were imposed during World War II, when no new housing could be built. They were lifted soon after the war ended and were abolished in most places, but not in New York, Stone explained. Instead, the state took over the program, a political decision, but then found that no developer would build new housing to meet the pent-up demand as long as rents were still controlled. In a compromise, existing rent-controlled apartments would stay rent-controlled. New units would not be controlled. In 1961, Republican attorney general Louis Lefkowitz ran for mayor of New York and was hounded by pro–rent control forces for supporting a 15 percent rent hike as attorney general. He lost, and convinced that rent control was a political albatross, urged the Rockefeller administration to turn it over to the city.

About that time, the city tightened its restrictions on how many units could be built on a site, so developers rushed to build ahead of the effective date and be grandfathered in. A housing surplus resulted, forcing some landlords to give concessions. By 1968 the glut had been absorbed and a housing shortage had developed, leading landlords to start hiking rents for units built after 1947.

Mayor John V. Lindsay responded by creating a new rent control program called rent stabilization for the uncontrolled units built between 1947 and 1959. He also tightened up enforcement of building codes for pre-1947 rent-controlled apartments, which were deteriorating because landlords had no incentive to keep them up.

"The Lindsay administration commissioned a study on rent-controlled housing," Stone explained. It showed that the rent control system was unsustainable, and would lead to a net loss in terms of housing abandonment and deterioration. The system was a pending, long-term disaster. "The only feasible solution was to raise rents," Stone said.

Only fifty draft copies of the report were produced, Stone said, and Lindsay himself denied it existed, but nonetheless acted on it. His administration developed a system that allowed slow increases in rents until they reached MBR—maximum base rent. That infuriated the renting public, who saw it as a sellout to landlords. The state law on rent control gave the city the power to pass local laws or conduct a referendum related to rent control. Rent control advocates called for a referendum to throw out the concept of maximum base rent.

At this point, Charles Urstadt, the State Commissioner of Housing and Community Renewal, met with Governor Rockefeller about the worsening situation. Urstadt had been a real estate developer and came from a real estate–owning family. Rockefeller had been the leasing agent for Rockefeller Center in his youth, so both understood the business and the incentives involved. That is when Rockefeller decided to take on rent control, to water it down or get rid of it to the extent possible, and above all to remove any possibility of the city reimposing even stricter controls.

Stone developed a memo outlining what became the four key elements of the new legislation. One element recognized that costs were costs—rents below the landlord's actual costs for such elements as taxes and utilities should be adjusted upward accordingly. A second element held that a rent-controlled apartment that was not the renter's primary residence could be decontrolled. A third component provided for vacancy decontrol—when a renter died or moved out for whatever reason, the apartment became decontrolled. And the fourth key element provided that the city could not establish rent controls more stringent than those provided by state law, thereby eliminating the threat from a popular but ill-advised referendum.

Despite howls of protest from busloads of tenants, the legislative package passed and took effect. It was dubbed the Urstadt Law. "I didn't want my name on the bill," Urstadt said, "but no assemblyman had the guts to put his name on the bill. And here it is, thirty-seven years later [forty as this is written], and they're still fighting it."

Thus in 2006, when Urstadt was scheduled to receive Bernard Baruch College's first Real Estate Man of the Year Award for his work developing Battery Park City, the event was picketed by protesters calling for repeal of the Urstadt Law. Few in attendance had ever even heard of the Urstadt Law.

But the legislation that Urstadt, Stone, and the governor pushed through has had a significant effect in reducing the inequities and market distortions inherent in government control of rent levels. As Stone noted, from 1,200,000 rent-controlled apartments when the legislation was enacted, the total number is down to a little over 50,000. Their occupants are still vociferous, though their numbers have dwindled. But as often happens with such contentious issues, it is a case of two steps forward, one step back. A subsequent bill passed by the legislature and signed by Governor Wilson allowed the city, in effect, to re-control many of the vacancy decontrolled apartments by shifting them to its rent stabilization program. With a city agency as the arbiter of allowable annual rent increases, the landlord-tenant battles are far from over.

Politics, Personalities, and Institutional Imperatives

New York City has always been the economic engine of New York State, as well as its cultural, intellectual, media, and political capital—not to mention its national and world stature. Yet despite its commercial and financial preeminence, New York City, like every upstate county, city, and town, is a municipality created by New York State and subject to laws enacted in Albany.

Home rule laws give the city broad authority to govern itself, yet many projects and proposals need legislative sanction, and many state activities impact the city directly or indirectly. New York City mayors, as a result, have large lobbying operations, and heavy agendas in Albany. Nonetheless, the mayor himself must often get directly involved, particularly in dealings with the governor.

When Nelson Rockefeller took office as governor in January 1959, Democrat Robert F. Wagner Jr. had already been mayor for five years. There were predictable institutional frictions, but in general, the two men got along and got things done. Both were pragmatic and more results-oriented than ideologically motivated. Wagner served three four-year terms, retiring at the end of 1965.

When John V. Lindsay, the tall, handsome Republican congressman from Manhattan's Upper East Side "Silk Stocking" district, was elected mayor that year, the first Republican mayor in twenty years, many predicted even smoother city-state relations. After all, Rockefeller and Lindsay were both liberal Republicans, and Rockefeller had strongly supported his candidacy.

Things did not turn out that way. The two men were oil and water, so to speak, almost from the time Lindsay took office.

Lindsay's swearing-in coincided with the onset of a twelve-day, city-wide transit strike, which critics claimed he had done nothing to try to head off or prepare for in the weeks before taking office. It essentially shut the city down. That was only the beginning of Lindsay's labor troubles. In 1968 there was a four-month teachers' strike prompted by the firing of several teachers in Brooklyn. As it dragged on, the city was hit by a Broadway theater strike, a police slowdown, and a disastrous nine-day garbage strike. News photos of garbage bags piled ten feet high on city sidewalks ran nationwide. The Lindsay administration's inability to resolve the public employee strikes inevitably led Governor Rockefeller and his administration to step in to try to settle them.

Michael Whiteman, as first assistant counsel and then counsel to the governor, saw the Lindsay-Rockefeller relationship at first hand.

> I sat through a great many negotiating sessions during the garbage strike and came to see him [Lindsay] through a different set of lenses. Lindsay and John DeLury, head of the Sanitation Workers Union, were in a stand-off. Garbage was piling up in the city and it was on the verge of a public health crisis. The governor intervened in an effort to broker a settlement of the strike. We had often had the feeling that Lindsay was just out there posturing on a whole range of issues, and that was certainly the feeling we had about him during the garbage strike.
>
> Lindsay asserted that he was standing on principle, and therein lay a big difference between Lindsay and Rockefeller. Among other reasons why they didn't get along was that Lindsay was wont to stand on principle in various situations, his principle, whatever it may have been in a given case, and to leave to others the hard work of reconciling differences and getting to yes.
>
> In contrast, the governor's approach was to recognize that in most disputes, both sides have principles and both sides have practical interests, and that to accomplish anything beyond having an unresolved argument, each side needs to recognize and respect the other side's interests and principles and to work to reconcile them.
>
> Thus they had fundamentally different negotiating strategies, styles and, it often seemed, objectives. As far as I could tell in the context of the garbage strike, Lindsay's objective was to win, and if he couldn't win, to be able to say that he had stood firm and that the governor had given in to the forces of evil. The governor's objective was to settle the strike, get garbage collections restarted, and enable people to get on with their lives. And to settle something, the governor's philosophy was, "the other guy needs to be able to take home some of the bacon."

First Deputy Mayor Robert Sweet handled negotiations for the Lindsay administration. Whiteman continued,

> I learned something from those negotiations, and I think the governor did, too, and it was probably more obvious to him than it was to me. And that is that you've got to negotiate with the decision-

maker, and not with somebody who could only be a messenger. If the other side is going to send a messenger to the table, then send your messenger to the table. The negotiations were asymmetrical in that Bob Sweet—nice guy, sincere, capable—was essentially without power. I don't think we realized that when he was sitting at the table across from the governor, and Sweet may not have either. In any event, we would reach a conclusion on some issue, and we'd go back to the office and then we'd learn that, ah, the agreement didn't hold, that he [Lindsay] wasn't accepting it—he was essentially repudiating his own negotiator.

I think it was that characteristic more than anything else that rankled the governor about Lindsay. As far as the governor was concerned, you couldn't pin Lindsay down. The governor's view of political negotiating was, you negotiate hard and when you shake hands on something, it's a deal and you stand by it. And his perception was that if Lindsay didn't stand by a deal that he shook hands on, and was so slippery that you could never get him to shake hands on anything, you couldn't rely on him.

Charles Urstadt recalled the tension when the governor and the mayor came face to face. "Rockefeller called him 'Johnny Boy,' and I could see Lindsay grabbing onto a chair, his knuckles white." Urstadt's lingering image of the garbage strike is of stopping in at the governor's Manhattan office on a Friday, the day after the garbage strike began. "Lindsay dumped the hot potato in Rockefeller's lap, and Rockefeller met all night with both sides at his Fifty-Fifth Street office in an effort to settle the strike," Urstadt said. "For some reason, I was there at eight o'clock in the morning. Lindsay was asleep on the couch, Bob Sweet on the floor, while Rockefeller was negotiating."

When Lindsay washed his hands of the garbage strike, he urged the governor to call out the National Guard, "if necessary." The local media joined in the clamor for troops, and the words, "if necessary," were quickly overlooked. But Rockefeller had been informed that even if all his National Guard units could be mobilized, collections would still fall short by four thousand tons of garbage a day, leaving a worsening mess. Meanwhile, the union representing workers at the private carters who collected trash from commercial enterprises threatened to join the strike if troops were brought in. And the state health commissioner was fearful of a cholera epidemic if the situation continued.

The governor worked out a proposed settlement that would have cost the city $250,000, a relative pittance.[7] But the *New York Times* lambasted him for refusing to call out the troops. "Next thing you know, on Saturday morning," Urstadt said, "Lindsay denounces the settlement. And the two of them were supposed to appear at [New York County Republican leader] Vincent Albano's dinner that night, at different times." But the strike was over.

Enter the Taylor Law

The damaging 1966 transit strike reopened the politically charged issue of how to prevent, settle, and punish strikes by public employees. The existing Condon-Wadlin Law made it a felony for public employees to strike, and workers were to be fired and their leaders jailed. Statewide, it did deter smaller unions from striking, but not the big, powerful New York City unions that could bring the city to its knees by withholding vital services. Their political clout was sufficient that they would never agree to end a strike without amnesty legislation in Albany, preventing application of the Condon-Wadlin Law's penalties. The end result of the discussion, however, was enactment of the Taylor Law—about which more later—which governs relations between government entities and their unions fairly effectively to this day.

Trade Center Tussle

Rockefeller and Lindsay were frequently at odds over housing and redevelopment plans for New York City, particularly Manhattan, including housing, Battery Park City, and the World Trade Center, which both wanted built. Although the Port Authority of New York and New Jersey actually did the construction, it was Governor Rockefeller and his brother, David, vice chairman of the Chase Manhattan Bank, who were responsible for putting the World Trade Center in lower Manhattan. In the early 1960s, many Wall Street banks and investment banks were beginning to move up to Midtown, threatening the economic vitality of the downtown area. David Rockefeller persuaded the bank's board of directors to put down an anchor by building a new headquarters building for Chase downtown. Nelson Rockefeller threw his weight behind the World Trade Center project. Financing this huge addition of office space was difficult, given the glut of downtown office space at the time. Mayor Lindsay wanted the state to agree to rent a huge block of space to house state agencies that were scattered all over the city. Rockefeller was against it. OGS commissioner John Egan recalled the circumstances:

We had to write an analysis of going into the trade center. General Schuyler [Commissioner of the Office of General Services] came to us—I was a planner at that time—and he told us what the governor wanted. The governor wanted all the arguments for not going into the Trade Center. So we spent a lot of time doing an analysis of why we should not go in, the fiscal implications, the congestion it would cause and so on, and gave it to him.

Whenever he and John Lindsay were at loggerheads, we knew it. So we weren't going to go into the trade center. Lindsay wanted us in the trade center, Rocky didn't. Suddenly, out of the blue, came the notice: now make an argument to go in. So we sat down and we made an argument to go in, and he took that one. So we went into the trade center, fifty-nine floors.

We didn't like the buildings. I had to testify after they fell down. They found a report I'd written about the safety of them that fortunately never saw the light of day with the press. We knew they weren't built as state buildings were normally built. They weren't built strong and rugged—they were very fragile. You could do the same thing with this building [crash an airliner into the Corning Tower] and it wouldn't fall down. It has a huge concrete core and it's very rugged.

Ten years after we moved in, the market had changed, so we moved out. So there was only one State agency left in there when 9/11 came along. Earlier, we had over twelve thousand [state employees] in there."

Expanding Manhattan

A subsequent large-scale project in that end of Manhattan, which was not a collaboration with David, was Battery Park City, built on land created in the Hudson River. As Douglass described it:

The governor was really strongly motivated by wanting to demonstrate that you could do things in New York, including building a modern city, in spite of financial problems and racial problems, such as [Mayor] John Lindsay was dealing with and [that left him] unable to leave any kind of an architectural or institutional legacy.

And the governor said, "I'm going to prove it to him." I said, "Well, Governor, you don't have a lot of power over the city because of the City Home Rule Law and independence. As a matter of fact, the only thing the state owns in the city is an office building on Lower Broadway."

He said, "Well, there must be something we can do to prove this point." And [Secretary to the Governor] Bill Ronan or someone said, "Well, we do own half-way out in the Hudson River." And the governor said, "That's a great idea!" And so with that was born the notion of Battery Park City.

At the time, said Douglass, Lindsay was trying to assemble a site on the Lower East Side of Manhattan for a project to be called Manhattan Landing, and it was progressing. Douglass continued:

> And Brother David was a great supporter of that with Lindsay. That was an easier deal, though it would have to be done with platforms, rather than fill like Battery Park City.
>
> The governor never told his brother what he was up to, and one day he was down in lower Manhattan and stopped in to see him. And he used to call him Dave—I don't know anyone else who called him Dave—and he was asked by his brother, "What brings you down here?"
>
> "Well," the governor said, "I'm going to announce a big new project over on the Hudson River."
>
> "Well, what's that?"
>
> "Battery Park City." And I think David, in a sibling way, never forgave him for that. But it worked out fine, and then David became a supporter of it. But it certainly was a surprise.

To create Battery Park City, coffer dams were built out in the Hudson and filled, partly with fill from the excavation of the World Trade Center site, but mostly with sand brought over from Staten Island. Construction and operation of the two-hundred-plus acre development was handled by the Battery Park City Authority, headed initially by Charles Urstadt in addition to his duties as state housing commissioner and chairman of the Housing Finance Agency.

The development is now home to some nine thousand families, and about fifty thousand people work in its offices and commercial buildings. It is now called the Hugh L. Carey Battery Park City Authority, after the governor who was in office when it was completed.[8]

Rockefeller and Lindsay: Always a Story

For the New York City and Albany press corps, the prickly relations between Rockefeller and Lindsay were a mother lode of good copy. While institutional conflicts between a governor and a mayor of New York could have explained some of the animosity, it was clear to anyone who saw them together that there was more to it than that.

Some observers believed there was envy on both sides, and they may have been right. Lindsay could well have been envious of Rockefeller's wealth, connections, power, and effectiveness as a political and governmental operator. Rockefeller, in turn, could envy the youthful Lindsay's godlike good looks and telegenic charm. Various Rockefeller insiders have said there was also an element of resentment on the part of the governor because Lindsay would never publicly acknowledge or say thank you for Rockefeller family support and contributions of $500,000 to his election campaigns. This included the first, successful run for Congress that put him on the path to political stardom. Lindsay presumably did not want to be viewed as a protégé of Rockefeller, or as beholden to him. Rockefeller, who could be very generous, nonetheless expected to be thanked.

Whatever the cause, Rockefeller was privately disdainful of the mayor, and didn't mind taking him down a peg on occasion, as the following two stories illustrate.

One involved the highly controversial "commuter tax"—legislation Lindsay sought in 1966 to help plug mounting deficits in the city budget. The idea was that people who worked in the city but lived in the suburbs should pay at least some New York City income tax, helping to fund the many city services they used or benefited from. Not surprisingly, suburban legislators of both parties opposed it, contending that they had to pay high suburban property taxes and the mounting cost of commuting by rail, bus, or car.

At one point Lindsay asked Rockefeller to set up a meeting with a group of Long Island assemblymen to discuss their objections to the tax proposal, which the governor did. As former assemblyman Arthur J. Kremer, remembered it:

> The governor called the five assembly members from Long Island, all Democrats, to attend the meeting, as they were the majority party in that house. The group of five arrived promptly at 1 p.m. and the governor ushered Mayor Lindsay into the Red Room [the governor's ceremonial office]. After the mayor was introduced, the governor told Lindsay: "Okay, John, you're on your own. I'm getting out of here."
>
> Obviously, the governor wanted no part of Liberal Lindsay and his agenda. If anybody knew how to convey a message, it was Nelson A. Rockefeller.

But the commuter tax bill did ultimately pass that year, and the governor signed it. It was in effect until 1999, when the legislature voted to exempt state residents from it while continuing to levy the tax on out-of-state residents—primarily from Connecticut and New Jersey. State courts held that to be discriminatory and unconstitutional, thus killing the tax altogether.

The Water Route to Albany

Another incident, recounted here by Jacob Underhill, a deputy press secretary at the time, involved an unscheduled Lindsay trip to Albany.

> One morning just before noon in the first week of Lindsay's term, a reporter from City Hall called our press office in Albany, where the staff was encamped during the legislative session.
>
> "What time is Lindsay going to see Rockefeller today?" the reporter asked. I explained that I hadn't seen the mayor's name on the governor's schedule.
>
> "Lindsay just left here to fly to Albany to see him," the reporter said. I put him on hold and went next door to tell Ann Whitman, NAR's secretary, the news. She said the governor was fully booked until nightfall. "I don't know how we can fit him in."
>
> I went back to the reporter to tell him that Lindsay didn't have an appointment on this crowded day. Lindsay arrived just after lunch with his aides and a group of reporters. Ann made the mayoral party comfortable in an anteroom outside the governor's second-floor office. There they cooled their heels until about 8 p.m. It surely showed who ran Albany. Later, the joke in the third-floor press room was: "How did Lindsay come to Albany?" The answer: "He walked up the Hudson."

The mutual distrust between these two giants of New York's political firmament is believed by many to have cost Lindsay a U.S. Senate seat. After Senator Robert F. Kennedy was assassinated in June, 1968, it was up to the governor to appoint someone to fill out the remaining two-and-a-half years of the term. Lindsay, beset by problems in his third year as mayor, was said to want the senate seat, but would not ask for it publicly or even say he would accept it if offered, lest Rockefeller snub him and appoint someone else. Rockefeller, widely believed to favor Lindsay for the seat, would not say so publicly, apparently lest Lindsay reject the offer, which would not only insult the governor but diminish whoever was ultimately chosen. Rockefeller eventually appointed a young upstate congressman, Charles E. Goodell of Jamestown, to the position.

5

The Indefatigable Campaigner

If Nelson Rockefeller was not a born campaigner, he was certainly the next best thing—a quick learner whose energy, enthusiasm, and electric presence generated crowds from the outset of his political career. As he grew accustomed to the role of glad-handing politician, he often seemed to relish the rigors and rituals of running for office and to enjoy the people he encountered.

It wasn't always enjoyable, of course; far from it. The travel was endless and exhausting, often in weather ranging from uncomfortable to abominable. Crowds were sometimes sparse, and occasionally hostile. Too many commitments or unanticipated obstacles could play havoc with the most carefully planned schedules. After slogging through heavy rain and ankle-deep mud in the 1964 New Hampshire primary, he grumpily remarked to an advance-man that if this was what it took to get elected president, maybe he should reconsider.

Nevertheless, he had already grown to regard personal campaigning as not just a necessary chore, but rather an activity that he was good at, and that could help him achieve his objectives. Unlike many politicians, he was undaunted by the near-endless round of county fairs and rubber-chicken political dinners (although he seldom ate anything at them). Like everything else he did, he went at campaigning with all his impressive physical energy and relentless determination and seemed to draw renewed energy from the response of the crowds he saw or addressed. And on many occasions he seemed truly to be enjoying himself.

During his fifteen years as governor, as noted previously, there was always a campaign of some sort. In addition, there was a steady stream of public appearances intended to promote or dramatize his projects, programs, or proposals.

The media loved it. Rockefeller was always good copy, and drew heavy media coverage wherever he went, not only because of what he did, but also because of the things he sometimes disclosed. He was famous for discarding his speech texts and speaking off the cuff, a practice particularly frustrating to his principal speech writer, Joseph E. Persico, who labored hard to put style and substance, as well as news, into the governor's speeches. (Disclosure: having been in charge of the speechwriting function for Governor Hugh L. Carey for a time, I can sympathize with Persico's frustration.) Rockefeller typically would say he stood by everything that was in this fine speech prepared by his staff (he sometimes cited Persico by name), but that he wanted to discuss something else. And off he would go. As a practical matter, this usually meant that whatever news was in the written speech didn't make the papers, as Rockefeller's impromptu remarks were almost always good copy. Often the governor let slip things his administration didn't want revealed just yet, or at all.

As Lieutenant Governor Wilson once quipped: "We have the only Ship of State that leaks from the top."

Style and Substance

Rockefeller's campaigning style evolved over the years. Jacob Underhill, then deputy press secretary, recalled Rockefeller telling him: "When I started campaigning in 1958, I found that when I waved one hand at a crowd, they'd respond by waving one hand back at me. When I waved my whole arm, they'd respond by waving a whole arm back at me. And when I waved two arms over my head, they'd reply by waving their two arms up in the air in response. So I started to use two arms." It made for great pictures.

"NAR was proud of his ability to communicate with Puerto Rican citizens in what one aide characterized as 'street Spanish,'" Underhill remembered. "He was in great linguistic form during the Sunday Puerto Rican Day Parade on Fifth Avenue in 1966 when he was running for reelection." Underhill continued,

I was marching along with him to keep the press and TV people reasonably orderly. NYPD detective Walter Karpowicz was along for protection, but the crowd was happy and enthusiastic. "El Rocky," they chanted. Both arms high, NAR sang out some appropriate Spanish greeting.

Somewhere in the East Seventies, he looked down a side street and dropped out of the parade, motioning to Walter and me to follow. There we found Judge Frank O'Connor with a similar political entourage, totally surrounded by happy Puerto Ricans.

The judge had not yet received the Democratic nomination

to oppose Rockefeller, but he was considered a shoo-in for the party's nod. Yet this wooden campaigner was standing stock still, surrounded by cheering Puerto Ricans. He had the bemused air of an Irish Catholic priest trapped in a New Orleans Mardi Gras parade.

El Rocky to the rescue! In street Spanish, the Republican governor explained to the crowd that he knew they were all Democraticos, and that the judge was their Democratico candidate. He was the man they were going to support in November.

"Viva O'Connor," NAR shouted. "Viva O'Connor," the crowd replied. And so we returned to the parade with the O'Connor entourage behind us in the line of march. By the time we passed the Rockefeller apartment at 812 Fifth, I was pretty sure the election campaign was over. The judge didn't have campaigning skills he needed for modern ethnic campaigning.

Robert Stone, at the time deputy commissioner of the Office of General Services, recalled a visit to New York City with his wife that October, when things still looked bleak for Rockefeller, and the *Daily News* was predicting his defeat. Back in that era, when most New York taxi drivers were local natives, out-of-town reporters and others used to pick their brains at election time, to get a sense (however limited) of local sentiment and political wisdom.

"Upon our arrival in Gotham," Stone said, "I asked the cab driver, 'Who do you like in the election?' He immediately responded: 'Rocky's my man.' 'Why?' I asked. 'Because he's for the cabbies,' he responded. [The governor was on the right side of a taxi medallion dispute.].

"Later, at a restaurant, I asked our waitress what she thought about the election. 'Rockefeller!' she said with enthusiasm. 'Why?' I asked. 'Because he's putting my daughter through college.'" Stone said he couldn't recall whether she was referring to the much-expanded state university or the governor's TAP [tuition assistance program] grants, "but NAR had the attention of the man in the street. And I told my bride, 'Don't worry. He's in.'"

And so he was.

Just as the lack of campaigning skills helped do in Frank O'Connor in 1966, it also contributed to the demise of Rockefeller's 1970 opponent, Arthur Goldberg. Despite his stature as a former justice of the U.S. Supreme Court and ambassador to the UN, and his long career as legal counsel to the AFL-CIO, Goldberg never gained sufficient traction to offset Rockefeller's organization, financial advantage, public record, and campaigning ability. He barely dented Rockefeller's labor support, particularly in the construction trades. Goldberg was neither a dynamic personality nor a particularly good public speaker, and his unfamiliarity with New York State became embarrassingly apparent when he referred to the Hudson River city of Poughkeepsie (pronounced "Puh-KIP-see") as "PUFF-kip-see." The media gave it prominent coverage.

The Advance-Man Riseth

The craft of the advance-man took a big leap forward during the Rockefeller years. Recall that during his first campaign for governor, in 1958, Rockefeller had a single advance-man—Jack Vandervort, a Republican Party organizer. Later, on a West Coast trip, the press described Vandervort's function as organizing "spontaneous demonstrations."

With the onset of Rockefeller's campaigns for the Republican presidential nomination, the ranks of advance-men grew and grew. Rockefeller's people recruited young men from all over as the governor's travel schedule expanded beyond the borders of New York State. Many were young lawyers, but there were also hotel people, bankers, Young Republican leaders, party loyalists, and people from all kinds of professions. Some served in a single campaign, many re-upped again and again. They were valuable resources that could be kept in reserve and mobilized when needed. One advance-man who subsequently made a name for himself in the political arena was George Pataki. His political "rabbi" was R. Burdell Bixby, a partner at the Dewey law firm where Pataki (Yale and Columbia Law School) worked. Pataki, who went into elective politics, was elected mayor of the village of Peekskill, assemblyman, and then senator from districts in the lower Hudson Valley before successfully running for governor in 1994. His memories of advance work, he told Judge Lewis Bart Stone, included the continuing requirement to provide the governor with Oreos and Dubonnet at every overnight stop.

Not surprisingly, the advance crew came away with vivid recollections of Rockefeller campaigns, and of the memorable, illustrative, or humorous incidents that occurred on their sorties around the country.

For example, Jack Vandervort recalled a trip Rockefeller took in December, 1959, to test the political waters in the nation's heartland. After a stop in Madison, Wisconsin, the entourage headed for St. Louis, Missouri, where local Republicans were planning a reception for Rockefeller in the ballroom at the Chase Hotel. How many people would attend, the governor's staff asked Vandervort, the sole advance-man.

I said, 'I don't know whether there are going to be ten people at this function or a thousand.' Well, it was closer to three thousand people who showed up at the ballroom. The local people whom I'd been working with hadn't really organized it, so Carl Spad, who was then appointments officer to the governor, and Ed Galvin [the governor's state police bodyguard] and I were funneling people in to shake hands with the governor. And he looked everybody in the eye—all the famous 'hiya fella' and what have you. Next morning I had black and blue marks on my back and all over.

Even without such mob scenes, routine campaign events were punishing for the governor as well. Robert Malito, who was president of the Queens County Young Republicans at the time, once made a campaign swing through that borough of New York City with Rockefeller. "I was stunned by the sheer energy that Rocky had in shaking hands on beaches, in shopping centers, and at Republican Club gatherings," Malito said, in recalling the occasion for Joe Boyd, who had been there as chief of advance. "When he got back into the bus, I saw how you would have a bucket of shaved ice on the seat next to Rocky and he would immerse his 'Pillsbury Dough Boy' hand into the ice and keep it there until the next stop, at which time you would hand him a towel and he would dry his hand and then bound off the bus for another session of handshaking."

(Avoiding or coping with the pain inflicted by hours of hand-shaking is a problem for many politicians, particularly where campaigns are protracted or frequent. One technique, favored by Richard Nixon, among others, is to relax the hand and make sure the hand-shaker grabs the fingers, rather than the whole hand. This avoids pain but comes off as a limp handshake. Minnesota senator Eugene McCarthy, seeking the presidency in 1968, told a reporter his painful tennis elbow was the result of shaking too many hands. By the same token, I also recall a member of the New York State Assembly, a rugged, young former paratrooper, whose grip was so vigorous and powerful that he hurt everyone whose hand he shook. Colleagues and others learned to avoid shaking hands at all costs.)

Seeing the World in Advance

Because of Rockefeller's constant travel and public appearances in his capacity as governor or as a candidate, he needed more advance-men than in the early days, and when on duty they were expected to work around the clock, if necessary. Their job was to do whatever it took to assure that the governor had a successful event or appearance, and that his personal needs (Oreos, etc.) were efficiently met. They were also expected to smooth ruffled local feathers when a campaign plane was late, a schedule changed, or a long-sought meeting canceled.

For many members of this ever-changing fraternity, the years with Rockefeller were a high point in their lives.

Ron Abney, a Southerner who was part of the advance team for Rockefeller's Latin American trips for President Nixon in 1969, as well as various other campaigns, described working for the governor as "a great experience and a supreme honor. It was truly the most exciting time of my professional life. Nothing excited or elevated me more than to arrive in a foreign country or an upstate New York town and be referred to as 'Nelson Rockefeller's man.' I still get chill-bumps."

Abney recounted the following story, as passed on to him via a colleague on the advance team, George Humphreys. "Advance-men were always ready to throw themselves in front of the governor if need be. It did rankle us a bit though that we were never sure he knew exactly who we were or what our names were. Example: two advance guys with about a year's experience on the upstate New York team did their preparatory work in one city and were united with the Man on his arrival. The governor, recognizing the faces of these two staff stalwarts, gushed: 'Hey, there's what's-his-name . . . and his friend!'"

Advance people sometimes felt unappreciated by some members of the governor's staff, and relished such incidents as this one. On one upstate campaign swing, Abney said, the governor agreed to a quick, unscheduled radio interview that was not on the "pink"—the daily schedule. "Hugh Morrow, longtime communications director, pronounced proudly: 'We don't need no stinking advance-men—I'll do it. How hard can it be if all these rednecks are doing it?' So off they went.

"Once at the station, Hugh, leading his champion through the halls of the small station, bullied his way past the receptionist to the door inside the building. The overwhelmed young woman shrieked at him but old Hugh trudged on. What she was trying to tell him was that the door he was now walking into was a broom closet."

Courting Votes in the Catskills

In the 1950s and 1960s, the big resort hotels in the Catskills were still going strong. Grossinger's, one of the best known, was a regular stop for campaigning politicians courting the Jewish vote. In the fall of 1960, Governor Rockefeller was campaigning for the Republican national ticket of Richard Nixon and former UN ambassador Henry Cabot Lodge. Joe Boyd recalled that one of his first advance assignments was to assist with a planned visit to Grossinger's by Rockefeller and Lodge. They were to attend a cocktail reception and luncheon at the home of the hotel's matriarch, Jennie Grossinger, located on the hotel grounds.

When the meal bell rang, Jennie turned to Joe: "Young man, may I have your arm and will you escort us to my table?" Commented Joe: "We entered the dining room to standing applause, followed the red carpet, with Ambassador Lodge and Governor Rockefeller following. Later the governor remarked to me that he didn't know I was running for office.

"After lunch," Joe said, "most of the guests adjourned to chairs on the patio. Mrs. Grossinger introduced Rockefeller, who introduced Lodge. As Ambassador Lodge started to speak, a woman in the front row raised her hand and called out, 'Mr. Ambassador!' Lodge stopped and said, 'Yes, ma'am.' She replied: 'You're standing in my sun.'

Rockefeller quickly moved the podium so that the sun shone on the woman's face. "She said, 'Okay, Mr. Ambassador—you can continue.'"

In the 1966 gubernatorial campaign, Rockefeller spoke at a banquet at Grossinger's, and at one point had to leave the dais to take a telephone call. Advance-man William McDevitt recalled that as he waited outside the private room where the governor was taking the call, two elderly women approached him and asked if they could meet the governor. McDevitt agreed to arrange it, and just then the governor emerged. McDevitt introduced the two women. Rockefeller was gracious, even when the women said they could not vote for him. "But if we could, you'd carry Ontario and Quebec!" The governor howled with laughter, McDevitt said, and later used the quote on several occasions.

If It Quacks . . .

Life on the campaign trail could be challenging in many ways for advance-men. McDevitt recalled a luncheon put on by the Long Island Association—Long Island's principal business organization—at which the governor was presented with a live duck. It was a gimmick reflecting Long Island's reputation for commercial duck farming.

"As he took off by helicopter for the next event," McDevitt recalled, "he asked me to look after the duck and get it to the helicopter for the trip home. He wanted the duck for his two sons, Nelson and Mark.

I drove to the next event, arriving as it was ending, and then continued on to the field where the helicopter was waiting. Upon arriving, I noticed that the duck was silent. It had died, either because of the heat of that summer day, or the fright of its life or whatever. Now I had to tell the governor.

"When his entourage arrived, I walked over to the aircraft and broke the bad news. 'Well,' he said, 'Happy will be happy.' It dawned on me that he had been thinking how he would explain bringing home a live duck."

Uncomfortable moments sometimes make for treasured memories. Joe Boyd recalled a helicopter trip with the governor in the summer of 1966 from Albany to a spot just south of the city of Hudson, at the east end of the Rip Van Winkle Bridge over the Hudson River. Rockefeller was there for a dedication marking the state's purchase of nearby Olana, the historic Hudson River estate of painter Frederic Church, high on a bluff overlooking the river. One reason for going was to help his first cousin, Alexander "Sam" Aldrich, the commissioner of Parks and Recreation, who was running in a Republican primary for Congress that year.

The dirt road winding uphill from the estate entrance was very dusty. "I was in the last car, a Corvette convertible with the top down, holding the governor's speech in my lap," Joe said. "The car was driven by Craig Thorn of Hudson, who would later become a key Rockefeller campaign and travel aide. When we reached the house I proceeded to the reception on the porch, where Nelson Rockefeller took one look at me and started laughing. My face and clothes were covered with dust. When I took off my sunglasses, I looked like a raccoon. The light brown envelope was now dark brown and there was a light rectangular area on my suit where the speech had been held. Of course, Rockefeller had to talk about my ride in his opening remarks," Joe added.

Christmas Shopping, Rockefeller Style

Staff members who traveled with Rockefeller, advance-men included, knew that he never carried any money, and that it was prudent to carry a lot of cash in case the governor decided to buy something along the way.

Vandervort, again recalling that pulse-taking tour of the heartland in early December, 1959, noted that it ended up in Dallas, where the famous Neiman Marcus store was located. The governor and his wife, Mary—the first Mrs. Rockefeller—decided to go Christmas shopping. Vandervort described the scene:

As we were walking around Neiman Marcus, the governor would say, well, that's very nice—can we block this out for so-and-so and all the kids? And I could see the manager and the sales people were unhappy with that, and the manager said, "Well, are you taking these with you?" I said no, you should ship them to Room 5600, 30 Rockefeller Plaza, in New York. [Room 5600 was the site of the Rockefeller family office, which handled the financial affairs for the entire Rockefeller clan.]

And he said, "Well, who's going to pay for them?" I'm not even sure I had a credit card, and of course they [the Rockefellers] never have any money. Neither Mary Todhunter Clark Rockefeller nor the governor ever had any money.

And the guy said, "Well, we don't normally do this—you don't have an account here." And I said, "The governor of New York, who's paying this, is synonymous with money," or something like that, and I added, "I wouldn't worry about it." Then Mrs. Rockefeller said, "Jack, I would like you to take care of this one present." So I was entrusted with one present. Problem solved.

For that and other expenses, needless to say, Vandervort was reimbursed.[1]

Advance-men were also expected to be quick-thinking opportunists, as was Rockefeller himself, when it came to generating press coverage. McDevitt told of another occasion in the 1966 gubernatorial campaign when the governor attended an elaborate dedication for a new chemical plant in Rockland County.

"As people were leaving the ceremony," McDevitt said, "the company had arranged for a local high school band to be playing. They happened to be from nearby New Jersey—Bergenfield High School.

"The governor stopped politely to listen a little, when I pointed out a girl in the front row with a full leg cast on her right leg, leaning on her crutches and playing the flute. He went right up to the band, talked to her a bit, knelt down in the grass and autographed the cast, to her delight and that of the band. That picture made papers in both states the next day."

The Sound of Music

Joe Boyd recalled that Rockefeller loved jazz, in particular, Dixieland. His favorite song was "Sweet Georgia Brown." Advance-men were instructed to hire local Dixieland bands at each stop to greet the governor at the airport, ride in the motorcade, and perform at campaign events. In October, 1966, with the governor considered an underdog in the gubernatorial race, his campaign manager decided a Rockefeller noontime jazz rally outside Macy's in Herald Square was just the thing to provide a boost to the campaign. The executives at Radio City Music Hall were in charge of obtaining the musicians. Joe recalled that he sent three advance-men to put up signs and recruit the crowd with bullhorns and sound trucks.

> When the campaign bus arrived at Herald Square, the platform was set in the middle of Seventh Avenue and surrounded by people as far as the eye could see. On the platform were four musicians playing swing music.
>
> They weren't just any musicians. They were Benny Goodman on clarinet, Lionel Hampton on vibes, Teddy Wilson piano, and a drummer who I think was Gene Krupa. Rockefeller bounded from the bus, shook hands with the musicians and said into the microphone, "Let's hear the music."
>
> The quartet played one tune after another for maybe ten minutes more and the crowd started swinging, with some people dancing in the street.

The rally was a big success. Benny Goodman appeared at several Rockefeller events over the next few years, Joe said. Lionel Hampton became a close friend of Rockefeller's.

"After the Macy's rally, Lionel was a regular on the Rockefeller campaign bus," Joe said. He continued,

> Two weeks later, while campaigning in Harlem, Lionel convinced the governor to go into the world-famous Apollo Theater on 125th Street, where soul singer James Brown was appearing. Brown was thirty-three at the time.
>
> I accompanied Rockefeller and Hampton backstage. Brown was singing. Rockefeller told Hampton not to interfere. The stage manager sent a note to Brown, who called Hampton out on stage. Lionel told Brown that he had Nelson Rockefeller backstage and they both, with enthusiasm, invited Nelson out. The primarily black crowd stood and cheered. The governor spoke three or four minutes about Hampton, Brown, and the importance of music. The crowd cheered, stood again, and Rockefeller, with one arm waving, left with his other arm around Lionel's shoulder. The media reported with special interest the impromptu stop at the Apollo.
>
> Once back on the bus, Lionel said to Nelson that he had them

cheering in the balcony, which was a good luck sign for any performer and meant the governor was going to win reelection.

In the 1968 Republican presidential primaries, Lionel and his band traveled with the campaign around the country, appearing at big events while a small group played Dixieland at special receptions. Lionel and his band were there for Rockefeller in Miami in 1972 at the Republican National Convention. In fact, Hampton cut a record called "Rock-e-feller." I still have the 45 rpm.

Lionel was also there for Rockefeller at the governor's funeral at Manhattan's Riverside Church, February 2, 1979. His Dixieland band performed a musical tribute during the service and then played the recessional music following the ceremony—to no one's surprise, it was "Sweet Georgia Brown."

A Dynamic Campaigner

Unlike the rest of his very private family, Nelson Rockefeller was comfortable being in the limelight, and often enjoyed the very physical public activities that go with campaigning. Winnie Thorn, wife of Craig Thorn, recalled taking her three small children to the Columbia County Fair in Chatham, New York, on Labor Day weekend in 1966 so they could see the man their father was working so hard to get reelected.

"The governor arrived as scheduled," she said, "and I will never forget how he bounded off the helicopter, his sleeves rolled up, and moved right into the crowd. You have to understand that the people there were really down-home folk, farmers for the most part, not the New York sophisticated type. And here was their governor, walking through the field on a hot day, shaking hands, answering their questions and responding to their concerns with complete knowledge of their problems. And there was no question, he was enjoying himself. What I remember is that one of the local farmers standing behind me and the children commented that the governor was 'an all-right guy—I like him.' That to me is what made Nelson Rockefeller so special. He was comfortable meeting with people, he could field questions thrown at him about almost any topic, and with his response, you knew he knew what he was talking about. There weren't and aren't many people in politics who can do that. And our kids liked the man Daddy was working for."

On one occasion Rockefeller was to speak at a local political dinner in Schuyler County, in south-central New York, with a press conference scheduled beforehand. The governor let it be known he was going to drop in on "Don and Flossie"—Donald J. Wickham was his commissioner of Agriculture and Markets, and was also a successful fruit farmer and businessman in nearby Hector. As Wickham's son William recalled: "The scheduled time for his press conference passed, and several frantic calls were received in the Hector area. The governor was finally located. He and my Dad were riding on our family's mechanical grape harvester as it worked! As the governor put it later, 'This was a lot more fun!'"

William Wickham cited the mutual respect and strong personal relationship between the two men during Rockefeller's years as governor. "I think that my father showed the governor a side of New York life that wasn't completely familiar to him. He also gave the governor a new respect for those who worked in production agriculture, and those who were engaged in the processing and marketing of New York–grown products. These two men made a great team, and New York agriculture benefited from their efforts."

Charles Urstadt, at the time Rockefeller's commissioner of Housing and Community Renewal, recalled another occasion when the governor threw caution to the winds and enjoyed himself playing with a large mechanical toy, in this case, a wrecking ball.

The state was to begin demolishing some dilapidated townhouses in Harlem to make way for a large housing project, and Urstadt arranged to have Rockefeller inaugurate the project by swinging the ball at a particular house. Clearly, this would make great copy and pictures in the newspapers, and it did. Rockefeller maneuvered the machine and swung the ball with gusto into the side of the building—the wrong building. "But it didn't make any difference," said Urstadt. "That building was coming down, too."

Rockefeller never lost that willingness to plunge into such activities with enthusiasm. I recall covering a 1968 campaign trip to Oregon when the Rockefeller entourage visited a big county fair. This was lumbering country, and there were various kinds of competitions testing lumberjacks' skills at tree-climbing, log-rolling, and chopping. One contest required participants to chop a foot-thick pine log while standing on it, the axe blade biting into the wood between their feet. Someone handed Rockefeller a razor-sharp, double-bladed axe, and he took off his coat, climbed onto the log, and began hacking away vigorously. As I remember it, he quit after about thirty seconds, much to the relief of his staff, but it made for great news photos. The professionals, of course, took not much longer than that to cut through the whole log, scarcely missing a beat as they spun 180 degrees halfway through in order to cut from the other side.

Fergus Reid was an advance-man responsible for rounding up delegates in the Rocky Mountain states at that time, and he remembered being on a bus en route to a campaign stop in Salem, Oregon.

"The moment I remember so clearly as the bus sped through a spectacular countryside of meadows and mountains," said Reid, "was that of NAR standing in the entry well by the driver, waving tirelessly to absolutely no one but a sheepherder and a couple of cows.

"To me this epitomized Nelson's indefatigable campaign enthusiasm, without which he couldn't have accomplished the endless political victories that he achieved," Reid said.

Well, the victories weren't really endless, and in fact, when it came to running for president, they were all too few. The 1964 Republican Convention at the Cow Palace in San Francisco springs to mind.

The Unreachable Nomination

In 1960, when Rockefeller was a fresh face on the national political scene, he had decided to pass up a full-scale run at the GOP nomination to avoid a party-splitting battle with Vice President Richard Nixon. In retrospect, it was almost certainly his best shot at obtaining the nomination.

Nixon having lost in 1960 and "retired" from politics after losing a run for governor of California in 1962, Rockefeller undertook an all-out assault on the nomination in 1964. But by that time, the party had already begun to move to the right, its center of gravity shifting westward, away from the more moderate East. Senator Barry Goldwater of Arizona was the conservatives' champion. By 1964, Rockefeller was already widely perceived as a big spender and taxer. He had also created political problems for himself with his divorce from Mary Rockefeller and subsequent marriage to Happy. Compounding this was the birth of their son, Nelson Junior, on the Saturday before the all-important California primary.

Having bested Goldwater in the West Virginia primary, Rockefeller had expected to win in California, as well as in Oregon, and hoped the resulting momentum would carry him to the nomination. It was not to be, with conservative strength in southern California narrowly outpacing Rockefeller's support in the more liberal northern part of the state. He did carry Oregon, but it was not enough. Rockefeller then pulled out of the race, but got Pennsylvania governor William Scranton to take his place.

With the conservative faction calling the shots, the GOP convention, and even San Francisco itself, seemed like hostile territory to the

Rockefeller operatives sent to make arrangements for the convention. Recalled Deputy Press Secretary Jake Underhill: "As we packed up to go to the convention, I think most of us figured that he was going to have a lot of trouble. When we got to San Francisco, there were a bunch of protesters. Two weeks earlier, at our headquarters at the Palace Hotel, people would spit at us if we had Rockefeller buttons on."

Vandervort picked up the convention story: "By this time the extreme right had really gotten involved. It was unfortunate, because a lot of it was being led by these old Young Republicans—Clif White was involved and what have you. [Clifton White, a former president of the New York Young Republicans, and erstwhile GOP chairman of Tompkins County, was not a Rockefeller fan, and in fact, was Goldwater's campaign manager.]

"We went out to San Francisco for a month, and I was stopped by some of Goldwater's people at every move that I made. Yeah, I mean it was scary," Vandervort said. He continued,

> So anyhow, we went out to the convention where Rockefeller gave that famous speech. And the governor's photographer, Bob Wands, said, "Jack, would you just take pictures? Just keep snapping pictures, with this camera (which he gave me), of the boos and the catcalls and the whole nine yards."
>
> Well, one of my assignments was to watch out for Ken Keating [U.S. senator Kenneth B. Keating of Rochester]. And Ken Keating decided to leave. I went out into the audience, to the delegates and alternates, because we wanted to show some protest. And there were a couple of people who had voted against Goldwater in the final tally.
>
> So Keating decided he wanted to leave and get dinner. I said, "You can't leave right now." And he said, "I can, too." And I said, "They're going to watch you leaving, and we're going to have every reporter in the world and all these TV cameras wondering where you're going." He said, "Jack, we're leaving." So I advised the governor that I was accompanying him [Keating] to the men's room. And yes, two or three of the media were following us right along, wondering what was going on. And I directed him to the men's room, and he said, "I don't have to go. I'm leaving—take me out to my car." And I said, "No. Whether you like it or not, you're going to the bathroom, whether you have to go or not." And then he did leave, but by that time, they [the press] had gone off.

Joe Boyd has understandably vivid memories of that convention.

As personal aide to the governor, I had the responsibility of putting the governor's speech on the dais podium while he made his way up shaking hands. This was Goldwater country. When Rockefeller was introduced to the convention, which was broadcast on national television, the hall erupted into loud boos, particularly the balconies, which had been stacked with Goldwater youth.

Senator Thruston Morton of Kentucky, a large man, was the convention chair and emcee. He waited a few minutes and when the booing and throwing of paper did not stop, Senator Morton said to Rockefeller: "Why don't you come back later?" Rockefeller said no. Then Morton tried to push Rockefeller away from the microphone with his body. Rockefeller resisted, put his hand over the mike and told Morton that if he tried to push him again he would "cold-cock" Morton [punch him out] right there on the stage in front of the TV audience.

In the meantime, Clif White, Goldwater's campaign manager, who was directing the Goldwater delegates and supporters from a trailer outside the Cow Palace, was yelling into his phone to his lieutenants inside to quickly stop the demonstrations, which could hurt Goldwater in the general election. They did so.

New York state police major Ed Galvin and I were the only Rockefeller people on the podium. Ed directed me to "stop kids from throwing things at Rockefeller's back." I ventured into the stand, where I found a high school student on an aisle who was about to throw something. I picked him up by the lapels and, with his forward motion, brought over me [sending him tumbling] down the steps. He hit his eye, which began to bleed profusely. I turned to the crowd, asked who was next, and slowly back-stepped to the podium.

The crowd finally became quiet and Rockefeller gave his speech, which was highly acclaimed by the media, and left for the Palace Hotel.

Once back in New York, the Rockefeller forces were ostensibly backing the GOP ticket of Barry Goldwater and William Miller, a congressman from Niagara Falls. But the principal focus was on the various New York races—Senator Keating, and Republican candidates for Congress, the state senate, and the assembly. The effort on behalf of the top of the ticket was understandably unenthusiastic. Jake Under-hill recalled dropping in on state GOP chairman Michael Scelsi at the

Republican Party's New York office and seeing a Teleflex machine sitting silently in a corner. "I said, 'What's that?' and he said, 'Oh, the Goldwater people sent that to us to keep us alert and to write speeches for us.' And I said, 'well, what does it say?' And he said, 'I don't know, I've never turned it on.'"

In the election that November, President Lyndon B. Johnson defeated Senator Goldwater in a landslide, with the Republican winning only his own state of Arizona—narrowly—and four Deep South states: Georgia, Louisiana, Mississippi, and South Carolina. In New York, Johnson won by 1,670,000 votes out of more than 7,160,000 votes cast, a margin of better than two to one. Goldwater carried not a single one of New York's sixty-two counties, a good measure of his widespread unpopularity.

The result was a disaster for the rest of the Republican ticket and for the New York GOP as a whole: Robert F. Kennedy easily captured Keating's senate seat, despite running roughly a million votes behind President Johnson. Democrats gained congressional seats and captured both houses of the legislature.

Last Hurrah

One of the most interesting stories to come out of the 1968 presidential election did not actually surface until more than decade after the fact. It answers the question that intrigued so much of the nation's political community during that trauma-fraught election year: Why did Nelson Rockefeller get ready to run for president, then quit the race, and later, when it was essentially too late to succeed, jump back in?

As 1968 opened, Richard Nixon was the clear favorite to win the Republican presidential nomination, despite having "retired" grumpily from politics after losing the 1962 election for governor of California. As Barry Goldwater bore the GOP standard bravely over the cliff in the 1964 election, Nixon was hard at work rehabilitating his standing in the party. By 1968, having campaigned vigorously for Republican candidates all over the country and spoken at innumerable GOP "rubber chicken" fund-raising dinners, he had succeeded in winning the loyalty of many of the party faithful. It was from their ranks that delegates to the party's nominating convention in Miami Beach would largely be chosen.

But Nelson Rockefeller was weighing his options as well. After all, Nixon had a losing track record and had been out of office since 1960, whereas Rockefeller had been running one of the largest states skillfully the whole time and had won a third term as governor. And the conservative element that had booed and hooted at Rockefeller at the San Francisco convention in 1964 had been repudiated, temporarily at least, by the Goldwater debacle. Rockefeller began taking soundings across the country.

Meanwhile, as public opinion soured on the Vietnam War, Democratic senator Eugene McCarthy of Minnesota announced he would run against President Lyndon Johnson, who, despite his landslide triumph of 1964 was looking increasingly vulnerable. The presidential race was soon in turmoil. The outpouring of support for McCarthy led Senator Robert F. Kennedy of New York to jump into the race as well. In March, 1968, Johnson announced he would not seek reelection. Alabama governor George Wallace threw his hat in the ring. President Johnson's withdrawal cleared the way for Vice President Hubert H. Humphrey to do the same.

Rockefeller scheduled a press conference in New York City, setting the stage for what most expected would be a formal announcement of his candidacy. Instead, he announced that he was not going to run. Clay Richards, an Albany-based United Press International reporter who was covering Rockefeller at the time, picks up the story from there.

"Nelson Rockefeller surprised the political world when he announced he would not run for president in 1968, in part out of respect for his wife, Happy, who was humiliated when he was booed off the stage at the 1964 Republican convention shortly after their marriage," Richards said. "Rockefeller surprised everyone again a few months later when he announced he would run after all. The difference: an encounter with Lyndon Johnson after he dropped out of the race." Explained Richards:

The story was told by [Attorney General] Louis Lefkowitz to Kirt King [Kirtland I. King was UPI's Albany bureau chief], who told it to me. One night after a party at the [Executive] Mansion, Carol [Clay's wife, a reporter for Gannett News Service] and I rode with a somewhat tipsy Rockefeller in his state car to Jack's [restaurant], where we were all going to have dinner. I recounted the story as Kirt had told it to me, and he confirmed it, filling in the blanks, but saying he would deny it if I ever printed it while he was still alive. I wrote it for UPI when Rockefeller died, and it got wide play in hundreds of newspapers around the country.

It seems Johnson summoned Rockefeller and Happy to a private dinner at the White House. They had been friends for years, having bonded when they went hunting at the King Ranch in Texas years before.

Rockefeller said, "He [Johnson] told me he could not sleep at night if Nixon was president and he wasn't all that sure about Hubert [Vice President Humphrey] either." Johnson said he could only sleep well if Nelson Rockefeller were president. Rockefeller responded that Happy did not want him to run and he had promised her he would not.

"'Let me talk to Happy,'" LBJ responded, and the two left the table and went wandering through the private quarters of the White House. Rockefeller said: "They came back a half hour later and Lyndon said, 'I've talked her into letting you run.'" Rockefeller returned to Albany and the following week called a news conference and announced he had changed his mind and was running for president.

Also encouraging Rockefeller to change his mind during this interim period were several former GOP national chairmen and other party leaders. Recalled Robert Douglass: "(Senator) Thruston Morton of Kentucky came to him and said, 'Nelson, you've got to run. Running Nixon again is like putting on a pair of socks that you've worn for a couple of days.'

"Then he [Rockefeller] said, 'Look, the Republican Party doesn't want me. I hear you, and I'm most grateful.'" Whether their support was a factor in his subsequent decision to run is not clear, but the governor was glad to have it.

The Rockefeller campaign that followed had a quixotic feel to it from the start because of its late start and the fact that Nixon had used the time effectively to nail down commitments from a near-majority of the delegates.

The Rockefeller campaign plane, a chartered American Airlines Boeing 727, became known to the press entourage as the "727 Flying Circus." At most campaign stops in key states, Rockefeller was cordially received, but sorry, no delegates.

Still, in the wake of the assassinations of Martin Luther King Jr. and then senator Robert Kennedy, the Democrats' situation was chaotic. Governor Wallace, a defiant segregationist, seemed likely to capture voters in both parties throughout the Southern states. Vice President Humphrey was avoiding a firm stand on the Vietnam War, and President Johnson in turn was dragging his feet about endorsing Humphrey. Senator McCarthy was leading a third party.

Poll results continued to buoy Rockefeller's hopes in the run-up to the GOP convention. "He was ahead in the polls over Nixon as the choice for the party to make if they wanted to win," Douglass said. "And then, surprisingly enough, two weeks or so before the Miami convention, a poll came out showing just the opposite. It showed that Nixon could actually win. And the integrity of that poll has always been a real question. Gallup [George Gallup, head of the Gallup Poll] was out of the country at the time. And by the time they did a re-do of that poll, which showed basically what had been shown all the time—that Rockefeller had a better chance to win than Nixon—the momentum was totally lost. All the air went out of the tires at Miami. And by that time the Nixon people and [campaign manager John] Mitchell had so well organized the convention that he [Rockefeller] didn't have a prayer." Nixon won the nomination on the second ballot.[2]

With voters turned off by the ongoing bloodshed of the Vietnam War and by the rioting that marred Humphrey's nomination at the Democratic convention in Chicago, Nixon looked like an easy winner. President Johnson's move in halting the bombing of Vietnam two weeks before the election nearly turned the tide for Humphrey, but it came too late and Nixon won.

1. Rockefeller, Joe Boyd, and Bob Cleveland taken at Colgate, fall of 1958.

2. An ebullient Governor Nelson Rockefeller in campaign mode, circa 1966.

3. On chartered flight in Oregon, Rockefeller gives Joe Boyd a birthday cake, with Major Galvin (bodyguard) on right, May 13, 1964.

4. Rockefeller, Margaret (Peggy) Mayes, and Joe Boyd at Sheraton in June 1967. Margaret later became Mrs. Boyd.

5. Power and experience: the official photograph of Governor Rockefeller, circa 1970.

6. Nixon, Rockefeller, and Joe Boyd taken in the fall of 1972.

7. Patriarchs of wealth and position. Nelson Rockefeller chats with his predecessor as governor and fellow Hudson Valley resident, W. Averell Harriman.

8. Governor Rockefeller dedicates the renamed South Mall as the Empire State Plaza, as key players look on. *From left to right:* Wallace K. Harrison, the architect; Lieutenant Governor Malcolm Wilson; Albany Mayor Erastus Corning II, Attorney General Louis J. Lefkowitz; Assembly Speaker Perry B. Duryea Jr., and Senate Majority Leader and Temporary President of the Senate Warren M. Anderson.

9. Governor Rockefeller, in hard hat on a tour of the South Mall construction site, is interviewed by a television reporter. Such tours generally made for good television coverage, although reporters' questions tended to focus on the lengthening schedule for completion and escalating costs.

10. With the Capitol as a backdrop, Governor Rockefeller talks with a construction worker at the South Mall site in 1973. Rockefeller often disappeared from his office for unscheduled visits to the labyrinthine project, where Joe Boyd or other staff members would typically find him chatting with construction workers.

11. Another formal portrait of Governor Rockefeller, circa 1970.

12. If it walks like a duck . . . Campaigning on Long Island during his 1962 run for a second term, Governor Rockefeller, accompanied by members of the Long Island Association, visited the Long Island Duck Cooperative in Riverhead. Duck farming was a major Long Island industry in that era.

13. Flanked by Republican Senate Majority Leader Earl W. Brydges and Democratic Assembly Speaker Anthony J. Travia, among others, Governor Rockefeller signs the controversial bill creating the powerful Urban Development Corporation in early 1968.

14. In the Capitol, Governor Rockefeller, with Albany Mayor Erastus Corning II and Lieutenant Governor Malcolm Wilson, unveils an architect's model of the planned South Mall project.

15. Governor Rockefeller, with Mayor Erastus Corning II and State University board chairman Frank C. Moore (holding pipe), points to a model of the planned new SUNY campus in Albany.

16. In his final year as governor, Rockefeller receives a medallion from Republican Senator John Dunne for his contributions to the environment.

6

The Rockefeller Air Force

Ready access to his family's fleet of aircraft was one of Nelson Rockefeller's earliest and most useful assets, both in campaigning and in governing. The fleet was jointly owned with Time Inc. through a company called Wayfarer Ketch and based at Westchester County Airport, conveniently close to the Rockefeller family estate at Pocantico Hills.

Joe Boyd recalled that when he first started traveling with the governor in 1962, the plane most used was a two-engine Convair that could hold thirteen to sixteen people. But later the "workhorse" was a two-engine Fairchild F-27 prop-jet, with high wings and the cabin slung underneath. "It took Rockefeller around the sixty-two counties of New York and back and forth across the country in 1964," Joe recalled. Wayfarer also had a fast, six-passenger Lear jet. Later the F-27 was replaced by a faster Gulfstream II jet. In addition, aircraft were sometimes chartered for a campaign.

One regular passenger aboard every plane the governor used during a campaign was a court stenographer named Arthur Mann, whose job was to take down every public word the governor uttered. Jake Underhill recalled him as "a short, wiry gentleman with a mustache that made him look something like a gigolo from Queens Village." Mann loved to dance. "In most cities NAR campaigned in throughout the nation, Mann would find a dance floor and a willing partner.

"Departure time from cities where we had overnight stays was absolute," Underhill said. "When the governor and Happy got aboard the plane, the plane departed. It was the press secretary's job to make sure all reporters and Arthur Mann were aboard before the governor. That meant waking them up on time at the local hotel and getting them to the plane. Usually all ran like clockwork.

"But on one campaign overnight stop when I was duty press secretary," said Underhill, "the governor came aboard, and Arthur Mann still hadn't arrived. With my heart in my mouth because I was responsible for Mann, I reported his absence to NAR.

"'Tell the pilots to take off,' he ordered. We droned into a taxiway on the way to the runway. Suddenly the plane halted and I looked out the window. Lugging his heavy stenotype machine in one hand and his electric typewriter in the other, Arthur was puffing down the taxiway. I heard the forward cargo hatch open. I could see sweat-soaked Arthur crawl aboard, and he silently took a seat forward.

"We took off. NAR knew perfectly well what had happened to his romantic stenotypist, but we were on time. So the governor never mentioned the incident."

The Helicopter Advantage

In the 1966 campaign for governor, the use of helicopters was still a bit of a novelty. Joe recalled one morning that fall when the governor appeared live on a CBS Sunday morning TV show. He was scheduled to travel back to Pocantico, thirty miles up the Hudson, in a helicopter that awaited at a helicopter pad on Manhattan's west side.

This was an eight-passenger craft which Craig Thorn of the Rockefeller campaign had chartered from an outfit in Louisiana. It was used to ferry workers to the offshore oil rigs in the Gulf, and was equipped with pontoons rather than skis. To my knowledge it was the first time a gubernatorial candidate had used a helicopter to traverse the state of New York.

We boarded and pilots took off, following the Hudson River north. It became apparent quickly that something was mechanically wrong with the helicopter, as the governor and I were bouncing around and would have hit our heads repeatedly on the ceiling if we had not been secured by the seat belts. The pilots assured us that they had the chopper in hand and it was safe.

However, when we approached the George Washington Bridge, the copilot turned around and asked us if we would prefer to go over the bridge or under. We said under, and that is exactly what we did. While I was scared silly, Rockefeller was looking out the window at the architecture and the structure of the underbelly of the bridge, saying, "Fabulous . . . fabulous . . . fabulous."

For the rest of the way, we followed the river, waving to boaters who somehow knew we were the helicopter that had just flown under the bridge. We landed near Kykuit [the mansion on the estate], where Nelson told Happy and Nelson Jr., who welcomed us, about our trip. His instructions to me were to call the state police to get us cars for the rest of the day's activities. Then he suggested we go inside and have a brandy. It was 11 a.m. Sunday morning.

Joe said the helicopter, despite this inauspicious debut, was used effectively during the campaign in upstate New York. "The governor was able to reach many small counties and towns which otherwise would have been bypassed if highway driving was the principal method of transportation," he said.

"The only problem was that the pilots were unfamiliar with the landscape. On one occasion, the governor was in western New York going from the city of Salamanca [Cattaraugus County] to Fredonia [Chautauqua County] with a full load of state legislators and press. I was relayed by state police cars for the one-hour drive between cities. When I arrived in Fredonia I figured the shopping center rally would be over and it would be time to leave for our next stop, but lo and behold, the governor had never arrived. The local host, Assemblyman Bruce Manley, was frantic. About fifteen minutes later, the helicopter arrived with the governor and group. Most of the crowd had gone on their errands and shopping. The delay was caused by the pilots' following a railroad track between the two cities. When they came to a fork, they went left and landed shortly thereafter at a shopping center where people were gathered. Once the helicopter landed, Rockefeller jumped out and starting shaking hands with the crowd. Finally he started to wonder why there was no local host nor welcoming band." Then he found out why—they were in Pennsylvania!

Joe said the helicopter was a great asset in the 1966 campaign, but once the upstate area had been covered, the aircraft was returned to Louisiana, both because of its high daily cost and the fact that it was not heated. In late October it gets cold in upstate New York. In a sad footnote to this story, Joe recalled that the helicopter crashed six months later in the Gulf of Mexico and one of the pilots was killed.

Helicopters were also useful in getting the governor around to different events in New York City. Charlie Urstadt, commissioner of Housing and Community Renewal and chairman of the recently begun Battery Park City, recalled touring the governor around lower Manhattan, to look at sites where Urstadt wanted to build large housing projects, then to the Bronx, where Co-Op City was under construction. Co-Op City comprised some 15,500 cooperative units for middle-income families. Rockefeller asked the pilot to circle the buildings, and as they did so, flying at about 2,000 feet altitude, the steelworkers started to wave. The governor immediately began to wave back, calling out his traditional "Hiya, Fella!" as if they could hear him.

The next stop was Floyd Bennett Field in Brooklyn and then on to Staten Island. There a hydrofoil awaited for the trip to Battery Park City, on Manhattan's lower west side, where Urstadt had planned a "water-breaking." Because the project was going to be built on fill dumped in the river, instead of a ground-breaking ceremony, Urstadt had arranged to have the governor set off a dynamite charge in the river.

Meanwhile, the hydrofoil trip from Staten Island had been very rough, and the governor arrived very late besides. "Are we glad to see you!" said someone among the assembled press corps. "That makes two of us," replied the somewhat shaken governor.

When the governor pushed the plunger, the dynamite charge in the river went off with a loud boom, producing a huge geyser, recalled Urstadt. It was a perfect photo opportunity captured by all the TV cameras—except one. Gabe Pressman, a veteran reporter then working for NBC, called out: "Governor, would you mind repeating that? We missed that shot!"

Rides to Remember

The governor was an intrepid flyer, seldom fazed by traveling in bad weather or on small aircraft.

On one occasion, Joe Boyd said, the governor had gone to Cleveland, accompanied by Lieutenant Governor Malcolm Wilson and New York Republican National Committeeman George Hinman, to speak to a Republican gathering. The weather worsened, rain coming down in buckets, puddles building up on the runway as they prepared to depart. It would have made sense to stay overnight and leave in the morning, but Rockefeller wanted to get home to Pocantico. Wilson said he didn't think they should fly in such conditions.

"Don't worry," the governor commented. "I've survived three air crashes." And off they went.

For advance-men trying to keep the constantly traveling governor on schedule, weather was an ever-present concern. Bert Levine recalled a trip to an event in Plattsburgh, in the northern tip of New York, about twenty-five miles from the Canadian border. It was raining buckets. "Given the severe weather conditions, we were worried that flying back to Westchester Airport would be impossible," Levine said. "There had already been discussions among the security people and the advance team about finding a car and driver to get the governor home, at least

to Albany [160 miles away] that night. Apparently he had made it clear
that he was not going to overnight in Plattsburgh."

Arriving at the airport amid a worsening downpour, Levine got
some good news: the weather front was moving through and the
pilots figured that by the time the governor drove the twenty or thirty
minutes to the airport, his plane would be able to take off. Levine
continued,

> I spotted the one payphone in the terminal, hoping to relay the
> good news to the entourage—this was well before the cell phone
> age—only to see that the phone was in use. Some guy, not much
> younger than me, was on the phone trying to reach his parents. He
> needed to let them know that they should not go out to LaGuardia
> Airport to pick him up because the Mohawk Airlines flight for that
> night had just been cancelled. He would not be able to get home
> until the next morning. (I did not want to be rude but I could not
> help overhearing the conversation with what I judged to be a younger
> brother or sister. Apparently mom and dad had already left for the
> airport.)
>
> When I completed my call I found that I had nothing to do for
> an hour or so. That would be about how long it would take for the
> governor to arrive at the airport. The pilots had gone back out to the
> airplane. The only people left in the terminal, aside from one or two
> employees and me, were the stranded college kid and what I judged
> to be his friend and traveling mate. We struck up a conversation and I
> learned more about their no-flight plight. A friend had dropped them
> off at the airport, they had no car and very little cash—this was also
> the pre-plastic era. So, they had no ride, which didn't seem to matter
> too much because they had no place to go.
>
> Advance-men get paid to spot opportunities to make their
> principals look good. What an opportunity this was! "College Kids
> Hitch Ride Home with Rocky." I grabbed a raincoat from one of the
> Robinson Crusoes and dashed out to the G-2 [a Gulfstream II jet].
> Was there any reason why the kids could not fly down to the New
> York area with us? The pilots had no objection. Back in the airport,
> I called the entourage. Whoever I spoke to grasped the political
> potential immediately. By the time the small motorcade pulled up in
> front of the airport, the governor and the traveling press had already
> been clued in (a small press contingent frequently traveled with us on
> the G-2). The governor, much on his game that night, and probably
> buoyed by the rapidly improving weather and prospects for returning

home that night, wasted no time in virtually accosting the college students.

"I hear you need a ride home."

"Yes, sir, we do."

"Well, will getting you down to Westchester help?"

"A whole lot, sir."

"Great! Let's get on board. You first."

Flashbulbs were already beginning to pop and pens were scratching on pads. An advance-man's dream was coming true. On board, the governor invited the students to sit at his table. I did not hear the first part of their conversation because, as junior staff person on board, I was pouring beer and soft drinks for my fellow passengers. I did notice, though, that as soon as we got above the clouds the press people unbuckled their seat belts and eavesdropped on the governor's conversation. Apparently the young man told the governor that mom and dad had gone out to LaGuardia not knowing that the flight had been canceled. After some further discussion—I was just now beginning to overhear the back and forth—it was decided that he, the student, should try his parents again. His folks might have returned home from the airport to await word from their stranded son. The guess was a good one.

The G-2 was equipped with what, by today's standards, was a fairly primitive air-to-ground phone system. Placing a call was not easy and the reception at both ends, especially in unsettled weather, was never especially good. After some effort, a connection was made and the student handed the phone.

"Hello, Mom. It's me, Ralph. RALPH, MOM! Can you hear? Look, me and Ted got a ride down to Westchester Airport. WESTCHESTER! Yes, there's an airport there."

"I don't know, Mom—you'll have to find out where. But it's Westchester Airport."

"No, it's not Mohawk. It's a private plane. A PRIVATE PLANE, MOM!"

"Whose? Governor Rockefeller's. GOVERNOR ROCKE-FELLER'S, MOM!"

"NO, I SWEAR, I HAVEN'T BEEN!"

The governor, the staff, the press and Ted dissolved in laughter.

Not every airplane ride was quite so jolly. Jake Underhill, deputy press secretary at the time, recalled an earlier journey aboard Rocke-feller's F-27 turboprop to Buffalo for a speech.

"NAR was gentle with his aides, rarely firing anyone, but it was not wise to oppose his orders," Underhill said. He continued,

There were a number of aides, personal and state, on the trip. I believe Carol Uht, the personal art curator, was consulting with him about art auctions somewhere. There was an investment advisor from Room 5600, I recall. Aboard, too, was Harold Wilm, the state commissioner of conservation.

Our general route was north along the Hudson and then west across the state, but Rockefeller sensed that we had not turned west when he expected us to do so. He looked out the window to see that we were flying over the Adirondacks along the route of the Northway, then under construction. Commissioner Wilm arrived at the governor's seat, pointed out the window and started to describe to him how the Public Works people were raping the pristine landscape below.

NAR listened for a moment, then told me to go forward to tell the pilots to put us back on course to Buffalo. I did so, and when I returned to my seat, he asked who had told the pilots to fly up the Northway. It was Commissioner Wilm, I told the governor.

Two weeks later, we put out a press release announcing that the governor had "reluctantly" accepted the commissioner's resignation.

The lesson was not lost on the governor's staff or the heads of state departments or agencies.

7

Travels and Travails
South of the Border

Nelson Rockefeller had long had personal, business, and professional interests in Latin America. He owned a ranch in Venezuela. He had founded, with his brother Laurance, the International Basic Economy Corporation (IBEC) to foster economic development in Latin American countries. He spoke Spanish and was a well-known figure in Central and South America. During the Roosevelt administration, he had served as coordinator of Inter-American Affairs and during the Truman administration, as assistant secretary of state for Latin America. He had played a central role in rounding up the votes of Latin American delegates for the resolution that created the United Nations. The land on which the UN building stands, in Manhattan along the East River, was purchased and donated for that purpose by Nelson's father, John D. Rockefeller Jr.

The Goodwill Ambassador

So it perhaps made sense that Richard Nixon, on winning election as president in 1968, should ask his erstwhile rival, Nelson Rockefeller, to undertake a series of goodwill missions to Latin America on behalf of the new administration. Nelson Rockefeller's name, he was told, was still magic in the region.

Rockefeller agreed to undertake the project, perhaps in the belief that he could help shape United States policy in the region while reestablishing his own foreign policy credentials. He planned to make four trips during 1969, with visits to twenty countries. The first trip encompassed Mexico and the countries of Central America; the other three went to the Caribbean and South America. All were organized in typical, and elaborate, Rockefeller style by Joe Boyd and his advance crew, with a cadre of staff, advisors, and appropriate experts to observe, recommend, and lend substance to the effort. Among these were Dr. Alan Miller, state commissioner of Mental Hygiene, and Dr. Clifton R. Wharton Jr., a Spanish-speaking agricultural economist who later became chancellor of the State University of New York. Appropriate think tanks were consulted, and extensive briefing books prepared for each country by the State Department. On the ground, lavish arrangements were made, often with the help of the State Department, whose people cannot have been enthusiastic about Rockefeller's intrusion on their turf.[1]

In addition to the governor and his staff and advisors, there was a large press contingent—newspaper, magazine and wire service reporters, photographers, TV anchors, cameramen, and radio reporters—that required a second airplane.

Needless to say, the Rockefeller advance corps was mobilized to smooth the path for this outsized entourage. This was seldom easy and was sometimes impossible.

As an Albany reporter for Gannett News Service, I went on two of the four trips—the first one, which took in Mexico, Guatemala, Honduras, Panama, Nicaragua, and Costa Rica, and the third one, which encompassed Brazil, Uruguay, and Paraguay.

Welcomes: A Mixed Bag

Things went reasonably well on that first trip until we landed in Tegucigalpa, Honduras, where angry mobs were using the occasion to protest American influence and specifically American companies they felt had exploited the people of the region. Watching a furious demonstration outside our hotel, we saw protesters trying to scale the side of the building in order to tear down the American flag that flew there. One person died in the rioting. The hostility was unnerving.

The next morning, Rockefeller went to the palace for a meeting with the Honduran leadership. Police and soldiers kept the crowds back, and things were quiet but tense. When the meeting ended, Rockefeller and the leaders came marching out of the building into the square, and the crowd roared. Rockefeller took one look, decided that the crowd was friendly rather than hostile, and veered sharply to the left, into the crowd, where he began shaking hands. Major Galvin, his state police bodyguard—assigned to the Secret Service for this mission—struggled to stay with him as people swarmed around, and the Honduran police tried frantically to catch up with the man they were ostensibly protecting.

As cameras rolled and flashbulbs popped, Rockefeller gave a great bear hug to one grinning old crone. He may have known full well that this shot would make the papers everywhere. What he did not know, at least not until sometime later, was that she used the occasion to lift his wallet. In one sense, of course, the joke was on her, as Rockefeller, in typical fashion, carried neither money nor credit cards. But what a souvenir!

There were other memorable moments, such as the barbecue that Nicaraguan dictator Anastasio Somoza Debayle put on at his country house for the traveling press corps and the Rockefeller staff. Rockefeller, in his Roosevelt administration days, had developed a relationship with Somoza's father, Nicaragua's dictator at the time. Somoza's wife was part of the Nicaraguan host committee. And the advance team for the Nicaragua visit included Laurance Rockefeller's top aide, Henry David, who had been a classmate of Somoza's in prep school. The stage was thus set for an amicable visit.

The barbecue was sumptuous. The food was ample and excellent, and the drinks flowed. But I think many reporters, including this one, were uncomfortable being feted by a dictator. We were also feeling slightly intimidated by the presence of so many of Somoza's men—unsmiling, beefy fellows in black suits, with noticeable bulges under their armpits.

Joe recalled the visit in similar terms, but with a remarkable twist: it was the only time in his life, he said, that he was cornered by a rattlesnake! Somoza had to send his security people to rescue him.

The father-and-son Somoza dynasty, which began in 1937, ended in 1979 when the Sandinista National Liberation Front overthrew the government, ruling thereafter until 1990, when the Sandinistas lost at the polls.

The second trip, in which I did not participate, was scheduled to include stops in Columbia, Venezuela, Bolivia, and Peru, as well as Trinidad, Haiti, and the Dominican Republic. By this time, it appeared that everybody with an ax to grind—against the United States, against Nelson Rockefeller personally or as capitalist symbol, or against the current national government—had seen the publicity potential in making trouble for the Rockefeller mission. And some governments themselves had prickly relations with Big Brother to the north.

In Quito, Ecuador, Joe said, rioting was so severe that "the government was facing a revolution while Rockefeller was meeting with top officials. I went in and told him and we were escorted under a white flag back to our hotel, where we were told to stay for forty-eight hours. We had alerted the U.S. Southern Command in Panama, and they were going to send the marines with planes to get us out. We held them [the marines] up and they didn't come." The entourage was able to leave without interference.

"In Bolivia," Joe recalled, "we had to change the meeting place to meet at the airport, rather than La Paz. It was the safest place to meet." El Alto International Airport, twenty-five minutes from La Paz, the nation's administrative capital, is the world's highest international airport, at 13,300 feet altitude.

Scrubbed Visits

In Venezuela and Peru, the visits were cancelled altogether. Joe said that Rockefeller was notified while in Trinidad the night before departing for Caracas that the government of Venezuela had cancelled the visit. Rockefeller, who knew the oil-rich country well though he seldom visited his ranch there, sent Joe by Air Force plane to find out why they had been disinvited. Joe recalled having to descend from the plane via a rope ladder, under the watchful eyes of machine gunners aboard the plane. A black Mercedes waited on the tarmac, and Joe was told to get in.

"I was taken to a hotel, where the [U.S.] Secret Service and my advance-men, Craig Thorn and Dave Duffy, were. They were being moved every twenty minutes. They were told to go to the patio and join the party there. The problem was that the party was for a Japanese group, and the Americans were so tall that they had to bend their knees as they walked around so they wouldn't stand out."

Joe did find out why the visit had been cancelled. Along the route from the airport, the Secret Service advance team had found a secret machine-gun nest, obviously intended to ambush the entourage. The government cancelled because it concluded that it could not guarantee Rockefeller's safety.

As for Peru, Joe said he was told on the advance trip, designed to work out arrangements, that the mission would be disinvited. He met with the country's entire cabinet. "All they wanted to talk about was fishing rights," Joe said. Henry Kissinger, President Nixon's national security advisor at the time, called Joe to say that he was appointing Arthur K. Watson, chairman of IBM World Trade Corporation and vice chairman of the parent IBM, to negotiate the fishing problem. That ended the meeting. Arthur "Dick" Watson, who had prior business experience in Peru, was one of the private-sector participants in the Rockefeller mission.

Then, said Joe, "I was ushered into the defense secretary's office. I was told that if Rockefeller came as a private citizen or as governor of New York, they would declare a national holiday, but if he came representing Nixon or the United States, he would be disinvited."

Joe told the U.S. ambassador, a holdover from the Johnson administration, that Rockefeller was going to be disinvited. The ambassador didn't believe him and cabled Washington that the visit was all set. The Peruvian government formally cancelled the trip the following week.

Brazil: Vibrant, Suppressed

The third trip took us to Brazil, Uruguay, and Paraguay. Rio de Janeiro, the first stop, was magical and somewhat old world. Brasilia, the country's then-new capital city, carved out of the wilderness, was architecturally fascinating, quite empty, and had some overtones of the South Mall project underway in Albany. And São Paulo, known as the "engine" of Brazil's economy, seemed highly European—modern, busy, businesslike, huge. But again, there were major anti-American demonstrations in São Paulo, which the police put down with water cannons mounted on tanks. Police units, equipped with helmets and shields, wielded their sticks aggressively in breaking up the crowds.[2]

Advance-Man's Dream—Or Nightmare?

Asuncion, Paraguay, was the final stop. Paraguay, too, was run by a dictator, and the atmosphere seemed a bit tense and stifling compared with Uruguay and Brazil.

Advance-man Ron Abney, always on the lookout for opportunities to generate positive press, saw it differently, as he recalled years later.

Having had several almost disastrous stops due to local political problems, I finally arrived in a friendly country. Of course, the fact that Paraguay was then run by a tyrant/dictator who allowed no dissension didn't hurt. I decided this would be my crowning glory, the event that would catapult me into the advance-man's Hall of Fame.

With the governor and his very large party in one plane and a second plane for the press, arrival was set in Asuncion for noon—perfect. I had made a deal with the president's staff to have everyone with a heartbeat and a government link fill the airport and all its surroundings with masses of folks. Little ones, old ones, war veterans, army wives, school children, widows, Boy Scouts, government employees, and any low life wandering the streets. It helped that the president closed and emptied the schools, the churches, and what appeared to be the prisons. Businesses were closed, as it was proclaimed a state holiday. I had done all this—a twenty-seven-year-old South Georgia lad who literally caused a major Latin American country to completely shut down for one full day. It was surely legendary stuff!

My plan was, or course, to have the press plane land first, as it always had, and observe and photograph this mass of humanhood, all drooling to touch the governor's garment. I was beside myself.

Then it happened—my worst nightmare. The governor's plane, Air Force Two, was spotted breaking out of the clouds. It appeared that it would land first. But it couldn't—I wouldn't have it! I went ballistic. I ran to the tower and grabbed the radio headset and asked for Jim Cannon, who was traveling with the governor.

"You can't do this," I said. "History is being made here. Thousands are waiting—no, millions. The press must be allowed to land first—to record it, to marvel in it. Everything depends on it." By that time, I had come to the conclusion that everything I had done in my first twenty-seven years of life had led me to this moment. This epiphany made everything clear to me and caused me to be even more determined to redirect the order of airplane landings.

The voice came back: "The governor lands first and the press plane will land thirty minutes later. Make the arrangements."

"You can't do that," I screamed. "Ten million people are here. Everyone in Paraguay is here. I won't accept that decision." (I had apparently lost consciousness and had also temporarily lost my fear of being sent back to Macon, Georgia, on a Trailways bus.)

"Who made that #&*@# . . . decision?" I demanded to know. I was entitled, after all—I was speaking for thirty million Paraguayans. I blurted out: "It must have been a committee decision, as no one person is that stupid." Apparently at this point, I had decided that if fired I could always move to Paraguay and book sightseeing tours. My voice, almost gone now from screaming, gave forth with one final bark: "I must know who made that decision!"

The next voice I heard had a bit of authority to it and answered my question. "Nelson Aldrich Rockefeller made the decision." Without missing a beat and apparently with an instant moment of clarity, I yelled, "GOOD DECISION!"

The governor's plane landed. No speeches. The crowd instantly vanished into the hillside and thirty minutes later the press plane landed. An ABC reporter asked me why no people ever showed up at these events.

"It's a national holiday," I pointed out defiantly. "You don't expect them to be standing around at an airport all day on their day off, do you?" True story—every word of it.

Throughout these trips, Rockefeller's hardy advance-men scurried from country to country, working out plans and arrangements, smoothing feathers, and putting out brush fires. Language barriers, lack of sleep, confusing regulations, and the constant hassle of converting one currency into another wore them out. They were hard pressed to keep straight the name, country of origin, and value versus dollars of a dozen or more currencies. After awhile, they began to call any non-U.S. money "guzincas."[3]

Rockefeller and Papa Doc

Generally effective though the advance-men were at managing the schedule and arrangements for Rockefeller's visits—often under challenging political and linguistic conditions—they were also subject to a certain amount of manipulation by national leaders, who had agendas of their own. Haiti was a case in point. Dr. François "Papa Doc" Duvalier, elected president for life in violation of the constitution he himself had promulgated, ran the hemisphere's most repressive and isolated regime. Rockefeller's visit there, on the fourth of his trips, had to be adroitly handled so as not to give the impression that the United States was endorsing him or his government.

Advance-man Craig Thorn recalled his arrival at the airport at Port-au-Prince:

> I was met by our young ambassador, who had come to the airport in a nondescript, older model Chevrolet. The first question he asked me, once we were settled in the back seat, was: "Is Papa Doc still alive?" My answer was that I didn't think I would have been sent to Haiti if he were dead.
>
> In the course of the next few days, I worked on setting up the hotels we would be using and meeting with the foreign minister to start fleshing out the schedule for Rockefeller and his team of advisors. Because we were in Haiti, we expected more press than normal and we were right. This put a bit of a strain on our hotel accommodations, but we, in the end, managed to have rooms for everyone.
>
> When the governor's plane arrived in Haiti, I was very much relieved, since concerns had been expressed to me that both our embassy and the Haitian government were unsure that Nelson Rockefeller would show up. At the airport, the staff and the advisors left for the hotel, while the press and the governor left for Port-au-Prince, where the governor was to meet with Papa Doc.

Papa Doc had declared the day a national holiday, and had arranged transportation for thousands of Haitians to greet the governor. Somehow he cajoled Nelson Rockefeller to follow him through French doors out to a balcony, where several hundred thousand people cheered as Papa Doc grabbed Nelson's hand and greeted the crowd. The photographs and TV coverage of this event hit news organizations throughout the world, somewhat to the embarrassment of Nelson Rockefeller and the U.S. State Department.

During my negotiations with the foreign minister, I had turned down a request for the governor to visit the "new road to the south." It would be time-consuming and really served no purpose except to further inflate Papa Doc's image. Somehow, this managed to get on the schedule—not mine, Papa Doc's—and we had to squeeze it in. We suspected that Papa Doc thanked the governor for agreeing to make the trip, despite the fact that it was not on his schedule. We did make the trip and, as suspected, it really was a waste of time.

Rockefeller's linguistic skills surprised many, including Dr. Alan Miller, New York's commissioner of mental hygiene, who was one of the team of advisors. "I happened to be in the room when he was talking to Papa Doc," Miller said. "And they talked in French. He didn't make anything of it." Rockefeller also was essentially fluent in Portuguese, Miller learned on the subsequent visit to Brazil. But, he said, "I think he was more fluent in Spanish—he was totally comfortable in Spanish."

The Rockefeller entourage's departure from Haiti was memorable, as well, recalled Thorn. "We exited the hotel grounds very close to an art gallery, where the governor chose to stop his bus so he could see, and perhaps buy, some Haitian paintings. When something like this happened, the staff was trained to start collecting cash from each other so we could pay for whatever the governor bought. The governor never had any money with him," commented Thorn, sounding a much-repeated theme. "If you traveled as staff with Nelson Rockefeller, you carried cash. You would be reimbursed, but you'd better be flush."

Alan Miller vividly recollected a Rockefeller art-buying sortie in Port-au-Prince. "I remember when we were in Haiti, and there was some brief period between meetings when he had the time to go to one of the art galleries to buy art. He was followed by his entourage and someone was taking notes as he went, and he went flying through this place that was full of works of art of all kinds, and as he went by he would say 'that one, that one, that one.'" Small wonder his staff carried cash!

Thorn, despite the inevitable stress, had fond memories of Haiti. "One of the most enjoyable parts of my trip," Thorn said, "was being stopped on the street by Haitians who, once they realized I was from the United States, expressed great friendliness and warmth and let me know how glad they were that I was there and hoped that many more Americans would follow." Such positive sentiments were an anchor to windward against the hostility that greeted the mission in some other countries.

On that same trip, the Rockefeller mission visited the Republic of Trinidad and Tobago, and was in Port of Spain, on the island of Trinidad, preparing to head for nearby Venezuela, when he was informed that he had been disinvited.

James Kiepper, a twenty-eight-year-old faculty member at the State University at Albany, was part of the advance team for Port of Spain. He recalled that Rockefeller, before departing, dashed into a store adjacent to the Port of Spain Hilton to pick up some mementoes for his young sons Nelson Jr. and Mark. He chose some drums, and much to his staff's astonishment, hauled out a hundred-dollar American Express Traveler's check to pay for them.

In that era, before automated teller machines and credit and debit cards, traveler's checks, paid for in advance and already signed once by the purchaser, were regarded as the safest way to carry money when abroad. They could be cashed at banks (if open) and many hotels, restaurants, and retail stores would accept them.

As he watched Rockefeller scrawling his signature across the middle of the check, it occurred to Kiepper that he himself could have paid the merchant in cash and obtained the traveler's check with the governor's signature on it. Of course, he said forty years later, he wouldn't have cashed it—but what a souvenir! "How many people have a check with Nelson Rockefeller's signature on it?"

Back Page Material

Some of the reporters on these Rockefeller trips had full-time assignments in Latin America, and they were knowledgeable about the geography, history, culture, and politics of the various countries. Most of the rest of us, however, knew relatively little beyond the detail given in the briefing books provided by the State Department, and a few didn't even read those. They were there to cover Rockefeller and the spectacle provided both by the crowds that welcomed him and the crowds that rioted to protest his presence.

Fascinating as many of us found the history and current affairs of these countries, it did not take long to realize that our editors were little interested, perhaps because they sensed that so many of their readers were not interested at all. Many of the stories we filed with such effort were brutally cut or never got into print. America's focus—then as now—was predominantly eastward to Europe or westward to Asia—not southward. And that was true as well of the new president, Richard Nixon. The Rockefeller team toiled to produce an informed, comprehensive report detailing conditions throughout Latin America and recommending a broader, multilateral policy for the region in place of the existing unilateral policy. Both Congress and the Nixon White House largely ignored it. The report was quietly shelved, with minimum press coverage, and more or less forgotten. The Rockefeller mission was generally judged a public relations failure, and U.S. policy continued without change. Nixon had more pressing matters on his mind.

8

Ars Gratia Artis
and So Much More

Art was not only a passion for Nelson Rockefeller, it was an important part of his daily life, providing recreation and relaxation and a break from the unrelenting pressures of government and politics.

Robert Douglass, who, as counsel and later secretary to the governor, was probably closer to him personally than anyone else on the staff, recalled a scene typical of Rockefeller's campaigning in New York City.

> When the governor was campaigning on a weekend, we'd go to Astoria [Queens] and the Lower East Side and be all over New York, and he would go by car. He would be sitting in the back seat, and he'd either be working on a speech, or more likely, he had the latest Sotheby's catalogs with him. He would be sitting there, and I would be thinking, "I wonder how he's going to handle this—there's an angry crowd out there." And he would be going through the Sotheby's catalog. At the time he was collecting Korean pottery, and I think it was from the sixth or eighth century, mostly celadon green, beautiful stuff.
>
> I said, "Those are really attractive, governor." "Yes," he said, "there are a couple of big collections coming out now, and they're being auctioned, and the prices are really good. You know, I stopped collecting because the prices got so high—like Lowestoft [English porcelain] or Chinese Export. That's why I'm buying this. It's been tied up for years and it's just coming back on the market."
>
> And he would make little notes about how much to bid for it. He entertained himself and relaxed, and then he would jump out of the car and plunge into the rough and tumble of campaigning.

Joseph Persico, Rockefeller's speechwriter, who sometimes traveled with the governor so they could work on a speech en route, remembered similar scenes:

When we would be flying somewhere, part of his distraction would be to go through somebody's art catalog, Sotheby's or whatever. He had a code, and he'd put his code down, whether it would be an A, B, C, D, or an E. Then he would give the marked-up catalog to Carol Uht, who worked for him privately handling his art collection and sometimes traveled on the plane. Or he would give it to Joe Boyd, who in turn would give it to her. The code would tell her how interested he was in a piece, and whether to investigate its asking price and likely selling price.

And this was a pastime for him, this was a hobby, this was a great pleasure for him. Not that there was ever much leisure time, whether traveling or not. Nelson Rockefeller was a confirmed workaholic. There were very, very few wasted moments in the air in the Rockefeller administration. He had enormous mental energy. His mind was always roving to the next idea, the next crusade, the next campaign, and he was very blessed that he had the constitution of an ox that could bear up under these demands that he imposed on himself. Even when he achieved something major, it was, "Okay, what do we do tomorrow?" You didn't rest on your laurels for very long.

Rockefeller applied himself intensely to everything he did, including not only the process of governing New York, but also the collection and promotion of art. His lifelong absorption with art helped to shape not only his career but his legacy.

It Ran in the Family

Of the six children of John D. Rockefeller Jr., Nelson, the third and most ebullient child, was the one most interested in art. In this he took after his mother, Abby Aldrich Rockefeller, who was a founder of New York's Museum of Modern Art and a major influence on her son's artistic tastes, knowledge, and zeal for collecting. In his turn, Nelson became a trustee of the museum in 1932, serving nearly half a century until his death in 1979. He also served as its treasurer from 1935 to 1939, and as president from 1939 to 1941 and 1946 to 1953.

Although he loved and appreciated all kinds of art, including architecture, it was abstract modern and non-Western art that he preferred and primarily collected. As noted, this often included decorative art objects, such as the Korean porcelains and primitive pottery and sculpture from Africa, New Guinea, Mexico, and South America. Music and dance did not much interest him, although his stepmother,

Martha Baird Rockefeller, whom his widowed father married in 1951, had been a world-class concert pianist. He loved jazz, however, and had a very large collection of recordings.

Learning the Politics of Art: The Diego Rivera Affair

As a Rockefeller and a wealthy man, Nelson Rockefeller was involved in the art world at very high levels throughout his entire adult life, starting very early.

Cary Reich, in his excellent book on Nelson Rockefeller's first fifty years,[1] describes Rockefeller's involvement in a bruising controversy in 1933 over a mural that the flamboyant Mexican artist Diego Rivera painted in the main entrance lobby of the RCA building in Rockefeller Center. Rockefeller, a member of the committee selecting art for the center's buildings, had wanted Henri Matisse, but Matisse had turned down the assignment. Rockefeller—at the age of twenty-four a rising power in the management of the family-owned real estate complex—pushed to give the commission to some American muralists. Those artists' controversial and largely anticapitalist works had been reluctantly exhibited by the Museum of Modern Art under the auspices of a Junior Advisory Committee led by none other than Nelson Rockefeller. Getting nowhere in this effort, Rockefeller persuaded his starchy father, John D. ("Junior") Rockefeller Jr., to agree to give the commission to Rivera, an artist whose work his mother greatly admired in spite of the artist's overt leftist attitudes. In fact, says Reich, Rivera was a dedicated Communist who had been expelled from the party and was anxious to get back in its good graces. The thousand-square-foot fresco was supposed to depict the theme "Man at the Crossroads Looking with Hope and High Vision to the Choosing of a New and Better Future."

But as the mural took shape, onlookers saw a section showing airplanes, death rays, and soldiers with gas masks. Another section portrayed a May Day demonstration in Moscow's Red Square, and another section showed floating syphilis, gonorrhea, and tuberculosis microbes.

The final piece of the painting showed a soldier, a worker, and a black farmer holding hands with a figure whose face remained vague. On the day the building was opened to the public, Rivera gave the figure the clearly identifiable face of Vladimir Lenin. That was the last straw for Junior.

Amid the glare of publicity, Nelson himself wrote Rivera a letter saying the mural was beautifully painted, but that the Lenin portrait

would offend people and would have to be repainted with an anony-
mous face. Rivera refused. The artist was paid his fee and the mural
was then shrouded in canvas, where it remained until it was quietly
destroyed in early 1934. Rivera denounced its destruction as an act of
"cultural vandalism."

The Price of Vision

Rockefeller acquired some scar tissue, too, as a strong and early advocate of public support for the arts. On this subject he was way ahead
of his time. As Joseph Persico commented: "When he was serving in
the Eisenhower administration in a domestic policy capacity, he had
in mind a role for the federal government in support of the arts. But
when he encouraged the legislation in Congress, he was laughed at as
the promoter of the 'free piano lesson bill.'

"And that was a turning point for him," Persico said. "He realized
that as long as he was strictly an adviser, he couldn't bring to fruition
the things he believed in; that to have genuine power in government,
you had to have power derived from your election as a public official.
And that's when he came into New York State."

Obviously, that realization was greatly shaped as well by the frustrations of being constantly thwarted and undercut by entrenched bureau-
crats, politicians, and other powerful figures, such as the secretaries
of state Cordell Hull in the Roosevelt administration and John Foster
Dulles in the Eisenhower administration. To such people, Rockefeller's extraordinary energy, vision, and willingness to marshal private
resources to achieve his goals represented a continuing threat.

In any event, it was not too many years later, in 1960, that Governor
Rockefeller created the first State Council on the Arts. It became a
model, Persico said, for other states' arts councils and for the National
Endowment for the Arts.

Art for the Public

Promoting the arts and making both the performing and the visual
arts more accessible to the public would remain a continuing part of
Rockefeller's agenda.

One of his best-known efforts in this regard is the collection of
modern art works that line the long central corridor of the Nelson A.
Rockefeller Empire State Plaza, formerly known as the South Mall.

Of course, Rockefeller loved the architecture of the massive project,
and loved working with his good friend Wally Harrison, the archi-

tect, to refine its design. At the same time, and quite early in the mall's construction, he wanted to make sure that his concept of the corridor lined with art came to fruition. The ninety-two pieces were chosen by a committee, but its members knew and were keenly sensitive to what Rockefeller liked. So the artworks were acquired early on and stored for years until the project was sufficiently complete to put them in place.

Robert Douglass recalled a conversation one night in 1970 on a campaign trip to western New York, when Rockefeller thought he might lose to Arthur Goldberg in his bid for reelection to a fourth term.

> He called me up to the front of the bus, and he said, "I want you to make a promise. If I lose—and I think there's a good chance—I want you to help assure that the legislature continues to support, as long as you're up here, the state university budget."
>
> "And a footnote," he said, "the budget, which I have added to, covers the artwork, which it seems to me makes the campus across from the Capitol [i.e., the mall] a significant addition to the city of Albany. But without the art," he said, "it wouldn't be the same."

As it turned out, Rockefeller won handily and had another three years to shepherd his many undertakings along toward completion before he left office.

Wheeling and Dealing

One of Rockefeller's less well-known efforts on behalf of art for the citizenry of New York State involved his unsuccessful 1966 attempt to outbid the president of the United States for one of the world's outstanding art collections.

Jake Underhill explained that Joseph H. Hirschhorn, a wealthy financier and mining entrepreneur who lived in a twenty-two-acre estate atop Round Hill in Underhill's hometown of Greenwich, Connecticut, had assembled a huge collection of nineteenth- and twentieth-century paintings and sculptures.

"Rockefeller visited him there one Saturday," Underhill recalled.

> He was attempting to wrap up negotiations through which Hirschhorn would gift the collection of some six thousand items to the State University College at nearby Purchase. Rockefeller would agree to kick in various statues from his collection at Kykuit to pad out the college's art collection, which would become known as the Hirschhorn Collection at SUNY Purchase.

It was such a done deal that, as Hirschhorn and Rockefeller visited, I was stationed at my mother's house in Greenwich with a press release on a mimeograph stencil that I was to put out the instant the governor called me to tell me all was settled.

But LBJ [President Lyndon B. Johnson] had already called Hirschhorn that morning, and the president's fabled telephone charm had prevailed. The collection went to Washington to be housed in the gorgeous Joseph H. Hirschhorn Museum and Sculpture Garden, part of the Smithsonian Institution on the mall near the White House. I destroyed the mimeograph stencil.

When he died in 1981, Hirschhorn bequeathed the museum another six thousand works and added five million dollars to the original two-million-dollar endowment.

Rockefeller firmly believed that promoting the arts was both beneficial to the arts and good for the economy. The Saratoga Performing Arts Center (SPAC) is not only an expression of that belief but also a reflection of the governor's negotiating talents, and his ability to overcome opposition by giving in order to get.

Saratoga Springs, north of Albany, was long famous as a spa town, a summer resort, and a tourist destination, featuring hotels, sought-after mineral waters, harness racing, and thoroughbred racing in the month of August.

Joseph Persico, a keen observer of Rockefeller's deal-making skills, cited as an example a hypothetical negotiation between the governor and Senator Earl W. Brydges of Niagara Falls, a member of the state's ruling triumvirate as senate majority leader and a power in his own right.

"In the case of Earl Brydges, Nelson Rockefeller wants the Saratoga Performing Arts Center, a big deal here in our region. Earl Brydges says, well, then, I want an art park in Buffalo. Well, someone else might have become stiff-necked about that and said that's not what we're talking about. Nelson Rockefeller says, Earl, you get your art park, I get my Saratoga Performing Arts Center." Was there such a negotiation? "I was not privy to the discussion," said Persico, "but I know that Earl Brydges wanted that and it happened."

Living with Art

Rockefeller's own very large art collection, of course, included paintings, drawings, prints, and sculptures by a great many famous and not-so-famous artists, along with the spur-of-the-moment acquisitions he made when traveling and campaigning.

Indeed, the extended Rockefeller family, and in particular Nelson, lived with great art on an everyday basis. For example, tiny Union Church in Pocantico Hills, just outside the estate, is adorned with magnificent stained glass windows commissioned by the Rockefeller family. There are nine windows by Marc Chagall, primarily depicting the Stations of the Cross—the only such sequence of windows by that artist in the United States. There is also a beautiful rose window by Henri Matisse, commissioned in 1954 by Nelson as a memorial to his mother. It was Matisse's last work, and he died only a few days after completing the design.

The huge mansion on the Rockefeller family estate, "Kykuit," (which means lookout in Dutch), became Nelson's home after the death in 1971 of his stepmother, Martha Baird Rockefeller. (Brothers John, Laurance, and David had homes of their own on the sprawling estate. Winthrop, who died in 1973, lived in Arkansas.)

The property immediately around the mansion had long boasted a golf course, built for the enjoyment of John D. Rockefeller Sr. in his later years. This was a nine-hole course but was ingeniously designed so that it could also be played from different tees, in effect creating another nine holes.

Nelson Rockefeller placed giant sculptures—by Calder, Henry Moore, and many others—throughout this property, each carefully positioned by Rockefeller personally for maximum aesthetic effect.[2] Anyone playing golf on the course thus got a tour of a vast sculpture garden at the same time.

Robert Douglass, an excellent golfer who sometimes played a round with the governor on this course, described him as a decent player but impatient. "He was always disappearing in his golf cart to check on somebody's house or inspect some landscaping project," Douglass recalled.[3]

Rockefeller once invited the Legislative Correspondents Association—the Albany press corps—to an all-day party at the Pocantico Hills estate, a jaw-dropping experience for most. He was showing the newspaper reporters around his art collection in the basement of Kykuit when he stopped at a series of op-art pieces.

"But governor, what does this piece mean?" one bewildered reporter asked. "You writers are all alike," Rockefeller responded. "You have to analyze everything, to ask what it means. The question should be, 'What does it make you feel?'"

Rockefeller's own intense feelings for art and his trained eye are evident in a story told by advance-man William McDevitt.

NAR liked art not for its monetary value but for how it looked where it was placed. One day he asked me to fly down to Washington on the plane with him. He placed in my lap a tall box, and asked me to carry it carefully. When we landed at National, he had me carry it in the car to his home on Foxhall Road.

After we got to the house, he brought me to a circular stairway that went up two floors. From a nearby closet he removed a small pedestal table and placed it in the center of the circular stairwell. Then we unpacked the box, which contained a statue of a shepherd boy with his hand raised.

We then went up the stairs to the top floor, and he retrieved a small spotlight from a closet. Standing on a chair, NAR leaned over the railing to mount the light in a center fixture, turning it on. We went downstairs to see this perfectly lighted figure, with the rays of light shining down and amplifying its colors.

I was truly amazed at what he could imagine and the methods he used to collect his art. It was a lesson I never forgot.

Art of Persuasion

Rockefeller could be overpoweringly charming when he wanted something, and it was part of his toolkit for persuading people to see things his way.

"There were little things," Persico recalled. "He would bring into the office people he was wooing, like Ed Logue, whom he wanted to head the Urban Development Corporation. When they were sitting down, having a tête-à-tête, one of the staff would bring in the coffee, and Nelson Rockefeller would insist on serving. How much cream would you like? How much sugar? There were these little ways that he had of endearing himself to people, and to have a Rockefeller doing it is very powerful. It besots people."

Gifts of art were another tool he had at his disposal.

"He had an extraordinary capacity to get what he wanted from a legislature that was split," Persico recalled. "I remember vividly there was a Democratic leader named Meade Esposito. And Nelson Rockefeller invited him to dinner [at Rockefeller's apartment] at 812 Fifth Avenue. And Meade Esposito, who I doubt was a connoisseur of art, was admiring a Picasso drawing in the bathroom. The governor said, 'Meade, it's yours—here.' It's very hard for Meade Esposito after that not to feel seduced by this man. Of course, it was a copy. He didn't give him a genuine Picasso, but he had this capacity to woo people."

Others tell slightly different versions of the Esposito story, and have different views on whether the Picasso piece was a copy. Robert Douglass commented: "He [Esposito] loved getting it. 'God, he's given me this goddamned thing—I don't know what it is!' He knew what it was, all right. I would be astounded if it weren't signed. I think it was more special than something that was just a copy." The Picasso could well have been a drawing or a limited edition print, and in either case would have been signed by the artist, with whom Rockefeller had a longtime relationship. And would Rockefeller have had a mere copy hanging in his bathroom in the first place? Many who knew him well think not.

Longtime Republican state senator Roy Goodman, who represented Manhattan's East Side "Silk Stocking" District for thirty-three years, recalled a luncheon meeting with Esposito in 1973. Goodman had been city finance administrator during the first Lindsay administration, and the governor had asked him to accept an appointment as chairman of the Charter Revision Commission for New York City. Goodman described the circumstances:

> This commission would study the city government in detail and then recommend a course of action to the public, which would be presented in a referendum and voted up or down. It was a particularly complex and daunting task because the commission members would not be designated solely by the governor but rather by the mayor, the four Albany legislative leaders, the city council president, city council majority leader, and an appointee of each of the five borough presidents. The governor asked if I would go see, among others, Meade Esposito, the Brooklyn Democratic leader, to obtain his recommendations for members of the commission to represent Brooklyn. Meade invited me to lunch in "Little Italy," a section of lower Manhattan.
>
> As we sat there, he described his relationship with the governor. "This guy is some piece of work," Esposito said. "There's nothing like him that I've ever come across. Recently, when he needed a block of votes to carry his important sales tax legislation, he called on me for help and I was able to get the number of votes he needed to pass the bill. Shortly thereafter, what do you think he did?"
>
> I said, "I have no idea," and he said, "He sent me a Picasso by way of saying thank you. I didn't realize it at the time but that Picasso was worth many thousands of bucks. It was just the governor's way

of expressing his appreciation for what I had done to help him pass his sales tax bill. Imagine him sending a bum like me a Picasso! What a guy, what a guy!"

No Sale

Rockefeller was highly resourceful in applying his powers of persuasion in pursuit of his goals. But he did not always get his way. Albert B. Roberts, who as secretary of Ways and Means was the chief fiscal strategist for the Republican-controlled assembly at the time, told of one notable incident.

"You will recall the 1971 budget crisis, which started in my office," Roberts told an interviewer. His staff had convinced him that the trend lines for state expenditures and revenues were diverging dangerously. Spending was growing faster than revenues, meaning that unless the budget was cut significantly, the gap would continue to widen, forcing politically ruinous tax increases or draconian program cuts.

On the basis of the studies that his staff had done, Roberts persuaded assembly speaker Perry B. Duryea Jr. that government really had to be changed to slow spending growth. Said Roberts:

In those days, I had Bob Morgado[4] and a really heavyweight staff of twelve or fourteen, mostly Democrats. Duryea was smart enough so that he said just simply hire the best people, and in those days that normally meant Democrats.

And then ensued a major, major budget crisis. It ended up with firing sixteen thousand state employees—it was essentially a 10 percent cut in the state budget. And Rockefeller didn't take it seriously at first, and the senate certainly didn't take it seriously. But we had a pretty good strategy, I think, and after a while, it appeared that it was actually going to happen.

At that point, I believe Rockefeller began to focus on it for the first time. And I gather that someone said to Rockefeller that it was essentially my—Al Roberts'—doing, and if we could convince Al Roberts otherwise, then maybe the whole thing would go away.

So one day I got a call from the governor's office, and Ann Whitman, as I remember, asked me if I would come by. I assumed that it was a leaders' meeting, that Duryea was out of town and that I was invited to represent Duryea. It was not an unusual thing, that a leader would not be there and the principal staff people, for whatever area, would be invited. So I didn't think too much about it, but I looked around, and there was no one else there. I had a rationalization for that, and my rationalization was that sometimes leaders meet without staff, so I assumed that the governor and the other leaders were in some other room.

And in due course, nobody showed up, and Ann Whitman said, "The governor is ready," and I went in, and I was it. I had been told that it was going to be a luncheon meeting, so I think I got there at quarter of twelve or whatever. Anyway, it was Nelson and I, and I was ushered into a small room that I hadn't known existed, with a small square table, a table for four, and as I recall, there were two chairs adjoining, which I wasn't quite used to. In other words, you have a table for four, and there'll be someone across from you and someone next to you. I didn't realize that it was customary, particularly in the city and among the more intellectual and other circles, for people to sit next to one another, other than for romantic reasons.

A very handsome lunch was served, and about halfway through the lunch, the governor reached around and put his hand on my shoulder, and said, "This budget thing." He said, "I'm certain we can work it out." And so I started reciting the reasons that we couldn't. I was pretty well versed at the moment. So the luncheon was pleasant enough, but a sale was not made.

I went back, of course, and reported all this Duryea, and we didn't change our position at all. And about that same time, I had a report from someone on the governor's staff that [lieutenant governor] Malcolm Wilson, at one of Rockefeller's group meetings, had complained to the governor that he was letting Al Roberts run the state.

Roberts said he and Rockefeller often discussed art and collecting, in which he, too, had a strong interest. Shortly after the luncheon with Rockefeller, he got a call from the governor's office, asking if he was going to be in his office for the next hour. Roberts said he was. "In due course," said Roberts, "someone delivered a package." Roberts continued,

It was from the foremost dealer in Oriental porcelain. I think that before I opened it—I hope that before I opened it—I went out to see Duryea, and I asked, "Is it appropriate? Should we send it back?" And he said, "Hell, no—that's great."

And with it came this note: "Just a little souvenir of your visit to express my high esteem for your contribution to fiscal integrity and good government in New York State." So that was on top—in the package but on top. When I opened the package, there were two very handsome plates from something called the Bishop Sumner service, which is a well-known service, not of Chinese Export, which surprised me a little bit, because all of our conversations had been about Chinese Export. This was probably more valuable than a lot of Chinese Export, but it was made by Worcester in England. That was what was in the box. So I of course thanked him, and everything was fine.

It wasn't unique for him to give gifts. He had given a gift to [senate minority leader Joseph] Zaretzki of something having to do with Judaica—I remember that it was religious and that it was encrusted in silver, sort of like an icon with silver over it. So, as I say, this was not unique. I was very pleased to get it and I thought it was a very nice gesture. This followed a number of conversations that we had had, starting with an interesting one at Pocantico.

The first thing I ever collected was Chinese Export porcelain, so I was fairly knowledgeable about it. One day at Pocantico, the leaders were being served lunch, and it was either lobster or crabmeat. But it was being served on Portuguese Trade Chinese Export porcelain. And the thing about Chinese Export porcelain is that the decoration is fired as the last step, over the glaze, and fired at a very low temperature, and with your thumbnail you can remove the decoration. I was struck by the service that we were having for lunch at Pocantico.

The interesting thing was that the menu had been selected with reference to the porcelain, so there was nothing that needed to be cut. But a certain senator, who had had more than one martini, decided that there was a piece on his plate that needed to be cut, and as he spoke, he was grinding away with his knife on the piece of Portuguese Trade porcelain. I must have really shown my reaction, which Rockefeller saw, and I looked up at him, and he was looking at me, and he sort of shrugged his shoulders.

Well, after lunch, just after the leaders' meeting with the governor—this happened at leaders' meetings with the governor, that about once an hour we'd have a break for people to make their phone calls. So the lunch broke, and Rockefeller stayed in the room and we had a brief chat. I didn't talk about the incident but I did compliment him on the porcelain. He saw clearly that I knew what it was and volunteered that next time I was in New York, I should come by and see some Portuguese porcelain that he had collected.

Roberts then described a subsequent leaders' meeting, not too long afterward, at the governor's Fifth Avenue apartment.

You took an elevator that emptied into his drawing room, and he saw [to it] that people had their drinks. And I recall the art on the walls was striking. He took me into the hallway and flipped on the light, and there, floor to ceiling, were some glass cases and they were full of the rest of the world's supply of Chinese Export porcelain for the Portuguese Trade. And we talked, you know, and he showed me and told me about it and it was wonderful. And then he said he would make a call to the Metropolitan [Museum of Art] and that the author of a book that I had on Chinese Export was the curator there. And he said, "I'll call her and you'll go down and she'll show you," and in due course, I did that. And every once in a while we would chat about that, and the things that I was collecting, and he was very interested, even though the things I was collecting were so modest.

Rockefeller told Roberts at one point that if you were a serious collector of Chinese Export, the thing you had to have was a Hong bowl. Explained Roberts:

And a Hong bowl is just a big ceramic bowl but it's decorated with the various Hongs. And Hongs were the little factories that decorated the Chinese porcelain. So a Hong bowl would be decorated, inside and out, with depictions of the many factories, each with its flag.

He said, "I know where there is one in New York and you may want to acquire it." I was very excited about that. So I went down to the dealer, and he said, "Yes, come downstairs." And I'll never forget it. It was on metal shelving, this beautiful Hong bowl, and at some point, I had to ask how much it was. And he said it was eleven thousand dollars. Well, that's about what I was making per year at the time, and so I didn't do it. Now it's worth about four hundred thousand dollars. Strategically, it was perhaps a stupid thing to do [not to buy it], but he [Rockefeller] never quit talking to me about collecting and things like that.

Roberts also recalled flying to Washington on Rockefeller's F-27 airplane, whose cabin was "sort of like a living room," and being served crab imperial for lunch in Baccarat crystal cups. "It was little touches like that, especially, you know, with the upstate legislators. It probably had to do with impressions, and it worked. But in my case, it didn't."

Roberts said he thought the governor's staff would have had to view his private luncheon with Rockefeller at the Capitol during the budget crisis as "a disaster, because, for one thing the governor heard arguments that he hadn't heard before, and not only did he not make a sale, but I don't believe that his people were telling him some of the things that I told him."

Roberts added:

We operated sometimes with a majority of one, so we had to get every vote and everybody knew it. So when they were trying to get another penny on the sales tax, and Al Marshall [secretary to the governor] had come up [to the third floor of the Capitol, where the assembly and senate chambers are] with a yellow pad, I think that night we approved at least one and maybe two Thruway exits.

We had an assemblyman named Battista [Vito P.] from Brooklyn, and he was not about to deal with Al Marshall. He wanted to deal with Nelson Rockefeller. So Nelson came up, into Duryea's office. Well, Battista was telling Nelson—and I don't know how they got onto this subject—how athletic he was. He put his foot up on the chair and told the governor to feel his leg muscle. And Rockefeller said, "Oh, yes, that's good." I don't remember what else he wanted but that was very important to him.

Necessity as the Mother of Flexibility

In his art collecting, as in other things he did, Rockefeller wanted the best he could get, and was willing to pay for it. But on occasion, when something such as a sculpture or ceramic piece he particularly admired was not available, he was willing to substitute, and sometimes very cleverly. One such instance involved Picasso's famous painting *Guernica*, depicting the 1937 bombing of that Basque country town in Spain by German and Italian war planes at the behest of the Spanish Nationalist forces during the Spanish Civil War. The original painting, commissioned that same year by the Spanish Republican government, is some eleven feet high and more than twenty-five feet long. It hangs in the Museo Reina Sofía in Madrid.

Nelson Rockefeller, unable to have the original oil-on-canvas painting, arranged for Picasso to copy it in the form of a tapestry. As Robert Douglass explained, Picasso oversaw the whole project, choosing the weavers, creating the design, picking the yarns, and supervising the work. When finished, it was nearly identical to the painting—striking and powerful and unquestionably the *Guernica*, by the hand of Picasso.

For the *Guernica* tapestry, and similar woven reproductions of various other paintings, Picasso insisted on changing the dimensions, by plus or minus 15 percent, compared with the original paintings, Douglass said. He signed them all.

Many were surprised when Rockefeller, after leaving the governorship and then the vice presidency, set up a company, the Nelson Rockefeller Collection, Inc., to make and market high-quality reproductions of art works from his eclectic personal collection of some sixteen thousand items, including paintings, sculpture, pottery, and antique or ancient items. His rationale, however, was simple. The objects that were being copied were beautiful, high-quality pieces, and people who could not have or afford the originals could nonetheless enjoy their beauty by purchasing a reproduction.

But not all of the art so reproduced was of museum caliber. Advance-man Bill McDevitt recalled Rockefeller touring various county fairs during the 1970 campaign, "As we were touring the Tompkins County Fair, we were passing some displays of local arts and crafts when a sudden breeze came up and blew over some paintings of a local artist, one of which was punctured by a tent peg. The governor noticed the commotion and went over to her booth. She did nice work, and had one particularly good painting of three horses in a trotter's race. It was large—about four feet by seven feet. NAR was struck by the painting and asked to buy it. Her price was fifty dollars, cheap even at that time. Since he never carried money, we all chipped in and he bought it. He hung it in his collection in the Playhouse at Pocantico Hills, and it was contained in the 'Rockefeller Collection,' a venture of his that had copies of art made for public sale at a gallery he had on East Fifty-Seventh Street. I often wonder if she ever knew."

Al Roberts recalled Rockefeller telling him about his plan to reproduce works from his own collection. "I told him I didn't think it was a good idea," Roberts said. "And I think he had with him a picture, a copy of a copy of a Chinese Export teapot in his collection, and he said, 'We are going to reproduce these.' And I said, 'Well, how much are they going to cost?'

"He said, 'Well, they tell me we can sell it for $600.' And I said, 'But Governor, I can buy a real one for $200.' So he was a little out of touch."

Rockefeller had said he would not continue to operate the business if it did not become profitable. His sudden death in January 1979 effectively closed it down in any case.

Thus did Nelson Rockefeller, during his lifetime, go from being a major-league individual collector of fine art, to buying and promoting and often donating art for the enjoyment of the public, and finally to reproducing and selling items from his collection as a business.

Throughout Rockefeller's incredible and productive career, collecting and enjoying art remained a major personal focus, albeit mostly behind the scenes. Art gave him pleasure and much-needed relief from the pressures of a hectic governmental and political life. And he, in turn, with his vision, his vigorous support of the visual and performing arts, and his emphasis on the importance of the arts, contributed greatly to the public's access to and appreciation of art of all kinds. For a lesser man, that would have been enough of a contribution to society.

9

Legacy of a Leader

Assessing the legacy of a man of the scope and dimension of Nelson Rockefeller is no simple task, particularly given the astonishing variety of activities that characterized his life. He had a career in business, at Rockefeller Center and in business development in Latin America. He was a high-level bureaucrat and mover and shaker in Washington, in both foreign and domestic affairs. He was governor of New York State for fifteen years, elected four times, and potential presidential candidate three times. He was the nation's forty-first vice president, and the second one to be appointed rather than elected. And throughout his life, he was a major collector and force in the art world.

At this writing, more than three decades have passed since his death, and almost four decades since he left the governorship. It is fair to assume that a great many among New York State's population of eighteen million—say, those under forty-five and anyone who has moved into the state during the past forty years—have no direct recall of Rockefeller as governor or indeed as vice president. Even so, it may be too soon to expect definitive assessments of his life and legacy on the part of historians.

In any event, the goal here is to look primarily at his achievements during his years as governor, and mainly through the eyes of those whose recollections comprise the stories in this book—that is, people who were on his staff, who were commissioners, or who were legislators, other public officials, reporters, or political operatives.

I have also tapped the memories of some of these same people as they expressed them somewhat closer to the Rockefeller era. They were among about a hundred speakers at a two-day conference in 1982, put on by the Nelson A. Rockefeller Institute of Government, a state university unit. The transcript was edited into a book, *Rockefeller in Retrospect: The Governor's New York Legacy*, which usefully describes many of his achievements when they were fresher in everybody's mind.[1]

The range and number of Rockefeller's accomplishments as governor reflected his prodigious capacity for work and intense drive to get things done.

Joseph Persico, his speechwriter, recalled: "The day that he announced his resignation as governor, I came into the office, and knowing that was about to happen, I immediately called my researcher and my secretary together and I said, 'We're going to knock out the Rockefeller record.' We did it that morning. And we wound up with about ten single-spaced pages of the firsts the Rockefeller administration had achieved, the major-league accomplishments. I think it's an unmatchable record."

From his perspective today, how do those achievements stack up? "At the top of the list I would have to put the creation of the state university system," Persico said, "because when he came into office there was just a little chain of teachers colleges, which was not particularly impressive in the Empire State. When he left, you had this huge public education system, which today may be the largest in the world, maybe four hundred thousand students, so that has to be at the top of the list."

Former counsel and secretary to the governor Robert Douglass, when asked about Rockefeller's lasting legacy, said: "I think it is that of a strong executive who was a builder, and who wanted to leave a legacy that would last, whether it was through buildings or institutions. And I think, in his mind, one of the most important was the state university. To him that was enormously important."

Alexander (Sam) Aldrich, the governor's cousin, who held various state posts during the Rockefeller years, also saw the state university as Rockefeller's biggest achievement.

Very early in his administration, he realized that if some substantial money could be raised, the state university could become like the big state universities in the West. You know, it was a bundle of teachers colleges at the time, and not very good, and they were free. Nobody had tenure. And Nelson came up with the idea of giving all the professors tenure and charging tuition, and creating a university system with four major university centers—one on Long Island, one in Binghamton, one in Buffalo, and one in Albany. They would be honest-to-goodness graduate program universities and research centers. The teachers colleges would continue as undergraduate colleges, but would focus on different specialties, rather than simply training teachers.

The whole thing was his idea, and he put it through the legislature. Prior to Nelson's actions, the best universities in the state were private universities, and there were only four or five of them. But only about ten percent of New York State residents [i.e., graduating high school students] could get a first-class education in New York. They went to Massachusetts or states in the West. Nelson wanted to change that, and make it possible for New York students to have access to a first-class college education.

Creating a Modern State University

That Rockefeller should want to do something noteworthy in higher education is hardly surprising. It ran in the family, after all. His grandfather, John D. Rockefeller Sr., had given the major gift that in 1877 launched a Baptist seminary in Atlanta that became a leader in educating young black women in the post-Reconstruction South. Spelman Seminary was named after the family of his wife, Laura Spelman Rockefeller, and later was renamed Spelman College.

John D. also founded and supported two larger institutions—the University of Chicago and the Rockefeller Institute for Medical Research in New York City, now Rockefeller University.

Nelson Rockefeller, above all, loved to tackle big problems, and higher education was one of the most challenging ones he faced on becoming governor. Not only was the existing state university system inadequate for the current crop of college-ready students, but moving through the state's high schools was a tidal wave of baby-boom youngsters who would need colleges to attend.

Because of the complexity and scale of the task, and because it so well reflects Rockefeller's approach to major problems or issues, the process merits further treatment here.

Speaking at the Rockefeller in Retrospect conference, Dr. Oscar E. Lanford, the state university's vice chancellor for campus development and general manager of the State University Construction Fund, outlined the challenge. "New York State at the beginning of the Rockefeller administration," he said, "faced the need to accomplish in a period of a few years what most other states had required a century to accomplish, namely, to build a system of public higher education adequate to meet the needs of our society in this latter half of the twentieth century."

Lanford described the quintessential Rockefeller approach in dealing with the daunting physical, financial, educational, and political problems that creating such a system entailed.

It is apparent to all who lived through that period, as I did, that Governor Rockefeller undertook this challenge not only with a great deal of political and managerial skill, but also with a great deal of pizzazz.

First, the extent of need—for example, the definition of what needed to be done—was undertaken by a special commission chaired by Henry Heald, president of the Ford Foundation, in 1959. Its other two members were John Gardner, president of the Carnegie Corporation, and Marion B. Folsom, a former U.S. secretary of Health, Education, and Welfare. Such blue-ribbon commissions, designed to lay the groundwork for major programs, were a trademark of Rockefeller's *modus operandi*, honed back in his Washington days.

The Heald Commission report, together with the SUNY Master Plan of 1961, provided a blueprint for the statewide system of public higher education, which is strikingly similar to that which in fact exists today.

But how was this university to be constructed? Many said it could not be done in time to accommodate the large number of high school graduates who would be knocking on the door. The fact is that it was done, in spite of the obstacles that at the time seemed overwhelming. It was done so rapidly and successfully that, near the end of the Rockefeller administration, it was said that SUNY was then graduating, each year, more students than it had enrolled in its entirety when the Rockefeller administration took office.

Lanford cited three actions Rockefeller took that made this success possible. One was to work with former lieutenant governor Frank C. Moore, chairman of SUNY's Board of Trustees, and state budget director T. Norman Hurd to eliminate many of the regulatory restrictions that had hindered the university's growth. A second was to establish the State University Construction Fund, a public benefit corporation whose sole purpose was to plan, design, and build the university's capital plant. The third was an ingenious financing plan whereby bonds sold by the New York State Housing Finance Agency provided the funding for all of SUNY's academic facilities, with university tuition revenue pledged to pay debt service on the bonds.

Another speaker at the conference, James Lawrence, described Rockefeller's ability to focus on the broader higher education picture in New York State, not just the state university. Lawrence, at the time vice president for finance and administration at the City College of the City University of New York (CUNY), had previously been a state budget examiner responsible for the budgets of both the SUNY and CUNY. He noted that Rockefeller understood the politics of CUNY, which needed to expand and improve but lacked funding to do so because of its politically touchy tradition of free tuition, a classic Catch-22 situation. He also understood the power and the needs of the private institutions that had long dominated higher education in New York with the support of the State Board of Regents, which the state constitution charges with overseeing all education in the state. In the end he was able to build the huge and unified SUNY he envisioned while also expanding and strengthening the city university and the private colleges as well, plus vastly expanding scholarship and grant aid for students.

In accomplishing all this, Rockefeller repeatedly used his commission approach to great effect. There was the Muir Commission, dealing with higher education for the health professions; the Bundy Commission, which recommended per-graduate state grants to help private institutions, and the Keppel Commission, which focused on increasing need-based student aid and resulted in establishment of the Tuition Assistance Program. The TAP grants remain important today to students and their parents. Lawrence, who served as staff director of the Keppel Commission, summed it all up:

> The governor provided the leadership that altered this situation [New York's initial weakness in higher education] beyond recognition, making New York a national leader in higher education. The best statistical measure of this growth is seen in the expansion of enrollments [statewide] during his tenure from 380,000 students to 842,000, with increases in all sectors.
>
> The most remarkable achievement, of course, and one which ranks among the governor's most important contributions, is the remarkable expansion and the qualitative improvement in the state university system. To give some idea of the growth, the amount of university space rose from fourteen million square feet when the governor took office to sixty-five million when he left, and much more was being planned or constructed. New campuses had been built at Albany, Stony Brook, Buffalo, Old Westbury, Purchase, and Canton, and expansion occurred everywhere else. The country's leading architects were brought in to design those facilities, and many award-winning projects resulted.

A few current statistics reflect the lasting nature of the accomplishment. Today SUNY is the country's largest university system, with sixty-four campuses and some 467,000 students, of whom more than 41,000 are graduate students. It has 88,000 employees. In its relatively short lifespan, it has granted more than three million degrees, and has some two and a half million living alumni, of whom more than two million reside in New York State.

Creating a Cleaner Environment

It may well be, as some have suggested, that Nelson Rockefeller's brother Laurance, perhaps his closest confidant and a committed conservationist, sparked the governor's interest in cleaning up and protecting the environment.

In any event, Governor Rockefeller, despite his much-exercised fascination with development and big projects, proved himself a true conservationist during the course of his administration.[2]

One of his most successful efforts was the billion-dollar Pure Waters Bond Act of 1965. The bond issue, which had to be approved in a statewide referendum, was intended to help clean up the state's lakes, rivers, streams, and coastal waters. At the time, it seemed like a huge amount of money, but with the help of a clever advertising campaign featuring a cartoon fish, it passed overwhelmingly, suggesting that the concept had touched a public nerve.[3]

Robert Douglass gave an account that shed some light on the genesis of the effort to clean up New York's waters. The governor was at a Republican governors conference, he said, and was talking with Governor Ronald Reagan of California, a state notorious for water supply problems.

"They got talking about clean water," Douglass noted, "and Nelson said, 'Well, that's not a problem at all in our state—we've got the Great Lakes and great river systems and so forth.' And Reagan said, 'Yes, but are any of them polluted?' And the governor said, 'I don't really know.' And he went back and found that a lot of them were [polluted], and that communities just didn't have the money, locally, to pay for the clean-up. And he came up with some very good ways in which local governments could finance sewage treatment plants, and he embarked on cleaning up the waters, cleaning the Hudson River, and it was a terrific accomplishment."

Douglass added: "I remember one day that he mentioned, somewhere in a speech, the Pure Waters Bond, saying, 'And one of the most important things it will do, it will stop more affluents from going into the waterways.' I said, 'Governor, it's EFFLUENTS.' 'Oh, yes,' he said, 'but they'll know what I mean.'"

The governor's legacy of cleaning up the environment would be hard to overstate. That legacy greatly and benignly affects public health, drinking water, recreation, economic development, pride in New York's landscape, and tourism, among other things. One of the attractions for the high-tech employees for the Capitol District's growing nanotechnology industry is that the area, including the Adirondacks, is a nice place to live. The Hudson River is an important piece of that legacy. The river is tidal all the way to Albany, 140 miles from the ocean. Every high tide pushes water back upstream—the river sloshes back and forth. For over a century all the raw sewage dumped into the river by the towns and cities on its banks also sloshed back and forth, creating a giant, smelly, and unhealthy cesspool. The governor's programs created effective municipal sewage treatment plants.

While up to the 1970s the Hudson was a place to be avoided for recreation or most other uses, it is now regularly used by rowing clubs, sailors, canoers, swimmers, and tour boats, among others. The Hudson is also one of the principal spawning grounds for oceangoing striped bass, an important sport and commercial fishery. The fish that live in the river are also thriving, although previously high levels of PCBs (polychlorinated biphenyls) are only slowly declining, limiting the river's use for fishing.

Rockefeller, never one to hesitate about shaking up the organization chart, revamped the Conservation Department to be able to manage and enforce the mandates of the Pure Waters program, renaming it the Department of Environmental Conservation (DEC). Traditionally the department had focused on forest, wildlife and natural resource management, water resource planning, and the state park system. Rockefeller refocused it on the environment, adding a sizable piece of the Health Department in the bargain, and appointed Henry Diamond, a lawyer who had worked for his brother, Laurance, as commissioner.

"Creating DEC meant a principled approach to situations, not what was internally easy or to some extent, externally easy," said Ronald W. Pedersen, a program associate in the governor's office. "The Conservation Council and others knew they would be losing control of 'their department.' The Department of Health was antsy about losing water and air pollution. On Annual Message day, 1970, an absolutely livid Hollis Ingraham [commissioner of Health] approached me, saying, 'What do you mean, *strengthening the Health Department!*, which was the language in the message turning over about a third of the Department of Health to DEC."

In remarks delivered at a 2008 celebration marking the hundredth anniversary of Rockefeller's birth, Douglass said the governor's success in protecting the Adirondack Park was perhaps his greatest achievement in the area of conservation and the environment. He continued,

> The Adirondacks are, as you know, a mountainous region of nearly six million acres, or 20 percent of the state's land area. The state owns 2.3 million acres, which are designated a "preserve" and protected under the state constitution to be kept "forever wild"— where timber cutting, road building, and development of any kind are prohibited.
>
> Intermingled with the state-owned land are some 3.7 million acres of privately owned land, including small towns and villages, where considerable development was starting to take place. Some of the private landholdings amounted to thousands of acres and had been in family hands for generations. But the pressure to sell and develop was increasing and threatened the natural beauty of the region.
>
> In 1967, Laurance Rockefeller, who was chairman of the State Park Advisory Council, recommended that a part of the Adirondack Park become a national park, which could provide greater protection against unregulated development. Conservationists and local leaders and legislators were skeptical about the proposal. Many thought a national park might actually encourage even more visitors and intensive development.
>
> The governor, without taking a stand on the issue, created a temporary study commission on the future of the Adirondacks to take a broad look at all the facts and what might be done to preserve the area and to ensure that development on private land would be appropriate.

The commission's 1971 report stressed urgency, recommended sweeping powers for a new agency empowered to regulate the use and development of all land, public and private, within the six million-acre Adirondack Park.

"If necessary," Douglass added, "it could override zoning decisions of local communities and land use plans of private property holders." Without such an agency, the report asserted, rapid, unregulated growth would ruin the whole area in a generation.

A battle ensued, pitting conservationists against local public and private interests. Rockefeller created an Adirondack Park Agency to develop a master plan to regulate both public and private lands. Several large development companies sought to launch major housing projects in privately owned areas, and opponents of the commission argued for delay. The legislature passed a bill delaying implementation for a year. Rockefeller vetoed it. Finally, in 1973, Rockefeller persuaded the legislature to approve a slightly modified plan for the agency.

"In the end," said Douglass, "the governor won and had, in his words, 'established regional planning for the Adirondacks before, rather than after, serious damage was done.'"

Roads and Rails

It is not surprising that the second huge bond issue that Nelson Rockefeller proposed—after his success in winning strong voter approval of his one-billion-dollar Pure Waters bond issue—was for transportation. Improving New York's various transportation systems was always a high priority for the governor. He understood that New York's economy depended importantly on effectively moving goods and people. The two-and-a-half-billion-dollar Transportation Bond Issue of 1967, discussed earlier in this work, reflected that priority. It was billed as funding a variety of projects upstate and down, not merely because they all needed to be undertaken right away but because that was necessary to get voter support beyond the New York metropolitan area. It also passed, but by a much smaller margin than the first one, a clear signal that the voters were becoming leery of Rockefeller's penchant for borrowing. In 1971, the voters turned down an even larger transportation bond proposition, for three-and-a-half billion dollars.

But Rockefeller's achievements in transportation are undeniable and lasting. He created the Metropolitan Transportation Authority as an umbrella agency in 1965 to concentrate the ownership, planning, operations, and—very importantly—the revenues of the many agencies and authorities that operated transportation facilities in the region. This included the Triborough Bridge and Tunnel Authority, which was a cash cow that had enabled master builder Robert Moses to fund many transportation operations and projects. Along with various bridges and tunnels, the MTA also included the New York City Transit Authority (New York subways), various city and suburban bus operations, the commuter rail lines on the New York side of the Hudson, including Long Island, plus Stewart Airport near Newburgh and Republic Airport at Farmingdale, Long Island.

His enthusiasm for big transportation projects seemed to know no bounds. The purchase of the collapsing Long Island Rail Road, the nation's largest commuter line, handling more than two hundred thousand passengers a day, was a case in point.

In 1965, he arranged for the state to buy the Long Island Rail Road from the bankrupt Pennsylvania Railroad, funding the purchase initially with a temporary loan from the state itself, a so-called first instance loan. New electric cars were bought and Rockefeller promised that in sixty days, the LIRR would be the finest commuter railroad in the country. At the end of the sixty-day period, he rode out to one of the stations on Long Island, where he duly declared to a skeptical crowd that, sure enough, the Long Island Rail Road was indeed the finest commuter railroad in the country. The declaration was, at best, premature, but to give the devil his due, the improvements were palpable.[4]

Outside the metropolitan area, the emphasis was on highways. Rockefeller built or improved so many that a campaign commercial for a later transportation bond issue claimed he had built enough highways to go from New York to Hawaii and back. This contention, according to Douglass, led some letter-writers to suggest that the governor ought not to be building highways outside of New York State!

Rockefeller took office at a time when the Eisenhower administration was pushing to build a national network of limited access highways such as had not previously existed, so the emphasis on highway construction is somewhat understandable. (Having seen first-hand the effectiveness of Germany's Autobahns in moving troops and materiel quickly, President Eisenhower doubtless saw a cross-country network of new highways as important components of the defense, as well as the economic, infrastructure of the United States.)

Some of the highways Rockefeller built were spectacular. One of these was the Northway, Interstate 87, which ran north through the Adirondacks from Albany some two hundred miles to the Canadian border, where it connected with a highway to nearby Montreal. Completed in 1967, the Northway was designated "America's Most Scenic Highway" by *Parade* magazine.

But the governor was also keenly aware of the necessity of balancing his costly mass transportation and highway projects in and around New York City with projects that could win support from upstate legislators and their constituents. That meant roads—if not new ones, improvements to existing ones. Road improvements, new highway bridges, and new exits off the Thruway were frequently used as bargaining chips in the administration's efforts to enact legislation, not just in the field of transportation, but all kinds of program areas. Rockefeller saw to it that New York's highways were well engineered and well maintained, and that remains an important legacy.

Edifice Complex

As was evident as early as his years working on Rockefeller Center, Nelson Rockefeller loved building projects, particularly if scale and grandeur—or architectural merit, if you will—were involved.

The Nelson A. Rockefeller Empire State Plaza—called the South Mall project back in the day, as previously noted—surely stands as a lasting monument to Rockefeller's drive to modernize New York State government, and to his ability to work with friend and foe alike to achieve his goals. It is also a testament to his conviction that art, whether in the form of painting, sculpture, or architecture, was not only appropriate for a state capitol campus but uplifting and inspiring. Designing and building the massive complex occupied some share of his attention throughout his entire time as governor.

Among other large-scale monuments was the spectacular but ill-fated World Trade Center, which could not have been built without his support and that of his brother, David, then vice chairman of the Chase Manhattan Bank, as noted, and a strong advocate for efforts to revitalize lower Manhattan. Battery Park City was another major Rockefeller project that contributed to that revitalization by bringing some six thousand families to live in an area that might otherwise have remained a ghost town after business hours.

Pioneering Programs, Legislative Initiatives

Like the list of his building projects, the roster of programs and pioneering legislation that Rockefeller pushed through, or that occurred on his watch, is far too long to be discussed comprehensively here. But some of his legislative successes deserve to be added to those discussed previously because of their pace-setting nature, because they were far ahead of their time or modernized outdated laws, or because they aptly reflect Rockefeller's thinking and approach on social and other issues.

One of these was the 1966 reform of New York's draconian divorce law, under which adultery was the only grounds for divorce. Efforts to change the law had been thwarted for 150 years, largely because of the staunch opposition of the Catholic Church. But New York's law had not only forced many couples to live out their lives in connubial misery, but had spawned a new profession, that of the professional corespondent, as people connived to fabricate the necessary grounds for divorce. Public opinion increasingly favored reform because the law was blatantly discriminatory: the wealthy could take up temporary residence in Mexico or Nevada and obtain a divorce that would be recognized in New York State. A joint legislative committee's proposal was melded with a competing bill sponsored by legislative leaders, and the reform was passed. It set additional grounds for divorce, provided for no-fault divorce under certain circumstances, and established a conciliation procedure. Rockefeller, himself divorced four years earlier, signed the legislation into law.

Another piece of legislation that significantly changed New York's social environment was abortion reform, which was enacted in 1970, after the governor called for it a third straight year in his annual message. Since the early nineteenth century, abortions in New York and most other states had been permitted only to save the life of the mother. The growing nationwide movement for women's rights encouraged the legislature, despite the strong opposition of the Catholic Church, among other opponents, to pass a bill granting women the right to a legal abortion up to the twenty-fourth week of pregnancy. Rockefeller's approval of the bill earned him further enmity from the conservative wing of his party and the growing Right to Life movement.

Tanya Melich was a Rockefeller campaign staff member, alternate delegate to the 1972 Republican National Convention, women's rights advocate, and author of the book *The Republican War Against Women: An Insider's Report from Behind the Lines*. In a letter to Joe Boyd, she expressed strong opinions about the significance of the abortion reform law.

"The New York law is a balanced one and has been praised for years as a humanitarian step toward dealing with a serious medical problem and unfair laws," she wrote. "Across the world, not just the nation, New York's abortion reform legislation is heralded as the just way to deal with the discrimination that exists when wealthy women can always get a safe, legal abortion but women of modest means cannot. New York's previous law, as with most in the United States at that time, subjected women to cruel, nineteenth-century barbaric practices. These laws didn't stop women from seeking abortions; they hurt women and enhanced an ugly, unsafe, illegal abortion underground. The time for reform was way overdue. The governor knew that and acted."

Program associate Ronald Pedersen told a story that revealed some of Rockefeller's thinking on this controversial issue, as well as a rare gap in his historical knowledge.

After the legislature had passed the abortion bill, the governor was carefully looking at everything about the subject. My feeling was that he was conflicted about the bill, trying to balance the moral questions. One day my phone rang and I was summoned to the governor's office. He told me he needed my expertise on this issue because of my background (I had been a Catholic priest). He showed me a copy of an editorial in the *Niagara Falls Gazette*, quoting the eminent Catholic theologian Thomas Aquinas, whose treatise on pastoral theology held that there could be no moral culpability if anything happened to an unborn child during the first six months of pregnancy. I told him that Aquinas had written that in his book on how to counsel and teach women who suffered the loss of a child. He asked me if he could meet with or talk with Thomas Aquinas.

After a short, stunned silence, I informed him that Saint Thomas Aquinas had died in the late 1200s. He laughed. Then he asked if I could get that teaching for him. While the New York Public Library, of course, had the complete works of Aquinas, this volume was missing, so I went back to my former seminary and got copies of the relevant pages. He was most grateful.

The 1967 enactment of the Taylor Law, in the wake of the crippling New York City transit strike the year before, was one of Governor Rockefeller's more important legislative accomplishments. Rockefeller, true to form, created a high-level committee to make a study and recommendations. It was headed by George W. Taylor, a renowned professor of labor and industrial relations at the Wharton School of the University of Pennsylvania, and an authority on negotiation, arbitration, and other forms of dispute resolution.

The Taylor Law—so named because no legislator wanted his name attached to it—for the first time gave public employees the right to participate as equals in negotiating the terms of employment, including not only wages but benefits and workplace policies. This, recalled Melvin Osterman at the Rockefeller in Retrospect conference, was a jolt to many state and municipal public officials, as it made them accountable to their employees, not just to the public. It also resulted in more uniform employment policies, which previously varied from one department to another.

Osterman's background was comprehensive: assistant counsel to the governor, counsel to the Taylor Committee, and special assistant to the governor in appearances before the Public Employee Relations Board created by the Taylor Law. The board became an independent agency adjudicating public employee disputes. Later Osterman became director of the state's Office of Employee Relations, which was established to deal with public employee unions representing state employees.

"During my tenure as director," Osterman told the conference, "I had essentially unlimited access to the governor for guidance as to the positions we were taking in collective negotiations. In short, the governor did not merely give lip service to the law he had brought into being; he cared deeply about its success. He was willing to allocate the resources and his own time and effort to make the process work. Whatever you may think of Nelson Rockefeller's political views, the Taylor Law today is a testament to the intelligence and commitment of a dedicated public servant."

Michael Whiteman, counsel to the governor in the administration's latter years, was asked in an interview for this book how he viewed the Taylor Law, particularly in light of pointed criticism from the *New York Post* at the time about the Taylor Law contributing to the high cost of government. Whiteman replied:

> Is it Nirvana? No. Are there problems? Well, there are problems in everything. But it seems to me it's a workable mechanism that in most cases does work and in most cases does facilitate getting to solutions. If the *New York Post* doesn't like salaries and benefits and thinks that government is too expensive, well, that's a negotiating thing and a question of whom they support.
>
> The worst raids on the retirement fund were circumventions of the Taylor Law. They weren't negotiated. The unions would go around to the legislature and get a bill through.
>
> And then—and this is post-Taylor Law—a legislator said to me, when I was counsel, "I've got to have this pension enhancement bill, it's the only way I can get reelected." The governor had, in fact, already vetoed this bill. As I recall, Malcolm [Lieutenant Governor Wilson], who had often been the most ardent supporter in the administration of pension enhancements, particularly for policemen and firemen, before having his epiphany about how expensive the retirement system was—Malcolm, the godfather of the Kinzel Commission [a commission to review and recommend changes in the retirement system]—had recommended disapproval of this bill, and the governor had disapproved it.[5]
>
> And I got word a couple of days later—we hadn't announced the veto—from this legislator that he absolutely had to have this bill, adding another special benefit to the retirement system, or he'd have a really hard time getting reelected. I went to the governor and told him this, and I said, "but you've already vetoed the bill." And he said, "Well, what's going to happen?" I said, "Well, I can't figure out why

he needs the bill anyway—he's already got four-party endorsement."
And the governor said, "Give him the bad news."[6]

Modernizing a Feudal Mental Health System

The scaling down and modernizing of New York's huge and unwieldy
Department of Mental Hygiene, the largest single state department
and the largest mental health system in the country, was a signature
Rockefeller achievement. It was also one that reflected his style of
leadership.

Dr. Alan Miller, commissioner of Mental Hygiene from 1966 to
1975, joined the state government's largest single department in 1964
as an associate commissioner, and two years later became the first
commissioner who had not come up through the ranks.

"When I came here, New York State had a highly evolved,
hospital-based system," Miller said in an interview. "An advanced
concept when New York pioneered it in the mid-nineteenth century, it
became increasingly hard to support and more and more a custodial
enterprise," he said. The hospitals were largely serving as nursing
homes for the elderly. There were eighty-two thousand patients in
the network of large state mental hospitals (down from a peak of
ninety-three thousand), and another forty thousand in schools for the
mentally retarded or developmentally disabled. There were also some
sixty thousand employees. The department's focus was on spending
as little as possible. Statewide, the department tried to limit food
costs to an average of eighty cents per patient per day.

When Rockefeller took office in 1958, New York State was already
the first state to encourage cities and counties, by means of matching
grants, to establish community-based mental health programs, as new
drugs improved treatment of mental illness. By the time Miller arrived,
some fifty of the state's sixty-two counties and a number of cities,
including New York City, were participating. For New York City, the
program was a natural—the state was simply picking up half the cost
of running large, existing local programs. But outside the city, coor-
dination between the hospitals and new community-based programs
was problematic.

"The hospitals were so large they functioned like towns," Miller
said in an interview. The largest was Pilgrim State in the center of
Long Island, with sixteen thousand patients, many of whom worked in
the hospital or on its grounds, cleaning, doing maintenance, working
in the gardens.

"I got him [the governor] to go to some of the state hospitals," Miller said. "We were down at Hudson River [State Hospital] at Poughkeepsie, and he was wandering around, doing his usual, shaking hands, and going into the crowds. And suddenly, there was a man, an African American, waving, trying to get his attention. When Rockefeller finally saw him, his face lit up, and he pushed through and they embraced. And this was a man who thirty years before had worked for his family. He apparently was very considerate of all the people that worked for the family."

The state hospitals were run like individual fiefdoms by powerful and entrenched directors, whom State Budget Division officials dubbed "the barons." The department had no real central staff, essentially just one physician and a secretary to oversee the hospitals, and another physician and secretary for the schools.

Miller said he sought to "build bridges" between the community programs and hospitals. When Rockefeller appointed him commissioner, the barons were quick to voice their disapproval of this outsider.

"They wrote a letter to the governor saying they didn't think I should be appointed, that I had no experience, that they didn't trust me and thought I was going to try to destroy the hospital system," Miller said. Rockefeller's response, in a written reply to the barons, was immediate and pointed: "Dr. Miller is my appointed commissioner," he wrote, "and if any of you don't like it, you can leave." Some did, Miller recalled.

Speaking at an Albany forum in 2009 to mark the hundredth anniversary of Rockefeller's birth, Miller said that when he was appointed, friends would ask what kind of boss Rockefeller was. "And my answer would be something like, 'He was the best boss I ever had, or could have.' I could not have asked for someone who was more supportive, more responsive. I don't mean he was a pushover, but you could always get to him, he would always listen, you could argue with him." Reminded that arguing with him was something Rockefeller seldom put up with from his staff or appointees, Miller said: "Well, he did from me."[7]

Some Darker Parts of the Legacy

The governor's legacy surely includes dozens of legislative triumphs and innovative programs that are not covered in this volume. He also had some fiascos, programs that didn't work or that in hindsight seemed silly, such as his backyard bomb shelter program. Robert Douglass, for example, thought his greatest mistake was overreaching on programs, trying to do too much, and incurring too much debt. Many would agree.

But most who knew him or remember him would probably say that the greatest negatives in his legacy were the drug laws he pushed through in 1973 and his handling of the September, 1971 Attica prison riot.

The Rockefeller Drug Laws, as they are still called, imposed stiff, mandatory penalties for possession of even small quantities of illegal drugs, such as heroin, cocaine, crack cocaine, or marijuana. That was an era of rising crime, rising drug use, and as a result of the Rockefeller crackdown, rising incarceration. The New York laws prompted a nationwide trend, which resulted in big increases in the prison population, a problem in itself.

Rockefeller's tough drug laws led many to accuse him of suddenly having become a conservative and ramming through a far-reaching program without adequate discussion or input from experts. But his approach really grew out of his frustration in trying for years to deal with a worsening problem in less draconian ways. This was his third attempt at a solution, according to his counsel, Michael Whiteman. Several years before, for example, he had created a new agency for treatment and detention for drug-users, supposedly separate from hardcore criminals. Despite putting $4 billion into it, the program didn't work and he shut it down.

And that is the very point many of Rockefeller's defenders make—that had Rockefeller been in office when the drug laws began to be seen as failing or excessively harsh, he would have changed them—several times, if necessary. But five governors came and went before the laws were changed. Eighteen legislative elections were held in that period—surely the laws could have been modified had there been the leadership, political will, and public demand to do so.

Attica was different, because it was a single incident. Rockefeller has been harshly judged by many on his refusal to go to the prison, and because of the large loss of life—forty-three people, including thirty-three inmates and ten hostages, almost all of them killed by state police gunfire. Many have puzzled over why Rockefeller did not go to Attica to negotiate with the uprising's leaders, as they had requested. Was he afraid to go? And would it have made any difference if he had gone?

Robert Douglass, who was the governor's point man at the scene, doesn't think so, on either count. As he told an interviewer:

I honestly believe that he wasn't afraid to go to Attica. He wasn't afraid of anything. He actually felt that there wasn't a prison anywhere where the inmates didn't so outnumber the guards that they could take over the prison. And the guards didn't carry weapons in the prisons.

As long as the guards were held hostage, under threat of death, it was not a matter of negotiation. You can't have a negotiation where one party says if you don't show up we are going to kill the guards. He felt that under this dynamic, they could bring the state government, or the federal government, to a halt by demanding that the president or the governor or the mayor show up. And so he stood fast on that, he wasn't going to bend, and he said, "All right, release the hostages, go back to your cells, and we have already had negotiations with you, but I'm not coming under the current situation." He also felt in the back of his mind that it was a bit of a spectacle and that they were itching for a fight and had no intention of really doing anything but disrupting the government. And the governor felt that once you start giving in to that kind of demands, with hostages, it would get worse.

At Attica, state officials agreed to almost all of the prisoners' demands for better conditions, but would not agree to amnesty for the rioters or their leaders for the uprising. The game changed after the death of one of the thirty-one guards held hostage, Douglass said. The rioters no longer cared about prison conditions but only wanted amnesty on the hostage's death, plus asylum in some other country. Tension built. After four days, the inmates presumably knew that time was running out and that their efforts to win their demands through an outside observer committee could not succeed. They threatened to kill the hostages, and displayed them blindfolded, with a knife-bearing executioner behind each. Then a state police helicopter dropped tear gas and the state troopers on the walls opened fire with riot guns. It was over in seconds, and the prison was retaken.

"It was initially heralded as a success," Douglass recalled. When the shooting stopped, twenty-nine inmates had been killed, along with nine hostages, who were initially thought to have had their throats cut. When a local coroner's report showed that the dead hostages had all been killed by police bullets—ricochets, Douglass said—the media felt they had been misled by state officials. Public opinion turned against the governor. Even some four decades later, many New Yorkers think Rockefeller should have gone to Attica.

"I was the only one with him during the assault," Budget Director Richard Dunham recalled. He and the governor had flown from Albany to New York's LaGuardia Airport en route to Puerto Rico for a governor's conference when the governor was informed that the state police were about to go in. The governor cancelled his trip but suggested Dunham continue on, but Dunham declined, and they went to Rockefeller's Fifty-Fifth Street office to await developments. Ann Whitman, the governor's secretary, later told Dunham that Rockefeller was alone in his office, and suggested he go in and sit with him.

"I never could understand why Rockefeller didn't go to Attica," Dunham said in an interview. "Much later, I asked George Hinman [Rockefeller's closest political adviser and New York's Republican National Committeeman]. Hinman said, 'You've forgotten your history,' and reminded me of the Ludlow Massacre."[8]

Douglass disagreed with Hinman's thesis. "Ludlow had nothing to do with his thinking," Douglass said, in answer to a question. But the governor's decision not to go still baffles many, and Attica remains a tragic part of his New York legacy.

Another Kind of Legacy

Nelson Rockefeller left another legacy that had less to do with his work as governor and more to do with his views as a wealthy, civic-minded citizen who was conscious of his own and his family's place in history.

And that legacy is Kykuit, the magnificent mansion at Pocantico Hills that was built by his grandfather and father, and occupied by four generations of Rockefellers. Nelson Rockefeller donated Kykuit to the National Trust for Historic Preservation. As a result, visitors can tour the house and the manicured grounds, which are dotted with the massive, modern sculptures the governor collected and carefully placed. Visitors can also see his underground art gallery that houses his Picasso tapestries, among other objects, and the cavernous coach barn containing his collection of carriages and antique automobiles. Part of the 3,400-acre family estate had already been given to New York State as the Rockefeller Park Preserve.

Rockefeller reportedly changed his will only a few weeks before his death to turn Kykuit over to the National Trust. How that all came about is somewhat murky, but Rockefeller had long spoken of the goal of enabling people to visit the many historic houses dotting the Hudson Valley, of which Kykuit was certainly one. Now they can.

Alan Miller believes he might have contributed to the process, having learned how the governor's mind worked in his years as commissioner of Mental Hygiene. "We actually became friends, which I never could figure out. It must have been in part because I didn't want anything from it," Miller said.

> I had decided early that if I wanted to influence what he was doing and his thought, if I introduced an idea to him, that first of all, he would listen, and secondly, that it would go into his head, and something would happen. But I didn't know exactly what would happen—it would come out in some different form or way, because there were a lot of different influences there, more than I could even know. But somehow what you said made a difference, but it might not be the way that you thought of it yourself.
>
> Once I remember specifically designing something that I hoped might get into his head, and he didn't do it, and I have only Happy's recollection that she thought it made a difference. I had been on vacation in Copenhagen. Well, there's a place about twenty-five miles outside of the city that's a tourist attraction. It's called "Louisiana." It's called Louisiana because it was the estate of a man whose two wives were both named Louise. He was a very, very wealthy man, and he had this magnificent estate overlooking the Skaggerak and had this beautiful home. Over the years he had bought world-class sculptures and artworks, which were placed around on various parts of the grounds. And he had added a gallery, which housed his great collection of paintings.
>
> And on his death, he had made a bequest to the state—that is, the country—giving this over. And they had put out a very handsome, bound book about this place and its collection. And so I'm thinking, now that's a book I should get for Nelson Rockefeller.
>
> First of all, he loves art books anyhow, and second, maybe he'll get the idea for Pocantico, to do the same thing. If I could put this into his head, something may come out of it.
>
> He was vice president then. I remember visiting him and bringing him this book, and how often do you find something to give to Nelson Rockefeller? He's always giving people presents, but what do you give Nelson Rockefeller? So I brought him this book, and I remember saying, "You certainly must have been there." And I remember what he said. He said, "You know, Alan, I never go anywhere just for fun." He'd never been there.

All I know is, six months later, there was a little announcement in the [New York] *Times* that the family had decided to do exactly that—and they have. They have had it go open—most of it, not all of it—in exactly the same way. And I've always wondered, "I wonder if this had anything to do with it?" Probably not, but Happy thinks it might have helped to influence it.

However it came about, Nelson Rockefeller's contribution of Kykuit to the American public, in effect, was entirely in keeping with the man, his upbringing, and his career in public life. It was a very large, very generous gift, and was given in a way that helps preserve the family's history and its important role in American life in the nineteenth and twentieth centuries. By turning it over to the National Trust for Historic Preservation rather than to the government directly, he was able to ensure that it would be well maintained and accessible to the public, but in such a way as not to intrude unduly on other members of his family still living on the estate. Part of the gift was his beloved collection of sculptures, paintings, drawings, and Picasso tapestries, reflecting his passion for art and for making it available for the public to view.

Given his long tenure as governor, and his incredible and diverse list of accomplishments—necessarily incomplete here—it is perhaps surprising that there are relatively few named monuments to his work. But three that seem particularly appropriate are the Nelson A. Rockefeller Empire State Plaza, originally the South Mall; the Rockefeller College of Public Affairs and Policy at SUNY Albany, and the Nelson A. Rockefeller Institute of Government, SUNY's public policy research arm.

The former surely reflects his broad vision, his proclivity for building and doing things on a very large scale, and his ability to work with various interests and even adversaries to achieve his goals. The latter reflects his dedication to governing effectively and honestly, not merely to further his own ambitions but because the people who elected him need it, deserve it and are paying the bill for it. The high standard he set, which those who served with him, worked for him, covered him in the press, or voted for him came to take for granted during his time in office, appears unlikely to be matched anytime soon.

Epilogue

Howard Ludington, a Rochester lawyer and campaign operative, said it all when he described the difference between 1958 and 1959 in the Rockefeller camp.

In 1958, Rockefeller had run for governor for the first time, and had won a huge victory. Ludington, who worked with campaign manager R. Burdell Bixby in that campaign, was soon called on again to work with Bixby and George Hinman to explore presidential possibilities.

"During the '58 campaign," wrote Ludington in a letter to Joe Boyd, "the word not to be mentioned was 'president.' During 1959–1960, the word to avoid was 'vice president.'"

An instant celebrity and player in the national political scene because of his election as governor, Rockefeller flatly refused, in his unsuccessful presidential efforts in 1960, 1964, and 1968, even to consider a vice presidential nomination that might sidetrack him from his goal. "I never wanted to be vice president of anything!" Rockefeller famously declared—often enough so that it became the title of an early biography.[1]

And so it is ironic that the closest Nelson Rockefeller ever came to becoming president was when he served as Gerald Ford's vice president, from December 19, 1974 to January 20, 1977.

The Road to Number Two

After Vice President Spiro T. Agnew was forced to resign in late 1973 because of federal tax fraud charges, President Richard Nixon appointed the Republican minority leader of the house, Gerald R. Ford Jr., to the position, under the terms of the Twenty-Fifth Amendment to the Constitution. Ford became the first unelected vice president, and when Nixon subsequently resigned in August 1974, he became the first unelected president.

Ford had been a solid, if not outstanding, congressman from Michigan for twenty-five years, the last eight as house minority leader. The country's relief at having a straightforward, what-you-see-is-what-you-get president, after nearly six years of the secretive Nixon and the prolonged trauma of Watergate, was almost palpable. But Ford was lacking in executive experience, foreign policy expertise, money, and charisma. In choosing Nelson Rockefeller, Ford filled in those gaps and gained a loyal and valuable ally and supporter.

Rockefeller had accepted the near certainty that his time—his opportunity to become president—had passed, but a spark of hope surely remained.[2] In any event, he had been given to believe he would have important responsibilities as vice president.

In the spring of 1975, Ford asked Rockefeller to take over the Domestic Council. Rockefeller installed his own people in key positions: James Cannon as head of the council, Arthur Quern as deputy, Richard Parsons as counsel. They moved from the vice president's payroll to the White House staff, and as such, worked for Ford's chief of staff, Donald Rumsfeld, and his deputy, Richard Cheney. After Rumsfeld became secretary of defense, Cheney became chief of staff.

Rumsfeld and Cheney, whom Ford had inherited from Nixon's staff, were determined to keep Rockefeller's hands away from the levers of power, and there was no love lost between them and Rockefeller. How was it to work for Rumsfeld and Cheney, knowing they were out to thwart Rockefeller, Parsons was asked in an interview.

"You know, one of my things is I get along with everybody—you have to make it work, you've got a job to do," Parsons said. "But it was always clear to everyone that fundamentally, Cannon and Quern and Parsons were Rockefeller people, and so they treated us all with some degree of distance. You know, they needed us because we were right in the middle of the whole domestic policy infrastructure."

Others from Albany days who came down to Washington to work for Rockefeller included former budget director Richard Dunham, Executive Secretary Ann Whitman, who became chief of staff, former chief of advance Joseph Canzeri, State Environmental Facilities Corporation head and former advance-man George Humphreys, adviser and communications director Hugh Morrow, and speechwriter Joe Persico. (Joe Boyd was also asked to come, but Governor Wilson, seeking to be elected governor in his own right, asked to have him remain in Albany as a member of the Racing and Wagering Board, and therefore available for campaign responsibilities.)

Dunham, recalling his days as an intern on Governor Dewey's staff, was struck by the differing approaches to decision-making among

Dewey, Rockefeller, and Nixon, as reflected by Rumsfeld and Cheney. "When Dewey met with his staff to discuss an idea or a proposal, he expected everybody to wade in and take it apart from every angle, and that argument would expose weaknesses or holes in the proposal. God help you if you agreed with others!"

When he later returned to Albany as Rockefeller's deputy budget director, Dunham used the same approach, which irritated the governor. "Finally, Bob Douglass, who was counsel to the governor, took me aside and said, 'Dick, you're going about it backwards.' The governor didn't want to be told why his idea wouldn't work. He wanted his staff to give him the facts and the law on whatever the proposal was. Only after that could political or other issues be brought up, and those were for the governor to decide. But he wouldn't act on it until after his secretary, counsel, and budget director had signed off—that was the same as with Dewey."

Dunham found that Ford's staff, holdovers inherited from Nixon, operated quite differently. "They prepared policy memos by having various staff members contribute sections, with no one's specific contribution or views identified in the final memo. Nixon didn't want to know who wrote which part of the memo. It was positioning, enabling staff members to hide their hand. It was a terrible system!"

Power Struggle

Joe Persico was a close observer of the power struggle between Rumsfeld and Rockefeller. "That was an interesting combat, because Don Rumsfeld was just a young fellow when he was chief of staff to Ford," Persico said. "Nelson Rockefeller was a power in both the political success he had achieved, and just in the power exerted by the Rockefeller family. And I think Rockefeller had the impression that when he became vice president he would have an enormous influence in domestic policy, and through Henry Kissinger, who had come into Ford's favor, he would have considerable influence over foreign policy. That this young, tough player named Don Rumsfeld managed to outbox him was to me like the young buck coming up against the old stag and the young buck winning."

Rumsfeld and Cheney's success in keeping Rockefeller from having much say about policy was somewhat surprising, Persico went on, "because I think President Ford had enormous admiration and gratitude toward Nelson Rockefeller, because the selection of Rockefeller, I think, was proof of the good judgment of Jerry Ford. And I think people felt very comfortable after the trials of Watergate to have a straight-shooter like Jerry Ford in the Number One spot and, in effect, a political giant like Rockefeller in the Number Two spot."

Once in office, to no one's surprise, Rockefeller chafed.

"In Washington, he was a misfit," said Dunham. "It was hard for him to be number two. He complained that 'All I ever do is go to funerals and dedicate things." Dunham said he and James Cannon were the senior staffers assigned to keep close tabs on Rockefeller so as to correct any mistakes immediately. He noted, "One day I flew to Detroit with him for a big, black-tie dinner for President Ford at Cobo Hall. During the flight on Air Force Two, Rockefeller went to his private cabin to get ready. He came out wearing a tuxedo with enormously wide lapels, and a yellow ruffled shirt. He explained that it was a tux he had bought before World War II, or nearly forty years earlier, and it was right in style at the time. He had no matching pocket handkerchief, but made do with some yellow toilet paper. If anyone noticed, I didn't hear about it." That in itself spoke volumes about Rockefeller's role.

Freedom of, with, and Sometimes for the Press

Carol Richards, a reporter in the Gannett Newspapers' Albany bureau, and her husband, Clay Richards, a United Press reporter also working in the State Capitol, got to know Governor Rockefeller during a number of years in Albany. They were transferred to assignments in Washington at about the time Rockefeller resigned as governor.

As a result, when he came to Washington as Ford's vice presidential pick, they were, of course, considered Rockefeller experts and assigned to cover his activities, including the protracted Senate confirmation hearings. The Democrats and Washington press corps had something of a field day with the hearings, which poked into almost every cranny of Rockefeller's finances, including gifts to staff members while in Albany. Carol recalled:

> After he came to Washington, both Clay and I had opportunities to have interviews with him, because at this point, we were old friends. He talked with us both with some frequency. He was candid about the fact that he never wanted to be vice president and wasn't cut out to be standby equipment. He said he would be famous for redesigning the vice presidential seal—the wingtips had dipped down, and he had them pointing up, so that the eagle didn't look as if it had been shot.
>
> He had a beautiful office. He gave us free access to the Old

Executive Office Building, now called the Eisenhower Building, since we had always had access [in Albany] to the Hall of Governors. People got very upset because they were not used to having press wander around that building. That was a practice that didn't last very long.

The Richardses and other reporters covering the confirmation hearings traveled with Rockefeller when he left on the weekends, in case some new and newsworthy angle developed. On a trip to Maine, where the governor had a modern house on a spit of land at Seal Harbor, near Mount Desert, he invited Carol and Clay Richards, Connie Chung of CBS, and another reporter to the house for a dinner of lobster stew. There were no available hotel rooms, so friends with cottages or extra room put up the traveling press. "Rockefeller was very gracious as vice president to those of us who had covered him before he became vice president," Carol Richards said.

Fleece Flipped

While Rockefeller was vice president, Dunham recalled, the former Naval Observatory was extensively remodeled as the official residence of the vice president, primarily at government expense, although Rockefeller himself paid for some of the work. (Rockefeller used it mainly for official functions, preferring to stay in the commodious 1790 house on twenty-six acres on Foxhall Road that he had owned since his years in the Roosevelt administration. Most weekends he and Happy went home to Pocantico.)

"Not long after," Dunham said, "Senator William Proxmire of Wisconsin put out a press release selecting the renovation for his Golden Fleece Award for the most wasteful government project." Proxmire, a Democrat, was chairman of the Senate's Banking, Housing, and Urban Affairs Committee.

"Rockefeller subsequently testified before Proxmire's committee. During his remarks, he mentioned the Golden Fleece Award, and asked Proxmire what it was given for. Proxmire replied that it was for the most wasteful government project. Further into his testimony, Rockefeller asked Proxmire if it wasn't true that Congress had appropriated the money for the renovation. Proxmire agreed that it was true.

Still later, Dunham said, Rockefeller asked Proxmire if he served on other Senate committees. Proxmire said, yes, he served on the Senate Finance Committee.

"By this time, everyone in the room knew what was happening," Dunham said. "Sure enough, Rockefeller asked Proxmire whether the Senate Finance Committee had considered the appropriation and approved it. Proxmire said it had. 'And how did you vote on that appropriation, Senator?' Rockefeller asked. And Proxmire had to admit that he had voted for the appropriation. The crowd loved it." Nelson Rockefeller was not about to be anybody's punching bag.

Hard Work and a High E-Q

Richard Parsons, who worked for Rockefeller under more and different circumstances than anyone else, was asked in an interview how it was to work for Nelson Rockefeller.

> I worked for him both in the state, as an assistant counsel, and in the federal government, and when he came back to New York State after the election of 1976, I worked as his personal counsel—yes, until he died. I had an office at 5600 [the family office at Room 5600, 30 Rockefeller Center, in Manhattan] and in fact I was given a house on the estate. I got to travel with him. He was a character—a real character.
>
> He was a good man to work for—he was a natural born politician. Now, what does that mean? It means he had a high E-quotient—a high emotional intelligence quotient. He had really good people skills, one of which is listening. Another is what I'll call well-timed humor—the things he could do and could talk about to advance his position. Another was empathy. He could—miraculously, in my opinion—actually understand where someone else was coming from. And a fourth was, I think, just a basic respect for people. So it didn't matter whether you were a cobbler or a king, Nelson treated you with respect.
>
> And he was that way with his employees. I never saw him intentionally embarrass anybody publicly. I never saw him abuse anybody. He might show a little disappointment, but that was it. And he was a man of genuine integrity, so that whether you agreed with him or not, nobody—I never met anyone who worked for Nelson or with Nelson in all those years who questioned his motives. They may have questioned his sanity at some times, but never his motives. Nobody ever said, well, he just did that for some personal or non-public agenda reason. We all believed that he was doing what he thought was right and in the public interest, even though we all didn't always agree with what he did.

And was Rockefeller a hard worker?

Oh, yes, a very hard worker, and he worked harder than it appeared, because the governor had a lot of trouble reading. But he would read everything. And you knew it, because when you got it back it would be all marked up. If he agreed with something he'd scribble Yes! in the margin. If he disagreed he'd put No! or he'd put exclamation marks or question marks, or he'd underscore something.

And when we were in Washington, for example, the day would start usually around nine o'clock because he'd have breakfast at home. But he'd start at nine o'clock with the staff, and he would go through the day, usually till about six, and he would be meeting with different people and so forth. And he had a habit: he always had one of his lawyers, Peter Wallison or me, at each meeting. And you would go through the day and it would get to be about six o'clock and he would decide that the day's work wasn't done. So he would take whoever it was that was still around, working on whatever it was we were working on, take them all out to Foxhall [his house on Foxhall Road]. And we'd sit around the dinner table and continue debating or discussing or working on whatever it was we were working on, and it would get to be around ten o'clock.

The governor would turn around and say, "Well, I think that pretty much does it for the day," and then he would turn to me: "Now, Dick, if you'd get this written up and give me a summary of the ground we've covered so I can read it in the morning, that would be great."

So I would be up till two o'clock every morning writing minutes and notes and summarizing everything, and we would start again the next day at nine o'clock. And he'd do the same thing day after day after day. Frankly, that's all he did, was work. He had an occasional state function or something, but the governor never went to the movies or anything like that. He just went from one meeting to the next, from one discussion to the next, from one event to the next, and when there wasn't one, he would create one by bringing the entire staff over to Foxhall for dinner and discussion of whatever issue he wanted to discuss.

Significant, Little-Known Achievements

Despite his frustrations and frequent complaints about not having anything to do other than attend ribbon-cuttings, make dinner speeches, and go to funerals on the president's behalf, Nelson

Rockefeller nonetheless had some genuine and important accomplishments as vice president.

One of these was in a field where Rockefeller's actions as governor of New York were even then becoming controversial: drug abuse. The Domestic Council, which he headed, spearheaded an interagency task force whose assignment was to develop an appropriate, comprehensive approach on narcotics control and interdiction. The resulting White Paper on Drug Abuse not only provided President Ford with balance and insight, but framed out the federal response in that area for the next twenty years, Parsons explained.

Reining in the Filibuster

Rockefeller's principal achievements, however, came in his role as president of the Senate, Parsons said, and "the most significant and least understood" of these involved reducing the number of votes needed to override a filibuster from sixty-seven votes to sixty.[3] Explained Parsons:

> When we got to Washington, it took sixty-seven senators, two-thirds of the Senate, to invoke cloture, that is, shut off debate. Today it takes sixty. It doesn't sound like a big move, but it was huge! Few today are aware of this achievement, except those of us who worked on it.
>
> What happened was, a few of the more moderate Republicans, led by, my recollection is, Senator [James B.] Pearson of Kansas, in conjunction with one of his Democratic colleagues [Senator Walter Mondale, Democrat of Minnesota] had proposed this "relaxation" or "diminution" of the cloture rule because it had been used by the Southern bloc to filibuster everything to death that they didn't want. And so, in a move to bring the Senate closer to a true democracy where the majority rules, they said, "let's relax it to sixty."
>
> The governor, presiding, knew exactly what was at stake. He liked going up to the Senate and sitting in the presiding officer's chair, because at least he had something to do—vice presidents don't have a mandate. So he would sit there every day and preside over this debate.
>
> And he had said to me—I was his lawyer at the time—he said, "Look, it's not for me to decide this issue—this is something that the Senate should decide for itself. There's a whole complicated set of issues that sit under it, in terms of whether the Senate is a continuing body, because it never turns over to the extent of 50 percent or more,

ever. One-third leave every two years, leaving two-thirds behind, so is it a continuing body or does the Senate make up every two years anew?"

So there was a whole bunch of legal issues and procedural issues, which they tried to submit to the presiding officer, and Nelson would have none of it. And he would just continually flip it back to the Senate to figure out themselves.

So this went on for six or seven weeks, and my recollection is pretty clear: the cloture rule, that's all they were debating. There was no legislation moving. So John Tower, a Republican senator from Texas [and Senate minority leader] came up to the White House and told the president that they weren't going to move any of the president's legislation unless and until the president got the vice president to climb on board and rule this thing out of order so they could move on. He should make some ruling that would shut the debate down.

This was communicated to Nelson Rockefeller by Jim Cannon, who had been at the meeting where Tower had come and essentially tried to bully the president into bullying the vice president. As Jim came to report, I remember I was sitting there, because I was the architect, as it were, of our strategy. And Nelson looked at him and said, "Nobody threatens Nelson Rockefeller." It wasn't a direct threat [from Tower to Ford] that "You've got to get your vice president in line," but the governor took it as a threat. And he turned to me and said, "Dick, we're going to shut this thing down today."

He had a predisposition for a lessening of the rule from sixty-seven to sixty senators, particularly given the way the filibuster had been used over the course of the last fifty years, mostly by Southern whites. He said, "We're shutting it down today and we're going with Pearson and Mondale—give me a road map."

So he went into the Senate and they started their usual foolishness of making procedural motions, which he had for the last six weeks been basically sort of ruling on in a way that didn't shut anything down, just kept it going. And he started making rulings that made it clear he wanted to tilt this thing in favor of the senators who wanted to impose the sixty-vote rule.

Jim Allen, the [Democratic] senator from Alabama, jumped to his feet, because he could see where this was going, and starting yelling and screaming, "You can't do this!" and "This is highly irregular!" and Nelson just followed the map, and they got the change in the rule. And after that, he really got blasted. And the funny thing is that the allies—the people whom he helped get over the finish line—just sat there. They never said anything. They just let their colleagues give the governor what for, because he wasn't really a senator and he had violated protocol. But we got it done.

If you go back and look at the transcript, you'll see that it was a hot issue. I don't know the actual vote—I'd have to go back and look it up—but it just crept over the line. And I don't think it would have happened but for Nelson. And it might not have happened if John Tower hadn't come up and tried to threaten the president. Oh, he [Rockefeller] was hot! You could tell by the set of his jaw. Nelson Rockefeller wasn't used to being pushed in this way or threatened.

Preventing a Sunset

Parsons described another important Rockefeller achievement as vice president that not only reflected his fundamental characteristics and beliefs as a man and political leader, but may also have cost him the vice presidential nomination in 1976. It all happened, Parsons said, when Rockefeller was presiding over the Senate, and the Voting Rights Act of 1965 was up for renewal. That seminal piece of legislation was one of President Lyndon Johnson's triumphs.

"Another thing that most people don't know," said Parsons, "when the Voting Rights Act was passed in 1965, it had a five-year sunset on it." He continued,

> And so it had to be renewed in 1970, which it was, and it had to be renewed in 1975. And there was a group of senators, mostly from the Southern states, who were angling to cut off the extension. It would sunset—it would die of its own terms—unless renewed. And they had adopted what they called the Southern Strategy, which they tried in 1970 with Dick Nixon but it didn't work. They tried it again in 1975 with Gerald Ford, and they actually had Ford convinced that this would be a good thing, because the Voting Rights Act, by the terms when it was first enacted in 1965, really only applied to seven states. Most people think it applies to everybody, but based on behavioral tests, it only applied to seven Southern states. And they were trying to get it expanded to apply to all fifty states.
>
> The argument they made is, what's good for the goose is good for the gander. If it was good for the Southern states, which was where the voting rights illegalities had been detected and documented, why shouldn't it apply to all fifty states?
>
> Now, by doing that, they knew that they had their core group, and there were enough representatives from other states that said, no,

we don't want that here because it will drive up the cost and make everything more cumbersome, that they might be able to muster enough votes to defeat the extension bill.

So they had convinced Jerry Ford that this was a good approach, a good plan. But it was very close in the Senate on this amendment, and the thinking was—the concern was—that it could come down to fifty-fifty, and that didn't include the tiebreaker, the president of the Senate, the vice president of the United States.

So Jerry Ford sent his attorney general, Edward Levy, up to see Nelson to explain to him why the Southern position was the right position. After Levy left him, he called me up—remember, I'm now on the White House staff—and he said, "Dick, can you get up here? I'd like to ask you something." And he said, "I'm confused. Clarence Mitchell (who was the chief lobbyist for the NAACP) was in here this morning, telling me that I should be against this particular approach. And then Ed Levy just told me that the president is FOR this approach. I'm confused. Now, will you tell me which direction I should go in?"

I said, "Well, that depends, governor—what do you want to do?" And he said, "Well, your people haven't been on the streets all this time for me to desert them now. What do you mean, what do I want to do?" And I said, "Then you've got to go with Clarence and the boys." He said, "Okay, I got it." He just wanted to know what the right thing to do was. So he sent the word out that that's the way he was going to go, and they didn't bring it [the amendment] to a vote that day and ultimately passed the extension. They thought they had some momentum for the amendment up that day, but they didn't.

And what was the fallout from Rockefeller's decision? "In my opinion? It cost him the vice presidency," said Parsons. He continued,

Clarke Reed was the Republican committee chairman from the state of Mississippi. He held together the coalition of Southern and border states—Tennessee, Kentucky, and so on. And he came, literally two days after that, to see Don Rumsfeld and told Rumsfeld that unless they bumped Nelson off the ticket, he, Clarke Reed, would deliver all those delegate votes to Ronald Reagan at the Republican convention.

And Ford subsequently had a meeting with Nelson where he basically repeated the Clarke Reed threat. And Nelson said, "I'll make it easy for you. Why don't I just step off the ticket?" And

somewhat to his surprise—because he was ashen when he came
back—Ford said, "Well, that's a good idea—why don't we do
that?"

Jack W. Germond, a longtime Washington reporter and syndicated
columnist who was one of the theme-setters at the 1982 Rockefeller in
Retrospect conference, said then that Ford's selection of Rockefeller to
be his vice president was a testament to the genuine regard in which
Rockefeller was held as a public official, and also to the remarkable
self-assurance of Ford, who never felt threatened by Rockefeller.

"Unfortunately, that same self-assurance did not translate itself to
Ford's staff or the party leaders," said Germond, who had covered
Rockefeller's campaigns in New York and nationally as an Albany
reporter and Washington bureau chief for the Gannett Newspapers,
and later as a political columnist for the *Baltimore Sun*. "It led to
Bo Callaway's famous statement, at a dinner meeting with a group
of reporters one night that I attended, that it might be the time for 'a
younger man.'" Callaway was Ford's campaign manager, a Georgia
businessman, former congressman, and former secretary of the army.
"And Rockefeller smiled and threw in the towel and allowed himself to
be dropped from the ticket."

In Germond's view, Ford would have been a much stronger candidate with Rockefeller on the ticket, and might have won the 1976
election. "The notion of heading off Ronald Reagan in the South never
had much of a shot, but everyone seemed to know that except the
people in the White House," Germond said.

A panelist in that same discussion, Richard M. Rosenbaum, a
former state supreme court justice from Rochester who served as
Republican state chairman in 1973 and 1974, described Rockefeller's
great loyalty as an impressive aspect of the man. "He was very loyal to
President Ford," Rosenbaum said. But he disagreed with Germond's
view that Rockefeller had simply let himself be dropped from the
ticket. "You know," said Rosenbaum, "somebody said he withdrew
as a vice presidential candidate. Politicians like to talk like that: he
didn't withdraw, he was bounced. But he was always loyal to Jerry
Ford even though he knew he had been forced out."

Rosenbaum said that during the primary season in the 1976
campaign, there was a day when six primaries were occurring, and
he was concerned that Reagan victories in these primaries would
precipitate a lemming-like flow of delegates into the Reagan camp.
Rosenbaum presented a memo to Rockefeller and his key advisers
arguing that New York and Rockefeller himself should come out

strongly for Ford. If that was done, they might yet stem the Reagan tide. If it was not done, and Ford lost the nomination, Rockefeller would be blamed for failing to support the president. The result: New York's delegation met the day before the primaries and gave most of its delegates to Ford. Ford won three of the six primaries, and fought Reagan almost to a draw in the other three.

"And that," said Rosenbaum, "was the end of the Reagan candidacy for all practical purposes—led, of course, by the governor's willingness to see the big picture."

During the general election campaign, Rockefeller campaigned hard for Ford and his running mate, Senator Robert Dole of Kansas, providing a major boost in the Northeastern states.

"I like to think," Rosenbaum said, "that I was the last person to get a letter of some political substance—as Hugh Morrow knows—the letter on the vice presidency, which he sent to me just a few days before he died. In it, he said that the vice presidency was strictly—and had to be—'standby equipment,' that the vice presidency was an office that had to be subdued, because the president had to be free to operate any way he could." That view, despite his personal frustrations, reflected Rockefeller's reverence for the office of president, and, said Rosenbaum, his loyalty to the president who had appointed him vice president.

Despite the inherent powerlessness of the vice presidency, which has frustrated the occupants of that position since John Adams first held it, Nelson Rockefeller achieved some significant things in his two years in that office. Given the take-no-prisoners partisanship of recent years, it seems likely that if it still took sixty-seven votes to end a filibuster, instead of the present sixty, the entire government might be locked in stalemate most of the time, unable to act on anything major or controversial. Reducing the number to sixty, in which Rockefeller was instrumental, was a signal achievement.

Similarly, using his leverage as the potential tie-breaking vote to thwart a subtle strategy aimed at scuttling the Voting Rights Act of 1965—a vital component of the civil and voting rights legislation President Johnson had been able to get passed a decade earlier—was a courageous step, particularly since he was going against the president's expressed wishes. It cost him dearly.

These noteworthy accomplishments notwithstanding, they pale before Rockefeller's record as the four-term, fifteen-year governor of New York, which is the principal focus of this book. The sharpest-edged and most vivid of memories may blur and recede with the passage of time, which could leave a recitation of works, deeds, achievements, and controversies dry and two-dimensional. The authors hope the recollections, accounts, and stories collected here will add depth and perspective to the portrait of Nelson Rockefeller the man, the leader, the politician, and the public servant. They are not intended to cast him as a candidate for sainthood, but it is not surprising that the memories of so many who worked for him or with him during his years as governor and thereafter should tend to show him in a favorable light. Many of the people quoted in these pages, like so many of their peers and colleagues, were attracted to public service—often from outside the state—by the personal magnetism of New York's dynamic governor. They were drawn by his drive to solve public problems, his determination to find the resources to do so, and his focus on creating educational and economic opportunities for New Yorkers.

John Hanna Jr. has marveled for decades at the caliber of people Rockefeller was able to attract and at how long they stayed. He himself left a Boston law practice to become the first counsel to Rockefeller's Office of Employee Relations following enactment of the Taylor Law, and later served as deputy commissioner and counsel of the Department of Environmental Conservation. He has been in law practice in Albany ever since.

"They were not just yes men," Hanna said of the Rockefeller recruits. "They saw something more important. I believe that most of us joined and stayed because NAR was leading an essential, and admittedly exciting, opportunity to make a difference in our generation in several significant areas. Education, the environment, housing, and others are not shabby, frivolous concentrations to be conducted before a Hall of Mirrors. It was more than just obeying orders from a strong-minded man. He thought and he did his homework."

Some of these people remained in state government their entire careers. Most moved on in due course, often after spending their most productive years in the Rockefeller administration. Yet it is a fair bet that for most of those who served with him, the years with Nelson Rockefeller were the most exciting, and in some ways the most rewarding, of their working lives.

As former Albany and Washington reporter Carol Richards fittingly commented: "I realized my expectations of people in government were unrealistic, because they had been ratcheted up by Nelson Rockefeller." Indeed.

Acknowledgments

The authors would like to acknowledge, with special thanks, Robert and Patricia Phillips, friends of Joe's, without whose philanthropy this book would not have been. Finally, we wish to thank the many people who helped in the protracted and sometimes tortuous process of creating this book. We are grateful, first of all, to those who gave us the personal stories and vignettes that add dimension and nuance to our portrait of Nelson Rockefeller. Many took the time to write their remembrances down and forward them to Joe; others allowed Charley to interview them at length. Doubtless we have missed some illuminating tales by not tapping every potential source, and we could not include every anecdote in any case. Some people we would have liked to interview unfortunately died before we could do so.

Joe is grateful for the strong support and encouragement received from his sons, Duncan and Andrew Boyd. The assistance provided him by Pat Marsh and Inge Schaefer in writing and organizing material in the early stages was instrumental in bringing this project to life. Deepest thanks are due as well to Joe's principal caregiver, Doreen Robinson, who has made it possible for Joe to convey his vision for the book and carry out his editing of the text. Charley is especially grateful to those who took the trouble to read all or parts of the several drafts with a keen eye for style, fact, and tone. These include John Hanna, who as chairman of the New York State Archives Trust brought Charley into the project in the wake of Joe's illness; Michael Whiteman, former counsel to Governor Rockefeller; State Supreme Court Justice Lewis Bart Stone, a former assistant counsel to the governor; and the ever-supportive Robert Bullock, president of the New York State Archives Partnership Trust, which sponsored this book. A special thank-you is in order for Rima Bostick, whose deep understanding of New York State government and sharp eye for detail were invaluable. In addition, the authors are grateful to State University of New York Press and its codirector, James Peltz; production editor, Ryan Morris; and marketing director, Fran Keneston, for their patience, professionalism, and encouragement.

Notes

Chapter 1. A Word of Introduction

1. Since the earliest days of the republic, governors of New York, a large, populous state, had usually figured importantly in national political life. George Clinton, the very first governor of the state of New York, was nominated for president in 1792, losing to incumbent George Washington. Later, Clinton was elected vice president in Thomas Jefferson's second term and in James Madison's first term, the only vice president to serve two presidents.

   Four New York governors have reached the presidency. Martin Van Buren was elected once, Grover Cleveland twice (but not consecutively), and Franklin D. Roosevelt, four times. Theodore Roosevelt, who had been elected vice president on William McKinley's ticket in 1900, became president after McKinley was assassinated and was elected in 1904 in his own right. A number of other sitting or former New York governors were nominated but did not win, including, in the twentieth century, Thomas E. Dewey, Alfred E. Smith, and Charles Evans Hughes. Daniel D. Tompkins, governor of New York from 1807 to 1817, was twice elected vice president on James Monroe's ticket. Levi P. Morton, a two-term Republican congressman, was asked by GOP presidential candidate James Garfield to be his running mate in the 1880 election, but turned it down. Had he accepted, he would have become the twenty-first president of the United States after Garfield's assassination. In 1888 he was elected vice president, running with Benjamin Harrison, but was dropped from the ticket in 1892. In 1892 he ran successfully for governor, serving one two-year term.

2. Reich died at forty-eight of pancreatic cancer in 1998, two years after the publication of the first volume. At the time of his death, he had completed the research and some of the writing for the second volume, covering Rockefeller's years as governor, vice president, and private citizen. George Mason University historian Richard Norton Smith has assumed the burden of completing the book.

3. Cary Reich, *The Life of Nelson A. Rockefeller: Worlds to Conquer* (New York: Doubleday, 1996).

4. Reich, *The Life of Nelson A. Rockefeller.*

Chapter 2. A Pivotal Encounter

1. Dubonnet, perhaps the world's most popular fortified wine, was created in 1846 by Parisian wine merchant and chemist Joseph Dubonnet. He won a government-sponsored competition for a new drink that would entice soldiers in the French Foreign Legion to take their anti-malaria drug, quinine, which was very bitter. His red wine–based aperitif, which

included herbs, spices, and additional alcohol along with the quinine, was
an immediate success. The family-owned company continued to make and
distribute the product, eventually adding a white wine version as well,
until the company was sold to Pernod Ricard SA in 1976. A gold version
has since been added.

    The British, whose own global empire also encompassed areas where malaria
was endemic, addressed the task of making quinine palatable at about the
same time as the French, and in somewhat similar fashion. They invented
the gin-and-tonic, which, like Dubonnet, became a popular favorite.

2. Even fifty years ago, Oreos seemed to have been around forever. In fact,
the National Biscuit Co.—Nabisco—launched the first Oreo in 1912.
The origin of the name remains a matter of speculation, even at Nabisco.
But the first Oreo was a very different cookie, mound-shaped and in two
flavors—meringue and cream. Made in Nabisco's Chelsea factory in New
York City, Oreos were initially aimed at the British market. The company
tried several formulations before hitting on a real winner in 1916—two
dark chocolate disks, with a design baked in, with a white cream frosting
sandwiched in between. It has been suggested that this cookie was very
similar to the Hydrox cookie introduced in 1908 by a company that later
became Sunshine Biscuit, Inc., one of whose founders had been a member
of the Nabisco board. The company had a plant in Binghamton, New York.
Hydrox cookies were a competitor until they were discontinued in 1998,
although current-owner Keebler Company, itself owned by the Kellogg
Company, has recently reintroduced them.

    In recent years, Nabisco, now owned by Kraft, has launched numerous
variations on the Oreo theme and pushed them in the United States and
abroad, but an estimated $362 billion of the traditional Oreos have been
sold in the United States making them the all-time best-selling cookie.

3. The symbiotic Rockefeller-Kissinger relationship goes back to 1955, when
Rockefeller, then a special assistant to President Eisenhower, hired the
brilliant, German-born academic to direct his Quantico II conference,
intended to develop new foreign policy proposals for the United States
in the wake of that year's Geneva Summit meeting. In 1957, Rockefeller
created (and family foundation money funded) a temporary think tank
called the Special Studies Project, which Kissinger also directed. Edward
Teller, a leading physicist best known as the theoretician behind the H-
bomb and an outspoken advocate of nuclear arms development, was also
part of the panel. That they were yelling at each other in German, in the
incident Joe Boyd recounted, is scarcely surprising, as Teller was an immi-
grant from Hungary. But that they were arguing at all is more surprising,
as Kissinger agreed with almost all of Teller's very conservative views on
foreign policy and other issues.

4. Princess Beatrix—now Queen Beatrix—of the Netherlands stayed at the
executive mansion as a guest of Governor Rockefeller and his first wife,
Mary Todhunter Clark Rockefeller, on the occasion of her visit to the
capital for the Albany Tulip Festival in 1959, marking the 350th anniversary of Captain Henry Hudson's 1609 voyage of discovery up the Hudson
River to what is now Albany. The princess is reported to have appeared
in a beaver coat, presumably symbolic of the brisk commerce in beaver
pelts and other furs that the Dutch carried on from trading posts they

subsequently established all along the river, including at Albany in 1614. Hudson's explorations on behalf of the Dutch East India Company failed to find a passage to Asia but enabled the Dutch to establish the colony of New Netherland. The colony, with its capital of New Amsterdam on the tip of Manhattan Island, encompassed the Hudson Valley from the river's mouth 140 miles north to Albany and beyond, as well as the western third of Connecticut, and Long Island east to Oyster Bay. The focus of the Dutch, however, remained primarily on trade rather than on settlement. Under pressure from faster-growing English settlements, some of them within nominally Dutch territory, and from English King Charles II, the Dutch surrendered New Amsterdam and the rest of the colony to the English in 1664. They recaptured New Amsterdam briefly later, but were forced to give up their claims in the region by treaty with the English in 1674. In the Hudson Valley, the Dutch legacy remains in architecture, place-names, family names and, particularly around Albany, even in local accents. But perhaps the most important legacy of the Dutch is New York City's ingrained tradition of tolerance of all races, creeds, colors, and ethnic groups, as well as its intense focus on commerce and trade.

Chapter 3. Getting the Governor's Ear, and Other Necessities

1. Wilson and Lefkowitz, universally referred to by staffers, legislators, and the press corps as "Malcolm" and "Louie," were very much part of the Republican leadership team, Wilson elected on the Rockefeller tickets and Lefkowitz elected separately but at the same time. The fourth statewide office-holder, longtime Comptroller Arthur Levitt, known, of course, as "Arthur," was a Democrat and did not reside at the mansion.

2. Joseph E. Persico, Rockefeller's speech writer, described the governor's departures from the Capitol as being "as electric as his arrivals." But even then, there was a pecking order keyed to Rockefeller's agenda for the day.

   "Warning telephone calls sounded up and down the second floor—the governor would be departing in five minutes," Persico recalled. "Aides traveling with him back to New York City threw on their coats and, with briefcases in hand, waited edgily in doorways until he burst out of his office, into the corridor and down in the elevator, creating a kind of suction that pulled people into his wake. All the while, he would be honking, 'Louie, Hughie, you sit with me. You, too, Al.' The seating in his car, or his plane, was never left to chance." (The reference is to Attorney General Louis Lefkowitz, Communications Director Hugh Morrow, and Secretary to the Governor Alton G. Marshall.)

3. Malcolm Wilson was conservative, cautious, precise, and lawyerly, a strong Roman Catholic, a heavy smoker but non-drinker (a rarity in Albany). He was extremely knowledgeable about the law, the legislature's rules and procedures, and about state politics and the people in it, especially upstate. A warm and thoughtful man, he not only remembered the name of all he met but, on meeting them again later, could instantly recall where they lived, what they did, the names and circumstances of their families. He also had a wicked sense of humor, as evidenced by his alleged response to a middle-aged woman who button-holed him at a Republican reception.

Woman, gushing: "It must be wonderfully exciting, working with Governor Rockefeller—solving big problems, creating new programs, dealing with Washington and national politics."

Wilson: "Yes, well, actually, it's a bit like being on a dog team: only the lead dog gets a change of view."

4. Trippe was assertive about what he wanted." Juan Terry Trippe was a founder and the driving force behind Pan American World Airways, one of the most successful and innovative international airlines of the pre– and post–World War II periods, from its creation in 1927 until his retirement in 1968. He also developed its then subsidiary, the InterContinental Hotels chain. Although he was widely but erroneously thought to have Cuban or Latin American antecedents because of his first name, he was actually named after Juanita Terry, the Venezuelan wife of his great-uncle.

5. Charles A. Schoeneck Jr. had been a Republican assemblyman from Syracuse, served as assembly majority leader in 1959–1960, and later was GOP state chairman. Vandervort, a self-described political junkie since his teens, held numerous party positions at the state level, including executive director of the state committee.

6. The transportation bond issue carried the state by roughly 2.8 million to 2.0 million votes, a 7 to 5 ratio, compared with a 4 to 1 ratio for Rockefeller's $1 billion Pure Waters bond issue proposition just two years earlier. New York City and suburban Westchester and Nassau counties, principal beneficiaries of heavy mass transit and commuter rail spending, provided the entire margin of victory. Elsewhere in the state, the proposition barely broke even despite strong support in several upstate urban counties. Thus Stone was clearly right about how well subways would sell upstate. Along with most other counties, Jefferson County, of which Watertown is the county seat, voted no.

Chapter 4. Governing New York

1. While in Albany, Truman made the rounds of the Capitol and even played the piano on "the Shelf," a sort of recreation area on a mezzanine adjacent to the cubicle offices of the Legislative Correspondents Association—the Capitol press corps. A signed photograph commemorates the occasion. The caption, which read "Harry Truman Played Here," was altered by Truman so it read, "Harry Truman Played The Piano Here," perhaps so no one would think the poker-loving president had participated in one of the reporters' regular after-hours games.

2. Jacob B. Underhill, then a deputy press secretary, recalled standing at the Mall site one morning with Rockefeller and General Schuyler. "The entire site had been cleared of the run-down buildings that began at State Street next to the Capitol. The governor was obviously pleased by the destruction, and proceeded to tell Schuyler and me of the military significance of the hilltop overlooking the Hudson. The site, he pointed out, controlled the river, a water highway from New York City and the Atlantic to the St. Lawrence and Canada. Burgoyne failed to reach it in the Revolutionary War, or U.S. history would have been different." In 1777, the British planned to isolate New England from the rest of the American colonies

by sending an army south from Canada to Albany and joining up with another army moving up the Hudson from New York City. British Major General John "Gentleman Johnnie" Burgoyne, commanding a force of some seven thousand British regulars, Hessian mercenaries, and Indians, moved down along Lake Champlain in late summer and built fortified positions at Saratoga while he struggled to gather supplies and clear roads through the wilderness. In the meantime, the Americans had gathered a force of twelve to fourteen thousand colonial regulars and militia under the command of Major General Horatio Gates. The British force coming up the Hudson from New York never arrived, and Burgoyne was defeated and captured at the Battle of Saratoga, October 17, 1777. The battle has been called the turning point in the war, as it galvanized the Americans and prompted France and Spain to declare war against England.

3. Joe Boyd said Attorney General Louis Lefkowitz told him the original plan for the Mall called for the Legislative Office Building to be located where the Justice Building now is, on the downhill side of the platform. The governor, Lefkowitz told him, had made the switch in order to get legislative backing for the Mall project. Joe also said that Transportation Commissioner Ray Schuler once told him he had, in a closet, a set of drawings for a North Mall, a replica of the South Mall that was never built.

4. Although Rockefeller's attendance at the Martin Luther King funeral and the battle he conducted from there and en route home to revive and pass the UDC bill were reported at the time, it is less widely known that Rockefeller actually paid for the funeral. Joseph Canzeri, deputy to Chief of Advance Joe Boyd, was dispatched to Atlanta to orchestrate the proceedings. Joe Boyd, who was in Arkansas at the time assisting Nelson's brother, Winthrop, in his gubernatorial campaign, also rushed to Atlanta to help with arrangements. His assignment was to look after senators, congressmen, and other Washington VIPs.

5. The governor loved grand schemes and was unfazed by obstacles. Bob Douglass, in a speech marking the hundredth anniversary of Rockefeller's birth, recounted how he had once been invited to sit in on a meeting between the governor and the futurist Herman Kahn, the brilliant director of the Hudson Institute. After initial pleasantries, Douglass said, Kahn addressed Rockefeller. "Governor: great bridges of the world! Can you name some?" The governor looked puzzled but replied, "The Brooklyn Bridge, the Golden Gate, the George Washington Bridge."

Herman's response was, "Very good, Nelson, very good. And what about the famous bridge in Florence?"

The governor quite proudly replied, "It's the Ponte Vecchio and it crosses the Arno. It has shops and vendors and buildings. It connects the city and you barely realize it's a bridge."

"Excellent, Nelson, excellent! Now, think for a moment: the East River, Manhattan, Forty-Second Street, Roosevelt Island and Queens."

Instantly, and with great excitement, the governor said, "Damn it, Herman, why didn't I think of that!"

I didn't have a clue what he meant, but it was soon clear that they were conceptualizing a New York City version of the Ponte Vecchio, merging Midtown Manhattan with Queens, with big buildings and shops from one end of the bridge to the other.

Before the governor got too excited, Herman warned him there was a slight problem. The East River was a "Navigable Waterway" and under the "Rivers and Harbors Act of 1899," a bridge at this location would have had to be at least 165 feet above the water at mid-span to allow for the passage of warships.

"The governor drew with his hand in the air the steep parabolic shape of what their future bridge would have to look like," Douglass said.

"Obviously, the bridge would be an impossibility without permission of the Coast Guard, or amending the act. Herman warned the governor that no one had ever been able to obtain an exception in a case like this. The governor was not dismayed. He thought it was a brilliant idea and he was confident that he could convince the Coast Guard and, if necessary, the Congress to amend the law.

"Over the next six months, he tried valiantly, contacting the Coast Guard and calling on friends in Congress, but without success. The height requirements still stand and no bridge could be built. The governor wasn't happy with the turn-down, but he had given it his all, and now it was time to move on to other big issues and big ideas."

6. After their law firms merged, John Mitchell became a friend of Richard Nixon, who persuaded him to be his campaign manager in 1968, then appointed him U.S. Attorney General, a post he held until he resigned to serve again as campaign manager in Nixon's 1972 campaign. Mitchell and campaign finance chairman Maurice H. Stans were indicted in 1973 for obstructing the investigation of fugitive Robert Vesco after Vesco made a $200,000 campaign contribution. Both were acquitted in 1974. Mitchell was later convicted of conspiracy, obstruction of justice, and perjury in the 1972 Watergate break-in and subsequent cover-up. He served nineteen months in federal prison.

7. At 5 a.m., with a settlement not quite reached, the union negotiator was hungry and wanted to leave. Rockefeller knew that if the union team left, they would not come back. So he told them breakfast was on the way. He then sent Joe Boyd, chief of advance, and Joe Canzeri, deputy chief, out to find eighteen meals. Advance-men are paid to be resourceful and Joe Canzeri was a hotel man to begin with. So, Boyd recalled, "We got the manager of the Gotham Hotel out of bed, and he cooked scrambled eggs, bacon, and toast." Boyd and Canzeri pushed a hotel table with eighteen breakfasts on it down Fifty-Fifth Street from the hotel to the governor's office, and the rest is history.

8. After Governor Hugh L. Carey, a Democrat and former Brooklyn congressman, took office at the start of 1975, Urstadt got word that Carey wanted to kill Battery Park City—it was not his project—and use the newly created land for park purposes. The Battery Park City Authority had issued some $200 million in "moral obligation" bonds, backed by revenue the project would generate when built, and buttressed in the meantime by the expectation that the state would back them up—the so-called moral obligation—if that was ever necessary. At this point, Urstadt needed to certify that the bonds were sound, which he could not do if Carey was going to halt the project.

"So I wrote a letter to Hugh," Urstadt said, "and I said you have to support these bonds." Because New York State's whole financial structure at that point depended on the credibility of billions of dollars of moral obligation bonds, Urstadt's letter sent tremors through the Capitol.

"I got a call from Judah Gribbetz" (counsel to the governor), Urstadt said. "Judah and I served on the same aircraft carrier."

"Take back the letter," Gribbetz said.

"I'll take back the letter only if the governor supports this thing," Urstadt told Gribbetz. "And I said, 'I'm going to find this project in default unless you support it.'" Urstadt said he then arranged to hold a press conference to announce the default, which would have toppled the whole house of cards. "At the last minute, Victor Marrero, who had my old job [as housing commissioner] came in and said 'Fine, the governor supports Battery Park City.'"

The concession by Governor Carey averted, for the moment, the financial crisis that later enveloped the city and the state.

Years later, when Urstadt heard that there was a movement in the legislature to name Battery Park City after Carey, he told then Republican governor George Pataki how Carey had tried to scuttle the project, but Pataki was unable to derail the naming legislation.

Chapter 5. Indefatigable Campaigner

1. Staff members handled the matter of reimbursement for expenses in different ways, for various reasons. Joe Boyd recalled a story told to him by an attractive young woman named Polly Weber, who worked in the 1970 gubernatorial campaign as assistant to the upstate director of Independents for Rockefeller, and was subsequently hired as administrative assistant to the appointments officer. Leaving the Fifty-Fifth Street office one evening about 6 p.m., she got on the elevator and came face to face with Nelson Rockefeller. "He was frantically going through his pockets," said Boyd. "Finally, not finding what he wanted, he asked her if she had any extra money. She gave him twenty dollars and he told her to collect from Ann Whitman, the governor's executive assistant and keeper of the access door and phone. Polly said she never pursued reimbursement since she didn't want to explain to Ann her meeting with the governor."

2. All's fair in love and politics. Former advance-man James Kiepper recalled that at the 1968 Miami convention, his assignment was to bring some two hundred college students to Miami and get them into the convention hall to cheer for Rockefeller. Getting them in was not easy, since access to the hall required a special identification tag tied with a red ribbon—and the Nixon people had seen to it that the Rockefeller supporters weren't getting any. Kiepper responded in kind by getting identical copies of the tickets printed up, but alas, could obtain only twenty of the telltale red ribbons. As time grew short, and no more red ribbons could be found, he resorted to a different tactic. Twenty students, equipped with beribboned but counterfeit tags with their names typed in, trooped into the hall and took seats. Kiepper cautioned them all to make no noise or do anything to call attention to themselves. Then one student—"a track star from Kansas State," Kiepper remembered—ferried the tickets and ribbons out of the hall to the Rockefeller trailer, where three campaign workers were busily typing up new tickets with the names of the next batch of students, whom the Kansas State student then guided in. And so it went until all two hundred were in place and ready to cheer when their candidate was nominated.

Chapter 7. Travels and Travails South of the Border

1. For old State Department hands, the Rockefeller missions may have seemed like déjà vu. In his youthful days as Roosevelt's coordinator of Inter-American affairs, Rockefeller was similarly a thorn in the State Department's side. He infuriated Secretary of State Cordell Hull and many of the U.S. ambassadors in the region with his freewheeling ways, insistence on independence, and determination to shake up a U.S. Foreign Service, many of whose people in Latin America he viewed as lazy, inept, or out of touch. Most troublesome of all was the fact that he had a direct reporting relationship to Roosevelt himself. Roosevelt, never reluctant to play one of his people off against another, valued Rockefeller's efforts to build goodwill in the Latin American countries and to constrain the Germans' attempts to increase their influence in the region.

   Rockefeller also ruffled enough feathers as assistant secretary of state for Latin America that President Truman fired him, although he later became Truman's principal salesman for the Point Four program for aid to third-world countries. And in the Eisenhower administration, as special assistant to the president for psychological warfare, Rockefeller sold the president on his "Open Skies" mutual inspection program as a new Cold War foreign policy initiative. Secretary of State John Foster Dulles, fiercely defending his turf, became an implacable foe, and ultimately Rockefeller was forced to resign.

2. Joe Boyd and Craig Thorn, the advance crew for São Paolo, were at the American embassy at the end of the Rockefeller visit, and were instructed by National Security Advisor Henry Kissinger's office to stay in São Paulo to resolve certain problems that had come up. Joe does not recall what they were.

   "We wanted to go home to our wives," Joe said. "We had been gone a month. We wanted to go home to New York with Rockefeller on his plane, and we did." Using the embassy's communications system, they sent a "flash" message to National Security Advisor Henry Kissinger, advising him of their decision.

   What they didn't know was that a "flash" message automatically activated the war room in the White House, the Pentagon, the Southern Command, and the Continental Command located in the Rockies.

   After the mission's final trip, a dinner was held at the Rockefeller mansion for the participants, and Kissinger was the speaker. As Joe recalled, Kissinger said, "I have a message for Joe Boyd and Craig Thorn: next time you want to get laid, call me collect!"

3. The shorthand term "guzincas" evolved from the process of trying to figure the dollar value of any sum in local currency by dividing it by the number of units of that currency there were to a dollar. To get a sense of the real cost of something priced at five hundred pesos (or whatever) in a country where the exchange rate was twelve pesos to a dollar, the advance-men would do the division the old-fashioned way—twelve "goes into" five hundred. Reflecting this daunting process, the result was soon being expressed as "guzincas" by harried advance-men leapfrogging from country to country to make the arrangements the large Rockefeller party required.

Chapter 8. Ars Gratia Artis and So Much More

1. Reich, *The Life of Nelson A. Rockefeller.*
2. Charles Urstadt, the former commissioner of Housing and Community Renewal and longtime chairman of the Battery Park City Authority, recalled with a chuckle an occasion when his wife drove him from his Westchester home to nearby Pocantico, whence he was to fly to Albany by helicopter with the governor. His mother-in-law came along for the ride, and was totally awed by the beauty of the estate. On meeting the governor, according to Urstadt, she said, "You have a wonderful place here!" "Yes," replied the governor, "aren't we lucky?"
3. I once played this course with Douglass and the governor and had the poor judgment or bad luck to bounce an errant shot off a large stone sculpture by an artist whose name I cannot recall. Nobody commented, and the lie was playable, which suggested to me that this was not the first time it had happened.
4. Robert J. Morgado later served as secretary to Democratic governor Hugh L. Carey (1975–1982), in effect the state government's chief operating officer. Carey, who had been a powerful congressman from Brooklyn but initially had limited knowledge of the legislature and state government generally, relied heavily on Morgado's expertise to keep the state running smoothly.

Chapter 9. Legacy of a Leader

1. The conference was run by Dr. T. Norman Hurd, who had been director of the budget for Rockefeller (as well as for Governor Dewey) and later served as director of state operations and secretary to the governor for both Rockefeller and Malcolm Wilson, and by Gerald Benjamin, a professor of political science at the State University College at New Paltz, and a faculty fellow at the institute.
2. Rockefeller loved large, innovative schemes. Robert Stone, deputy commissioner of the Office of General Services at the time, recalls his boss, Commissioner Cortlandt van Rensselaer Schuyler, describing to the governor a luxury housing project proposed by a developer along Cayuga Lake, one of the Finger Lakes. The plan: scrape off the top of the bluff and dump it into the lake to create new, waterfront property. "That's a great idea!" enthused Rockefeller. General Schuyler quickly pointed out that it was a bad idea environmentally and that the state was opposing it.
3. John Hanna, who was deputy commissioner and counsel to the Department of Environmental Conservation at the time, recalled another clever advertising and promotion campaign that helped assure passage of a later environmental bond issue—the Environmental Quality Bond Act of 1972. This one had DEC commissioner Henry Diamond riding a bicycle from Buffalo to Montauk, more than 350 miles, to promote the cause. Virginia Cairns-Callan, who later became head of the governor's Women's Unit, did much of the advance work and arranged for local politicians to join in. At one stop she had instructed a very little girl to run out and offer an ice cream cone to Diamond. The girl trotted out and handed it instead to a Democratic congressman, Rep. Samuel S. Stratton of Amsterdam, who knew a good photo-op when he saw one. He took one lick before Mrs. Cairns-Callan rushed out from behind a roadside advertising sign, snatched the cone away, and steered the girl to Diamond.

4. As an Albany-based reporter, I was determined to see firsthand how well he had delivered on that pledge. I rode out to the press conference on the train, not from Penn Station in Manhattan, but from the Hunter's Point Station in Queens, which was served only by diesel trains that could not use the tunnel that ran under the East River and most of Manhattan. Noting that the ancient car I rode on had no less than twenty-three cracked windows and plainly hadn't been cleaned in recent memory, I concluded that the governor, a congenital optimist, was sometimes a bit of an exaggerator as well.

But the railroad did get better, cleaner, and more reliable, if not actually faster. The new cars were easier to enter and exit. Tracks were improved, electrification was extended, fewer passengers had to change trains at Jamaica. Eventually, smoking cars were abolished, to the great relief of many nonsmokers who preferred to stand in a crowded car rather than take one of the vacant seats in the acrid smog of the smoker.

5. Lieutenant Governor Malcolm Wilson, although a conservative in most senses of the word, nonetheless was a strong advocate of improving pension benefits for policemen and firemen during his twenty years in the assembly and brought that viewpoint to the Rockefeller administration. Frustrated because so many one-year pension enhancement bills were being signed into law on Wilson's recommendation, Whiteman and a few others undertook to isolate him from the process, and also end the annual end-runs. (One-year bills, providing a temporary benefit, were deemed necessary to get around the state constitution's provision that public employee pension rights, once granted to an employee, can never be reduced or rescinded.)

John Hanna, at the time counsel to the Office of Employee Relations, recalled that he in effect became counsel to a small committee that met at night in a conference room next to Whiteman's office. The group included retirement system experts from throughout the government.

"We came up with a bill to close the retirement system and start it (anew) for new employees, with more limited benefits and ending a lot of the extra annual goodies," Hanna explained. "Malcolm Wilson was deliberately kept in the dark. Ultimately, our proposed bill was ready for prime time and Malcolm was invited to the governor's large conference room for a presentation. I believe NAR was present but am not certain," Hanna said. "Malcolm was ashen and quietly left the room. It was entirely possible that he would resign. He did not, though he obviously felt wronged."

The bill passed, and in due course, Wilson, perceiving the swelling burden of future pension costs, became a convert.

6. Governor Rockefeller was pragmatic about signing bills that he did not necessarily like or that were sponsored by legislators he had reason to be annoyed at. He was quite sensitive to the position of elected officials—whether a governor or a legislator—vis-à-vis their constituents.

Michael Whiteman recalled a telling conversation with Rockefeller: "Once, we were discussing some bill, and I said this was sponsored by Assemblyman so-and-so, who wasn't helpful on such-and-such an issue. And if you wanted to veto it, I could give you some reasons to do that. They're not very good reasons, but they'd pass. And he said, 'No, you've got to remember that his constituents are my constituents. If I veto that bill, he'll be a martyr and I'll be a meanie. And he'll go back to his constituents and say the governor is beating up on me and taking it out on you as a consequence. I can do that occasionally, if I see a bill that Assemblyman Jones wants passed because it assures that his brother is going to have a job. If you can narrow down the people who benefit from the bill to one or two, who are people who are close to Assemblyman Jones or Smith or whoever it might be, then you can get away with it. But this is a fiction that you can get away with vetoing bills as a form of vengeance—you're just shooting yourself in the foot.' The thing is, he was a shrewd politician and he understood that."

7. William Ronan could argue with Rockefeller. So could Alton Marshall, but he mostly did so circuitously rather than head-on, according to various observers. Robert Douglass could disagree as well, and sometimes teased Rockefeller in ways others could not get away with. Richard Parsons, a brilliant young black lawyer, came aboard as an assistant counsel near the end of Rockefeller's time in Albany but became a close adviser in Washington and for the rest of Rockefeller's life. He could also tell Rockefeller he was wrong on occasion.

Michael Whiteman, however, said he always felt that anyone could argue with Rockefeller, if he had knowledge and reason to offer—until the governor had made up his mind. "Once he had reached a conclusion, it was a far touchier business to argue. It wasn't that he didn't brook argument. What he disliked was re-argument and rehashing of issues that in his mind had been decided." Most staff members understood this process, but there were occasional outbursts.

Hugh Morrow, Rockefeller's longtime director of communications, told Alan Miller that he once got so angry and frustrated with his boss that he yelled: "You know, Governor, I don't have to do this for a living!" To which Rockefeller quietly replied: "No, neither do I, Hugh."

8. Nelson's father, John D. Rockefeller Jr., was a central figure in the 1914 Ludlow Massacre. In September, 1913, some nine thousand coal miners went on strike at Rockefeller-owned Colorado Fuel and Iron, headquartered in Ludlow, Colorado, after the company refused to accept the United Mine Workers as bargaining agent. Richard Dunham explained that when the strike began, the miners and their families were evicted from company-owned housing. They set up tent cities near the various mines they worked in, including Ludlow.

"John D. Rockefeller Jr. testified before a congressional committee, supporting the company's management and the principle of the open shop, in which workers could not be required to join a union," Dunham said. The strike dragged on through the winter, with sporadic violence, as the company imported strikebreakers and the governor of Colorado sent in troops. The killing of a strikebreaker near one of the tent colonies prompted the troops' commanding general to order the eviction of the strikers not only from that tent colony, but also all the other tent colonies, of which the one at Ludlow was the largest. On April 20, 1914, the troops began firing machine guns into the Ludlow camp, resulting in an all-day battle as the miners shot back. That night, under cover of darkness, the troops set the tent city on fire. Among the many dead were two women and ten children, who apparently asphyxiated while sheltering in a pit dug under a tent to shield them from gunfire. Public outrage was nationwide. It took many years of patient philanthropy and public relations efforts for that stain on the Rockefeller escutcheon to fade.

Epilogue

1. Michael Kramer and Sam Roberts, *"I Never Wanted to Be Vice-President of Anything!" An Investigative Biography of Nelson Rockefeller* (New York: Basic Books, 1976).

2. There was a moment in late 1973, after Agnew's resignation and before President Nixon chose Congressman Ford to replace him, when it appeared that

Nixon was going choose Rockefeller instead. Joe Boyd said Henry Kissinger, Nixon's national security advisor, called Rockefeller to say that he had just been with the president and Nixon was going to call and ask him to accept the vice presidency. The call never came.

Why did Nixon pick Ford over Rockefeller? The public reason was that Ford's reputation for integrity would reassure the American people (at a time when the administration seemed short on that characteristic). A view that insiders expressed privately was that Ford's long and uncontroversial tenure in Congress would make it easy to get him confirmed by the Senate.

But it is also possible that Nixon felt that his own survival of the burgeoning Watergate scandal would be jeopardized by having the highly capable and experienced Rockefeller waiting in the wings, ready to assume power if Nixon were forced to resign. Rockefeller was also controversial; nominating him might alienate his party's conservative wing, whose support Nixon would surely need. A protracted confirmation battle might further ensnarl the administration, already mired in Watergate.

In any event, history would have been quite different had Nixon chosen Rockefeller. He, not Ford, would have become the nation's first unelected president, and he would surely have been an energetic chief executive. He would almost certainly have been nominated for a full four-year term in 1976, and if so, would have been the odds-on favorite to win in November. Would he have lived to finish that term in January 1981? That is anybody's guess. As it was, he died in January 1979.

3. The word "filibuster" derives from the Dutch word *frijbuiter*, meaning freebooter or pirate. It evolved into the French word *filibustier* and then the Spanish word *filibustero*, a term applied in the mid-nineteenth century to American adventurers who tried to overthrow Central American governments. It was first used in the U.S. Senate in 1851, but the Senate's rules had always provided for unlimited debate, as, for a time, did those of the House of Representatives.

President Woodrow Wilson, who considered himself a congressional expert and had written his doctoral thesis on the filibuster, grew frustrated as the tactic thwarted passage of important legislation, including, in early 1917, a bill permitting the arming of merchant ships against the threat of German submarines. On March 4, in his second inaugural address, he blasted the Senate and called for a rule to provide cloture. "The Senate of the United States is the only legislative body in the world that cannot act when its majority is ready for action," he declared. "A little group of willful men, representing no opinion but their own, have rendered the great government of the United States helpless and contemptible."

The Constitution lets the Senate amend its rules only on the first legislative day of a new congressional term. Wilson got the change he sought, providing for cloture—shutting off debate—on a two-thirds majority vote. Over the next six decades, cloture was successfully invoked only a handful of times. The filibuster was used by Southern senators repeatedly to block civil rights legislation. The reduction in votes needed for cloture from sixty-seven to sixty thus has the potential for significant impact, even if it does not always allow the majority to rule.

Index

Note: Figure numbers refer to the photographs located after page 82 in the text.

Made in the USA
Charleston, SC
14 July 2014